Life and Teaching of Gautama Buddha

Life and Teaching of GAUTAMA BUDDHA

Shashi Bhushan Singh

PRASHANT PUBLISHING HOUSE
DELHI-110094

Published by :
Prashant Publishing House
C-34, 28 Foota Road, Gali-3,
West Karwal Nagar, Delhi-110094
Phone : 011-22963970, Mob. : 9810396373
e-mail.: prashantpublishinghouse@gmail.com

Life and Teaching of Gautama Buddha
Reserved
First Published 2019

ISBN 978-93-88526-15-9

PRINTED IN INDIA
Published by Mr. R.K. Jha M/s Prashant Publishing House and Published at H.S. Offset House Press, Delhi.

Contents

Preface

Buddha was born approximately 400 BCE in the district of Lumbini, which is now modern-day Nepal, close to the Indian border. He was brought up in a palace with all the comforts and luxuries possible. Growing up a young noble prince, it is said his father sought to shield the young prince Siddhartha from the pain and suffering of the world. It is said his father had a premonition that Siddhartha would one day renounce the world.

The Buddha would often give talks on enlightenment, but on one occasion, he simply held up a flower and maintained silence. Many left not understanding the point, but when later questioned, the Buddha replied that his real teaching could only be understood in silence. Talks could only give limited intellectual information which was not real enlightenment.

The Buddha sought to avoid deep philosophy, he avoided using the term God, preferring to talk about the practical way that a person may escape the cycle of birth and rebirth and attain enlightenment. Like many spiritual teachers, he often taught in parables to keep his teachings simple and practical.

Armed with his new knowledge, the Buddha was initially hesitant to teach, because what he now knew could not be communicated to others in words. According to legend, it was then the king of gods, Brahma, convinced Buddha to teach, and he got up from his spot under the Bodhi tree and set out to do just that.

For the remainder of his 80 years, Buddha traveled, preaching the Dharma (the name given to the teachings of the Buddha) in an effort to lead others to and along the path of enlightenment. When he died, it is said that he told his disciples that they should follow no leader.

The Buddha is undoubtedly one of the most influential figures in world history, and his teachings have affected everything from a variety of other faiths (as many find their origins in the words of the Buddha) to literature to philosophy, both within India and to the farthest reaches of the Western world.

This is a reference book. All the matter is just compiled and edited in nature, taken from the various sources which are in public domain.

The book is accompanied by introduction, preface, bibliography and general index. Besides these, an addition of glossary of Buddhist technical terms is another notable feature of this work. Hence, the present edition would be immensely useful to the students as well as researchers to understand the life of Lord Buddha.

—Editor

1

Biography

Siddhartha Gautama was a spiritual teacher from ancient India who founded Buddhism. In most Buddhist traditions, he is regarded as the Supreme Buddha (P. *sammasambuddha*, S. *samyaksambuddha*) of our age, "Buddha" meaning "awakened one" or "the enlightened one." The time of his birth and death are uncertain: most early 20th-century historians dated his lifetime as c. 563 BCE to 483 BCE, but more recent opinion dates his death to between 486 and 483 BCE or, according to some, between 411 and 400 BCE.

Gautama, also known as *Sakyamuni* ("Sage of the Uakyas"), is the primary figure in Buddhism, and accounts of his life, discourses, and monastic rules are believed by Buddhists to have been summarized after his death and memorized by his followers. Various collections of teachings attributed to him were passed down by oral tradition, and first committed to writing about 400 years later.

He is also regarded as a god or prophet in other religions such as Hinduism, the Ahmadiyya Muslim Community and the Baha'i faith.

CONCEPTION AND BIRTH

Siddhartha was born in Lumbini and raised in the small kingdom or principality of Kalpasutra, both of which are in modern day Nepal. At the time, a multitude of small city-states existed in Ancient India, called Janapadas. Republics and chiefdoms with diffused political power and limited social stratification, were not uncommon amongst them, and were referred to as gana-sanghas. The Buddha's community does not seem to have had a caste system, and their society was not structured according to Brahminical theory. It was not a monarchy, and seems to have been structured either as an oligarchy, or as a form of republic. The more egalitarian gana-sangha form of government, as a political alternative to the strongly hierarchical kingdoms, may have influenced the development of the Shramana type Jain and Buddhist sanghas, where monarchies tended toward Vedic Brahmanism.

According to the traditional biography, although not later writers such as Armstrong, his father was King Suddhodana, the leader of Shakya clan, whose capital was Kapilavastu, and who were later annexed by the growing Kingdom of Kosala during the Buddha's lifetime; Gautama was the family name. His mother, Queen Maha Maya (Mayadevi) and Suddhodana's wife, was a Koliyan princess. On the night Siddhartha was conceived, Queen Maya dreamt that a white elephant with six white tusks entered her right side, and ten months later Siddhartha was born. As was the Shakya tradition, when his mother Queen Maya became pregnant, she left Kalpasutra for her father's kingdom to give birth. However, she gave birth on the way, at Lumbini, in a garden beneath a sal tree.

The day of the Buddha's birth is widely celebrated in Theravada countries as Vesak. Various sources hold that the Buddha's mother died at his birth, a few days or seven days later. The infant was given the name Siddhartha (Pail: Siddhatta), meaning "he who achieves his aim". During the birth celebrations, the hermit seer Asita journeyed from his mountain abode and announced that the child would either become a great king (chakravartin) or a great holy man. This occurred after Siddhartha placed his feet in Asita's hair and Asita examined the birthmarks. Suddhodana held a naming ceremony on the fifth day, and invited eight brahmin scholars to read the future. All gave a dual prediction that the baby would either become a great king or a great holy man. Kaundinya

(Pail: Kondanna), the youngest, and later to be the first arahant, was the only one who unequivocally predicted that Siddhartha would become a Buddha.

While later tradition and legend characterized Œuddhodana as a hereditary monarch, the descendant of the Solar Dynasty of Ikcvku (Pail: Okkaka), many scholars believe that Uuddhodana was the elected chief of a tribal confederacy.

Early Life and Marriage

Siddhartha, said to have been destined to a luxurious life as a prince, had three palaces (for seasonal occupation) especially built for him. His father, King Œuddhodana, wishing for Siddhartha to be a great king, shielded his son from religious teachings or knowledge of human suffering. Siddhartha was brought up by his mother's younger sister, Maha Pajapati.

As the boy reached the age of 16, his father arranged his marriage to Yauodhara (Pail: Yasodhara), a cousin of the same age. According to the traditional account, in time, she gave birth to a son, Rahula. Siddhartha spent 29 years as a Prince in Kapilavastu. Although his father ensured that Siddhartha was provided with everything he could want or need, Siddhartha felt that material wealth was not the ultimate goal of life.

DEPARTURE AND ASCETIC LIFE

At the age of 29, Siddhartha left his palace in order to meet his subjects. Despite his father's effort to remove the sick, aged and suffering from the public view, Siddhartha was said to have seen an old man. Disturbed by this, when told that all people would eventually grow old by his charioteer Channa, the prince went on further trips where he encountered, variously, a diseased man, a decaying corpse, and an ascetic. Deeply depressed by these sights, he sought to overcome old age, illness, and death by living the life of an ascetic.

Siddhartha escaped his palace, accompanied by Channa aboard his horse Kanthaka, leaving behind this royal life to become a mendicant. It is said that, "the horse's hooves were muffled by the gods" to prevent guards from knowing the Bodhisatta's departure. This event is traditionally called "The Great Departure". Siddhartha initially went to Rajagaha and began his ascetic life by begging for alms in the street. Having been recognised by the men of King Bimbisara, Bimbisara offered him the throne after hearing of Siddhartha's quest. Siddhartha rejected the offer, but promised to visit his kingdom of Magadha first, upon attaining enlightenment.

Siddhartha left Rajagaha and practised under two hermit teachers. After mastering the teachings of Alara Kalama (Skr. Ara a Kalama), Siddhartha was asked by Kalama to succeed him, but moved on after being unsatisfied with his practices. He then became a student of Udaka Ramaputta (Skr. Udraka Ramaputtra), but although he achieved high levels of meditative consciousness and was asked to succeed Ramaputtra, he was still not satisfied with his path, and moved on.

Siddhartha and a group of five companions led by Kaundinya then set out to take their austerities even further. They tried to find enlightenment through near total deprivation of worldly goods, including food, practising self-mortification. After nearly starving himself to death by restricting his food intake to around a leaf or nut per day, he collapsed in a river while bathing and almost drowned. Siddhartha began to reconsider his path. Then, he remembered a moment in childhood in which he had been watching his father start the season's slowing, and he had fallen into a naturally concentrated and focused state that was blissful and refreshing, the jhana.

Enlightenment

After asceticism and concentrating on meditation and Anapana-sati (awareness of breathing in and out), Siddhartha is said to have discovered what Buddhists call the Middle Way—a path of moderation away from the extremes of self-indulgence and self-mortification. He accepted a little milk and rice pudding from a village girl named Sujata, who wrongly believed him to be the spirit that had granted her a wish, such was his emaciated appearance. Then, sitting under a pipal tree, now known as the Bodhi tree in Bodh Gaya, India, he vowed never to arise until he had found the Truth. Kaundinya and the other four companions, believing that he had abandoned his search and become undisciplined, left. After 49 days meditating, at the age of 35, he attained Enlightenment; according to some traditions, this occurred approximately in the fifth lunar month, and according to others in the twelfth. Gautama, from then on, was known as the *Buddha* or "Awakened One." Buddha is also sometimes translated as "The Enlightened One." Often, he is referred to in Buddhism as Shakyamuni Buddha or "The Awakened One of the Shakya Clan."

At this point, he is believed to have realized complete awakening and insight into the nature and cause of human suffering which was ignorance, along with steps necessary to eliminate it. This was then categorized into 'Four Noble Truths'; the state of supreme liberation—possible for any being—was called Nirvana. He then allegedly came to possess the Nine Characteristics, which are said to belong to every Buddha.

According to one of the stories in the *Ayacana Sutta* (Samyutta Nikaya VI.1), a scripture found in the Pail and other canons, immediately after his Enlightenment, the Buddha was wondering whether or not he should teach the *Dharma* to human beings. He was concerned that, as human beings were overpowered by greed, hatred and delusion, they would not be able to see the true *dharma*, which was subtle, deep and hard to understand. However, Brahma Sahampati, interceded and asked that he teach the *dharma* to the world, as "there will be those who will understand the *Dharma*". With his great compassion to all beings in the universe, the Buddha agreed to become a teacher.

Formation of the Sangha

After becoming enlightened, two merchants whom the Buddha met, named Tapussa and Bhallika became the first lay disciples. They are given some hairs from the Buddha's head, which are believed to now be enshrined in the Shwe Dagon

Temple in Rangoon, Burma. The Buddha intended to visit Asita, and his former teachers, Alara Kalama and Uddaka Ramaputta to explain his findings, but they had already died.

The Buddha thus journeyed to Deer Park near Varanasi (Benares) in northern India, he set in motion the Wheel of Dharma by delivering his first sermon to the group of five companions with whom he had previously sought enlightenment. They, together with the Buddha, formed the first sough, the company of Buddhist monks, and hence, the first formation of Triple Gem (Buddha, Dharma and Sangha) was completed, with Kaundinya becoming the first stream-enterer. All five soon become arahants, and with the conversion of Yasa and fifty four of his friends, the number of arahants swelled to 60 within the first two months. The conversion of the three Kassapa brothers and their 200, 300 and 500 disciples swelled the sangha over 1000, and they were dispatched to explain the dharma to the populace.

It is unknown what the Buddha's mother tongue was, and no conclusive documentation has been made at this point. It is likely that he preached and his teachings were originally preserved in a variety of closely related Middle Indo-Aryan dialects, of which Pail may be a standardization.

Travels and Teaching

For the remaining 45 years of his life, the Buddha is said to have travelled in the Gangetic Plain, in what is now Uttar Pradesh, Bihar and southern Nepal, teaching his doctrine and discipline to an extremely diverse range of people— from nobles to outcaste street sweepers, mass murderers such as Angulimala and cannibals such as Alavaka. This extended to many adherents of rival philosophies and religions. The Buddha founded the community of Buddhist monks and nuns (the *Sangha*) to continue the dispensation after his *Parinirvana* (Pail: Parinibbana) or "complete Nirvana", and made thousands of converts. His religion was open to all races and classes and had no caste structure. He was also subject to attack from opposition religious groups, including attempted murders and framings.

The sangha travelled from place to place in India, expounding the dharma. This occurred throughout the year, except during the four months of the vassana rainy season. Due to the heavy amount of flooding, travelling was difficult, and ascetics of all religions in that time did not travel, since it was more difficult to do so without stepping on submerged animal life, unwittingly killing them. During this period, the sangha would retreat to a monastery, public park or a forest and people would come to them.

The first vassana was spent at Varanasi when the sangha was first formed. After this, he travelled to Rajagaha, the capital of Magadha to visit King Bimbisara, in accordance with his promise after enlightenment. It was during this visit that Sariputta and Mahamoggallana were converted by Assaji, one of the first five disciples; they were to become the Buddha's two foremost disciples. The Buddha then spent the next three seasons at Veluvana Bamboo Grove monastery in Rajagaha, the capital of Magadha. The monastery, which was of a moderate distance from the city centre was donated by Bimbisara.

Upon hearing of the enlightenment, Suddhodana dispatched royal delegations to ask the Buddha to return to Kapilavastu. Nine delegations were sent in all, but the delegates joined the sangha and became arahants. Neglecting worldly matters, they did not convey their message. The tenth delegation, led by Kaludayi, a childhood friend, resulted in the message being successfully conveyed as well as becoming an arahant. Since it was not the vassana, the Buddha agreed, and two years after his enlightenment, took a two month journey to Kapilavastu by foot, preaching the dharma along the way. Upon his return, the royal palace had prepared the midday meal, but since no specific invitation had come, the sangha went for an alms round in Kapilavastu. Hearing this, Suddhodana hastened to approach the Buddha, stating "Ours is the warrior lineage of Mahamassata, and not a single warrior has gone seeking alms", to which the Buddha replied

That is not the custom of your royal lineage. But it is the custom of my Buddha lineage. Several thousands of Buddhas have gone by seeking alms Suddhodana invited the sangha back to the royal palace for the meal, followed by a dharma talk, after which he became a sotapanna. During the visit, many members of the royal family joined the sangha. His cousins Ananda and Anuruddha were to become two of his five chief disciples. His son Rahula also joined the sangha at the age of seven, and was one of the ten chief disciples. His half-brother Nanda also joined the sangha and became an arahant. Another cousin Devadatta also became a monk although he later became an enemy and tried to kill the Buddha on multiple occasions.

Of his disciples, Sariputta, Mahamoggallana, Mahakasyapa, Ananda and Anuruddha comprised the five chief disciples. His ten foremost disciples were completed by the quintet of Upali, Subhoti, Rahula, Mahakaccana and Punna.

In the fifth vassana, the Buddha was staying at Mahavana near Vesali. Hearing of the impending death of Suddhodana, the Buddha went to his father and preached the dharma, and Suddhodana became an arahant prior to death. The death and cremation led to the creation of the order of nuns. Buddhist texts record that he was reluctant to ordain women as nuns. His foster mother Maha Pajapati approached him asking to join the sangha, but the Buddha refused, and began the journey from Kapilavastu back to Rajagaha. Maha Pajapati was so intent on renouncing the world that she led a group of royal Sakyan and Koliyan ladies, following the sangha to Rajagaha. The Buddha eventually accepted them five years after the formation of the Sangha on the grounds that their capacity for enlightenment was equal to that of men, but he gave them certain additional rules (Vinaya) to follow. This occurred after Ananda interceded on their behalf. Yasodhara also became a nun, with both becoming arahants.

During his ministry, Devadatta (who was not an arahant) frequently tried to undermine the Buddha. At one point Devadatta asked the Buddha to stand aside to let him lead the sangha. The Buddha declined, and stated that Devadatta's actions did not reflect on the Triple Gem, but on him alone.

Devadatta conspired with Prince Ajatasattu, son of Bimbisara, so that they would kill and usurp the Buddha and Bimbisara respectively. Devadatta attempted three times to kill the Buddha. The first attempt involved the hiring of a group of archers, whom upon meeting the Buddha became disciples. A second attempt followed when Devadatta attempted to roll a large boulder down a hill. It hit another rock and splintered, only grazing the Buddha in the foot. A final attempt by plying an elephant with alcohol and setting it loose again failed. Failing this, Devadatta attempted to cause a schism in the sangha, by proposing extra restrictions on the vinaya. When the Buddha declined, Devadatta started a breakaway order, criticising the Buddha's laxity. At first, he managed to convert some of the bhikkhus, but Sariputta and Mahamoggallana expounded the dharma to them and succeeded in winning them back.

When the Buddha reached the age of 55, he made Ananda his chief attendant.

Death/Mahaparinirvana

According to the Mahaparinibbana Sutta of the Pail canon, at the age of 80, the Buddha announced that he would soon reach Parinirvana or the final deathless state abandoning the earthly body. After this, the Buddha ate his last meal, which he had received as an offering from a blacksmith named Cunda. Falling violently ill, Buddha instructed his attendant Ananda to convince Cunda that the meal eaten at his place had nothing to do with his passing and that his meal would be a source of the greatest merit as it provided the last meal for a Buddha. Mettanando and von Hinuber argue that the Buddha died of mesenteric infarction, a symptom of old age, rather than food poisoning. The precise contents of the Buddha's final meal are not clear, due to variant scriptural traditions and ambiguity over the translation of certain significant terms; the Theravada tradition generally believes that the Buddha was offered some kind of pork, while the Mahayana tradition believes that the Buddha consumed some sort of truffle or other mushroom.

The Mahayana Vimalakirti Sutra claims, in Chapter 3, that the Buddha doesn't really become ill or old but purposely presents such an appearance only to teach those born into samsara about the impermanence and pain of defiled worlds and to encourage them to strive for Nirvana.

"Reverend Ananda, the Tathagatas have the body of the Dharma—not a body that is sustained by material food. The Tathagatas have a transcendental body that has transcended all mundane qualities. There is no injury to the body of a Tathgata, as it is rid of all defilements. The body of a Tathagata is un-compounded and free of all formative activity. Reverend Ananda, to believe there can be illness in such a body is irrational and unseemly!' Nevertheless, since the Buddha has appeared during the time of the five corruptions, he disciplines living beings by acting lowly and humble."

Ananda protested Buddha's decision to enter Parinirvana in the abandoned jungles of Culinary (present-day Kushinagar, India) of the Malla kingdom. Buddha, however, reminded Ananda how Kushinara was a land once ruled by a righteous wheel-turning king that resounded with joy:

Kusavati, Ananda, resounded unceasingly day and night with ten sounds—the trumpeting of elephants, the neighing of horses, the rattling of chariots, the beating of drums and tabours, music and song, cheers, the clapping of hands, and cries of "Eat, drink, and be merry!"

Buddha then asked all the attendant Bhikshus to clarify any doubts or questions they had. They had none. He then finally entered Parinirvana. The Buddha's final words were, "All composite things pass away. Strive for your own liberation with diligence." The Buddha's body was cremated and the relics were placed in monuments or stupas, some of which are believed to have survived until the present. For example, The Temple of the Tooth or "Dalada Maligawa" in Sri Lanka is the place where the relic of the right tooth of Buddha is kept at present.

According to the Pail historical chronicles of Sri Lanka, the Dpavasa and Mahvacsa, the coronation of Ashoka (Pail: Ashoka) is 218 years after the death of Buddha. According to one Mahayana record in Chinese, the coronation of Hooka is 116 years after the death of Buddha. Therefore, the time of Buddha's passing is either 486 BCE according to The ravada record or 383 BCE according to Mahayana record. However, the actual date traditionally accepted as the date of the Buddha's death in The ravada countries is 544 or 543 BCE, because the reign of Hooka was traditionally reckoned to be about 60 years earlier than current estimates.

At his death, the Buddha told his disciples to follow no leader, but to follow his teachings (dharma). However, at the First Buddhist Council, Mahakasyapa was held by the sangha as their leader, with the two chief disciples Mahamoggallana and Sariputta having died before the Buddha.

HISTORICAL CONTEXT

The Buddha was born in Lumbini (Rummin-dei), near Kapilavastu (Kapilbastu) on the northern edge of the Ganges River basin, an area on the periphery of the civilization of North India, in what is today southern Nepal. Scholars speculate that during the late Vedic period the peoples of the region were organized into tribal republics, ruled by a council of elders or an elected leader; the grand palaces described in the traditional accounts of the life of the Buddha are not evident among the archaeological remains. It is unclear to what extent these groups at the periphery of the social order of the Ganges basin were incorporated into the caste system, but the Buddha's family is said to have belonged to the warrior (Kshatriya) caste. The central Ganges basin was organized into some 16 city-states, ruled by kings, often at war with each other.

The rise of these cities of central India, with their courts and their commerce, brought social, political, and economic changes that are often identified as key factors in the rise of Buddhism and other religious movements of the 6th and 5th centuries BCE. Buddhist texts identify a variety of itinerant teachers who attracted groups of disciples. Some of these taught forms of meditation, Yoga, and asceticism and set forth philosophical views, focusing often on the nature of the person and the question of whether human actions (karma) have future effects. Although the Buddha would become one of these teachers, Buddhists view him as quite different from the others. His place within the tradition, therefore, cannot be understood by focusing exclusively on the events of his life and times (even to the extent that they are available). Instead, he must be viewed within the context of Buddhist theories of time and history.

According to Buddhist doctrine, the universe is the product of karma, the law of the cause and effect of actions, according to which virtuous actions create pleasure in the future and nonvirtuous actions create pain. The beings of the universe are reborn without beginning in six realms: as gods, demigods, humans, animals, ghosts, and hell beings. The actions of these beings create not only their individual experiences but the domains in which they dwell. The cycle of rebirth, called samsara (literally "wandering"), is regarded as a domain of suffering, and the ultimate goal of Buddhist practice is to escape from that suffering. The means of escape remains unknown until, over the course of millions of lifetimes, a person perfects himself, ultimately gaining the power to discover the path out of samsara and then compassionately revealing that path to the world.

A person who has set out on the long journey to discover the path to freedom from suffering, and then to teach it to others, is called a bodhisattva. A person who has discovered that path, followed it to its end, and taught it to the world is called a buddha. Buddhas are not reborn after they die but enter a state beyond suffering called nirvana (literally "passing away"). Because buddhas appear so rarely over the course of time and because only they reveal the path to liberation (moksha) from suffering (dukkha), the appearance of a buddha in the world is considered a momentous event in the history of the universe.

The story of a particular buddha begins before his birth and extends beyond his death. It encompasses the millions of lives spent on the bodhisattva path before the achievement of buddhahood and the persistence of the buddha, in the form of both his teachings and his relics, after he has passed into nirvana. The historical Buddha is regarded as neither the first nor the last buddha to appear in the world. According to some traditions he is the 7th buddha; according to another he is the 25th; according to yet another he is the 4th. The next buddha, named Maitreya, will appear after Shakyamuni's teachings and relics have disappeared from the world. The traditional accounts of the events in the life of the Buddha must be considered from this perspective.

SOURCES OF THE LIFE OF THE BUDDHA

Accounts of the life of the Buddha appear in many forms. Perhaps the earliest are those found in the collections of sutras (Pali: suttas), discourses traditionally attributed to the Buddha. In the sutras, the Buddha recounts individual events in his life that occurred from the time that he renounced his life as a prince until he achieved enlightenment six years later. Several accounts of his enlightenment also appear in the sutras. One Pali text, the Mahaparinibbana-sutta ("Discourse on the Final Nirvana"), describes the Buddha's last days, his passage into nirvana, his funeral, and the distribution of his relics. Biographical accounts in the early sutras provide little detail about the Buddha's birth and childhood, although some sutras contain a detailed account of the life of a prehistoric buddha, Vipashyin.

Another category of early Buddhist literature, the vinaya (concerned ostensibly with the rules of monastic discipline), contains accounts of numerous incidents from the Buddha's life but rarely in the form of a continuous narrative; biographical sections that do occur often conclude with the conversion of one of his early disciples, Shariputra. While the sutras focus on the person of the Buddha (his previous lives, his practice of austerities, his enlightenment, and his passage into nirvana), the vinaya literature tends to emphasize his career as a teacher and the conversion of his early disciples. The sutras and vinaya texts, thus, reflect concerns with both the Buddha's life and his teachings, concerns that often are interdependent; early biographical accounts appear in doctrinal discourses, and points of doctrine and places of pilgrimage are legitimated through their connection to the life of the Buddha.

Near the beginning of the Common Era, independent accounts of the life of the Buddha were composed. They do not recount his life from birth to death, often ending with his triumphant return to his native city of Kapilavastu (Pali: Kapilavatthu), which is said to have taken place either one year or six years after his enlightenment. The partial biographies add stories that were to become well-known, such as the child prince's meditation under a rose-apple tree and his four momentous chariot rides outside the city.

These accounts typically make frequent reference to events from the previous lives of the Buddha. Indeed, collections of stories of the Buddha's past lives, called Jatakas, form one of the early categories of Buddhist literature. Here, an event reminds the Buddha of an event in a past life. He relates that story in order to illustrate a moral maxim, and, returning to the present, he identifies various members of his audience as the present incarnations of characters in his past-life tale, with himself as the main character.

The Jataka stories (one Pali collection contains 547 of them) have remained among the most popular forms of Buddhist literature. They are the source of some 32 stone carvings at the 2nd-century BCE stupa at Bharhut in northeastern Madhya Pradesh state; 15 stupa carvings depict the last life of the Buddha. Indeed, stone carvings in India provide an important source for identifying which events in the lives of the Buddha were considered most important by the community.

The Jataka stories are also well-known beyond India; in Southeast Asia, the story of Prince Vessantara (the Buddha's penultimate reincarnation)—who demonstrates his dedication to the virtue of charity by giving away his sacred elephant, his children, and finally his wife—is as well-known as that of his last lifetime.

Lives of the Buddha that trace events from his birth to his death appeared in the 2nd century CE. One of the most famous is the Sanskrit poem Buddhacharita ("Acts of the Buddha") by Ashvaghosa. Texts such as the Mulasarvastivada Vinaya (probably dating from the 4th or 5th century CE) attempt to gather the many stories of the Buddha into a single chronological account. The purpose of these biographies in many cases is less to detail the unique deeds of Shakyamuni's life than to demonstrate the ways in which the events of his life conform to a pattern that all buddhas of the past have followed. According to some, all past buddhas had left the life of the householder after observing the four sights, all had practiced austerities, all had achieved enlightenment at Bodh Gaya, all had preached in the deer park at Sarnath, and so on.

The life of the Buddha was written and rewritten in India and across the Buddhist world, elements added and subtracted as necessary. Sites that became important pilgrimage places but that had not been mentioned in previous accounts would be retrospectively sanctified by the addition of a story about the Buddha's presence there. Regions that Buddhism entered long after his death—such as Sri Lanka, Kashmir, and Burma (now Myanmar)—added narratives of his magical visitations to accounts of his life.

No single version of the life of the Buddha would be accepted by all Buddhist traditions. For more than a century, scholars have focused on the life of the Buddha, with the earliest investigations attempting to isolate and identify historical elements amid the many legends. Because of the centuries that had passed between the actual life and the composition of what might be termed a full biography, most scholars abandoned this line of inquiry as unfruitful. Instead they began to study the processes—social, political, institutional, and doctrinal—responsible for the regional differences among the narratives of the Buddha. The various uses made of the life of the Buddha are another topic of interest. In short, the efforts of scholars have shifted from an attempt to derive authentic information about the life of the Buddha to an effort to trace stages in and the motivations for the development of his biography. It is important to reiterate that the motivation to create a single life of the Buddha, beginning with his previous births and ending with his passage into nirvana, occurred rather late in the history of Buddhism. Instead, the biographical tradition of the Buddha developed through the synthesis of a number of earlier and independent fragments. And biographies of the Buddha have continued to be composed over the centuries and around the world.

During the modern period, for example, biographies have been written that seek to demythologize the Buddha and to emphasize his role in presaging modern ethical systems, social movements, or scientific discoveries. What follows is an account of the life of the Buddha that is well-known, yet synthetic, bringing together some of the more famous events from various accounts of his life, which often describe and interpret these events differently.

Previous Lives

Many biographies of the Buddha begin not with his birth in his last lifetime but in a lifetime millions of years before, when he first made the vow to become a buddha. According to a well-known version, many aeons ago there lived a Brahman named (in some accounts) Sumedha, who realized that life is characterized by suffering and then set out to find a state beyond death.

He retired to the mountains, where he became a hermit, practiced meditation, and gained yogic powers. While flying through the air one day, he noticed a great crowd around a teacher, whom Sumedha learned was the buddha Dipamkara. When he heard the word buddha he was overcome with joy.

Upon Dipamkara's approach, Sumedha loosened his yogin's matted locks and laid himself down to make a passage across the mud for the Buddha. Sumedha reflected that were he to practice the teachings of Dipamkara he could free himself from future rebirth in that very lifetime. But he concluded that it would be better to delay his liberation in order to traverse the longer path to buddhahood; as a buddha he could lead others across the ocean of suffering to the farther shore. Dipamkara paused before Sumedha and predicted that many aeons hence this yogin with matted locks would become a buddha. He also prophesied Sumedha's name in his last lifetime (Gautama) and the names of his parents and chief disciples and described the tree under which the future Buddha would sit on the night of his enlightenment.

Over the subsequent aeons, the bodhisattva would renew his vow in the presence of each of the buddhas who came after Dipamkara, before becoming the buddha Shakyamuni himself. Over the course of his lifetimes as a bodhisattva, he accumulated merit (punya) through the practice of 6 (or 10) virtues. After his death as Prince Vessantara, he was born in the Tusita Heaven, whence he surveyed the world to locate the proper site of his final birth.

DEATH AND THE IMPERMANENCE OF LIFE

In the teaching of the Buddha, all of us will pass away eventually as a part in the natural process of birth, old-age and death and that we should always keep in mind the impermanence of life. The life that we all cherish and wish to hold on.

To Buddhism, however, death is not the end of life, it is merely the end of the body we inhabit in this life, but our spirit will still remain and seek out through the need of attachment, attachment to a new body and new life. Where they will be born is a result of the past and the accumulation of positive and negative action, and the resultant karma (cause and effect) is a result of ones past actions.

This would lead to the person to be reborn in one of 6 realms which are; heaven, human beings, Asura, hungry ghost, animal and hell. Realms, according to the severity of ones karmic actions, Buddhists believe however, none of these places are permanent and one does not remain in any place indefinitely. So we can say that in Buddhism, life does not end, merely goes on in other forms that are the result of accumulated karma. Buddhism is a belief that emphasizes the impermanence of lives, including all those beyond the present life. With this in mind we should not fear death as it will lead to rebirth.

The fear of death stemmed from the fear of cease to be existent and losing ones identity and foothold in the world. We see our death coming long before its arrival, we notice impermanence in the changes we see around us and to us in the arrival of aging and the suffering due to losing our youth. Once we were strong and beautiful and as we age, as we approach our final moments of life we realize how fleeting such a comfortable place actually was.

2

Early Life of Siddhartha

THE BIRTH OF SIDDHARTHA

Months passed. Then, one day, the queen knew that the time was approaching for her son to be born. She went to King Suddhodana, and she said to him:

"My lord, I would wander through the happy gardens. Birds are singing in the trees, and the air is bright with flower-dust. I would wander through the happy gardens."

"But it will weary you, O queen," replied Suddhodana. "Are you not afraid?"

"The innocent being that I carry in my womb must be born amid the innocence of budding flowers. No, I will go, O master, I will go into the flower-gardens."

The king yielded to Maya's wish. He said to his servants:

"Go into the gardens and deck them out in silver and in gold. Drape the trees with precious hangings. Let everything be magnificent, for the queen will pass."

Then he addressed Maya:

"Array yourself, today, in great splendour, O Maya. Ride in a gorgeous palanquin; let your most beautiful maidens carry you. Order your servants to use rare perfumes; have them wear ropes of pearls and bracelets of precious stones; have them carry lutes and drums and flutes, and sing sweet songs that would delight the Gods themselves."

Ṡuddhodana was obeyed, and when the queen reached the palace-gates the guards greeted her with joyous cries. Bells peeled gaily, peacocks spread their gorgeous tail-feathers, and the song of swans throbbed in the air.

They came to a wood where the trees were in bloom, and Maya ordered them to set down the palanquin. She stepped out and began wandering about, aimlessly. She was happy. And behold! she found a rare tree, the branches drooping under their burden of blossoms. She went up to it; gracefully extending her hand, she drew down a branch. Suddenly, she stood very still. She smiled, and the maidens who were near her received a lovely child into their arms.

At that same moment all that was alive in the world trembled with joy. The earth quivered. Songs and the patter of dancing feet echoed in the sky. Trees of all seasons burst into flower, and ripe fruit hung from the branches. A pure, serene light appeared in the sky. The sick were rid of their suffering. The hungry were satisfied. Those to whom wine had played false became sober. Madmen recovered their reason, the weak their strength, the poor their wealth. Prisons opened their gates. The wicked were cleansed of all evil.

One of Maya's maidens hastened to King Suddhodana and joyously exclaimed:

"My lord, my lord, a son is born to you, a son who will bring great glory to your house!"

He was speechless. But his face was radiant with joy, and he knew great happiness.

Presently he summoned all the Sakyas, and he commanded them to accompany him into the garden where the child had been born. They obeyed, and, with a host of Brahmans in attendance, they formed a noble retinue as they gravely followed the king.

When he came near the child, the king made a deep obeisance, and he said:

"Do you bow as I bow before the prince, to whom I give the name Siddhartha."

They all bowed, and the Brahmans, inspired by the Gods, then sang:

> *"All creatures are happy, and they are no longer rough, those roads travelled by men, for he is born, he who gives happiness: he will bring happiness into the world. In the darkness a great light has dawned, the sun and the moon are like dying embers, for he is born, he who gives light: he will bring light into the world. The blind see, the deaf hear, the foolish have recovered their reason, for he is born, he who restores sight, and restores hearing, and restores the mind: he will bring sight, he will bring hearing, he will bring reason into the world. Perfumed zephyrs ease the suffering of mankind, for he is born, he who heals: he will bring health into the world. Flames are no longer pitiless, the flow of rivers has been stayed, the earth has trembled gently: he will be the one to see the truth."*

BIRTH AND EARLY LIFE

He determined that he should be born the son of the king Shuddhodana of the Shakya clan, whose capital was Kapilavastu. Shortly thereafter, his mother, the queen Maha Maya, dreamed that a white elephant had entered her womb. Ten lunar months later, as she strolled in the garden of Lumbini, the child emerged from under her right arm. He was able to walk and talk immediately. A lotus flower blossomed under his foot at each step, and he announced that this would be his last lifetime. The king summoned the court astrologers to predict the boy's future. Seven agreed that he would become either a universal monarch (chakravartin) or a buddha; one astrologer said that there was no doubt, the child would become a buddha. His mother died seven days after his birth, and so he was reared by his mother's sister, Mahaprajapati. As a young child, the prince was once left unattended during a festival. Later in the day he was discovered seated in meditation under a tree, whose shadow had remained motionless throughout the day to protect him from the sun.

The prince enjoyed an opulent life; his father shielded him from exposure to the ills of the world, including old age, sickness, and death, and provided him with palaces for summer, winter, and the rainy season, as well as all manner of enjoyments (including in some accounts 40,000 female attendants). At age 16 he married the beautiful princess Yashodhara. When the prince was 29, however, his life underwent a profound change. He asked to be taken on a ride through the city in his chariot. The king gave his permission but first had all the sick and old people removed from the route. One old man escaped notice. Not knowing what stood before him, the prince was told that this was an old man. He was informed, also, that this was not the only old man in the world; everyone—the prince, his father, his wife, and his kinsmen—would all one day grow old. The first trip was followed by three more excursions beyond the palace walls. On these trips he saw first a sick person, then a corpse being carried to the cremation ground, and finally a mendicant seated in meditation beneath a tree. Having been exposed to the various ills of human life, and the existence of those who seek a state beyond them, he asked the king for permission to leave the city and retire to the forest. The father offered his son anything if he would stay. The prince asked that his father ensure that he would never die, become ill, grow old, or lose his fortune. His father replied that he could not. The prince retired to his chambers, where he was entertained by beautiful women. Unmoved by the women, the prince resolved to go forth that night in search of a state beyond birth and death.

When he had been informed seven days earlier that his wife had given birth to a son, he said, "A fetter has arisen." The child was named Rahula, meaning "fetter." Before the prince left the palace, he went into his wife's chamber to look upon his sleeping wife and infant son. In another version of the story, Rahula had not yet been born on the night of the departure from the palace. Instead, the prince's final act was to conceive his son, whose gestation period extended over the six years of his father's search for enlightenment. According to these sources, Rahula was born on the night that his father achieved buddhahood.

The prince left Kapilavastu and the royal life behind and entered the forest, where he cut off his hair and exchanged his royal robes for the simple dress of a hunter. From that point on he ate whatever was placed in his begging bowl. Early in his wanderings he encountered Bimbisara, the king of Magadha and eventual patron of the Buddha, who, upon learning that the ascetic was a prince, asked him to share his kingdom. The prince declined but agreed to return when he had achieved enlightenment. Over the next six years, the prince studied meditation and learned to achieve deep states of blissful concentration. But he quickly matched the attainments of his teachers and concluded that despite their achievements, they would be reborn after their death. He next joined a group of five ascetics who had devoted themselves to the practice of extreme forms of self-mortification. The prince also became adept at their practices, eventually reducing his daily meal to one pea. Buddhist art often represents him seated in the meditative posture in an emaciated form, with sunken eyes and protruding ribs. He concluded that mortification of the flesh is not the path to liberation from suffering and rebirth and accepted a dish of rice and cream from a young woman.

The Enlightenment

His companions remained convinced of the efficacy of asceticism and abandoned the prince. Now without companions or a teacher, the prince vowed that he would sit under a tree and not rise until he had found the state beyond birth and death. On the full moon of May, six years after he had left his palace, he meditated until dawn. Mara, the god of desire, who knew that the prince was seeking to put an end to desire and thereby free himself from Mara's control, attacked him with wind, rain, rocks, weapons, hot coals, burning ashes, sand, mud, and darkness. The prince remained unmoved and meditated on love, thus transforming the hail of fury into a shower of blossoms. Mara then sent his three beautiful daughters, Lust, Thirst, and Discontent, to tempt the prince, but he remained impassive. In desperation, Mara challenged the prince's right to occupy the spot of earth upon which he sat, claiming that it belonged to him instead. Then, in a scene that would become the most famous depiction of the Buddha in Asian art, the prince, seated in the meditative posture, stretched out his right hand and touched the earth. By touching the earth, he was asking the goddess of the earth to confirm that a great gift that he had made as Prince Vessantara in his previous life had earned him the right to sit beneath the tree. She assented with a tremor, and Mara departed.

The prince sat in meditation through the night. During the first watch of the night, he had a vision of all of his past lives, recollecting his place of birth, name, caste, and even the food he had eaten.

During the second watch of the night, he saw how beings rise and fall through the cycle of rebirth as a consequence of their past deeds. In the third watch of the night, the hours before dawn, he was liberated. Accounts differ as to precisely what it was that he understood.

According to some versions it was the four truths: of suffering, the origin of suffering, the cessation of suffering, and the path to the cessation of suffering. According to others it was the sequence of dependent origination: how ignorance leads to action and eventually to birth, aging, and death, and how when ignorance is destroyed, so also are birth, aging, and death. Regardless of their differences, all accounts agree that on this night he became a buddha, an awakened one who had roused himself from the slumber of ignorance and extended his knowledge throughout the universe.

The experience of that night was sufficiently profound that the prince, now the Buddha, remained in the vicinity of the tree up to seven weeks, savouring his enlightenment. One of those weeks was rainy, and the serpent king came and spread his hood above the Buddha to protect him from the storm, a scene commonly depicted in Buddhist art. At the end of seven weeks, two merchants approached him and offered him honey and cakes. Knowing that it was improper for a buddha to receive food in his hands, the gods of the four directions each offered him a bowl. The Buddha magically collapsed the four bowls into one and received the gift of food. In return, the Buddha plucked some hairs from his head and gave them to the merchants.

THE MARRIAGE OF SIDDHARTHA

Suddhodana kept thinking of what Asita had told him. He did not want his family to die out, and he said to himself: "I will arouse in my son a desire for pleasure; then, perhaps, I shall have grandchildren, and they shall prosper."

So he sent for the prince, and he spoke to him in these words:

"My child, you are at an age when it would be well to think of marriage. If there is some maid that pleases you, tell me."

Siddhartha replied:

"Give me seven days to consider, father. In seven days you shall have my answer."

And he mused:

"Endless evil, I know, comes of desire. The trees that grow in the forest of desire have their roots are suffering and strife, and their leaves are poisonous. Desire burns like fire and wounds like a sword. I am not one of those who seek the company of women; it is my lot to live in the silence of the woods. There, through meditation, my mind will find peace, and I shall know happiness. But does not the lotus grow and flourish even amid the tangle of swamp-flowers? Have there not been men with wives and sons who found wisdom? Those who, before me, have sought supreme knowledge spent many years in the company of women. And when the time came to leave them for the delights of meditation, theirs was but a greater joy. I shall follow their example."

He thought of the qualities he would value most highly in a woman. Then, on the seventh day, he returned to his father.

"Father," said he, "she whom I shall marry must be a woman of rare merit. If you find one endowed with the natural gifts I shall enumerate, you may give her to me in marriage."

And he said:

"She whom I shall marry will be in the bloom of youth; she whom I shall marry will have the flower of beauty; yet her youth will not make her vain, nor will her beauty make her proud. She whom I shall marry will have a sister's affection, a mother's tenderness, for all living creatures. She will be sweet and truthful, and she will not know envy. Never, not even in her dreams, will she think of any other man but her husband. She will never use haughty language; her manner will be unassuming; she will be as meek as a slave. She will not covet that which belongs to others; she will make no inconsiderate demands, and she will be satisfied with her lot. She will care nothing for wines, and sweets will not tempt her. She will be insensible to music and perfume; she will be indifferent to plays and festivals. She will be kind to my attendants and to her maidens. She will be the first to awaken and the last to fall asleep. She whom I shall marry will be pure in body, in speech and in thought."

And he added:

"Father, if you know a maid who possesses these qualities, you may give her to me in marriage."

The king summoned the household priest. He enumerated the qualities the prince sought in the woman he would marry, then:

"Go," said he, "go, Brahman. Visit all the homes of Kapilavastu; observe the young girls and question them. And if you find one to possess the necessary qualities, bring her to the prince, even though she be of the lowest caste. For it is not rank nor riches my son seeks, but virtue."

The priest scoured the city of Kapilavastu. He entered the houses, he saw the young girls, he cleverly questioned them; but not one could he find worthy of Prince Siddhartha. Finally, he came to the home of Dandapani who was of the Sakya family. Dandapani had a daughter named Gopa. At the very sight of her, the priest's heart rejoiced, for she was beautiful and full of grace. He spoke a few words to her, and he doubted no longer.

The priest returned to King Suddhodana. "My lord," he exclaimed, "I have found a maid worthy of your son."

"Where did you find her?" asked the king. "She is the daughter of the Sakya, Dandapani," the Brahman replied.

Though he had great confidence in his household priest, Suddhodana hesitated to summon Gopa and Dandapani. "Even the wisest men can make mistakes," he thought. "The Brahman may be exaggerating her perfections. I must put the daughter of Dandapani to a further test, and my son himself shall judge her."

He had many jewels made out of gold and silver, and by royal command a herald was sent through the streets of Kapilavastu, crying:

"On the seventh day from this day, Prince Siddhartha, son of King Suddhodana, will present gifts to the young girls of the city. So may all the young girls appear at the palace on the seventh day!"

On the day announced, the prince sat on a throne in the great hall of the palace. All the young girls of the city were present, and they filed before him. To each one he presented a jewel, but, as they approached the throne, his striking beauty so intimidated them that they lowered their gaze or turned their heads away. They hardly took the time to receive their presents; some were even in such haste to leave that they merely touched the gift with the tips of their fingers, and it fell to the floor.

Gopa was the last one to appear. She advanced fearlessly, without even blinking her eyes. But the prince had not a single jewel left. Gopa smiled and said to him:

"Prince, in what way have I offended you?"

"You have not offended me," replied Siddhartha.

"Then why do you treat me with disdain?"

"I do not treat you with disdain," he replied. "You are the last one, and I have no jewel to give you."

But suddenly he remembered that on his finger he was wearing a ring of great value. He took it off and handed it to the young girl.

She would not take the ring.

She said, "Prince, must I accept this ring from you?"

"It was mine," replied the prince, "and you must accept it."

"No," said she, "I would not deprive you of your jewels. It is for me, rather, to give you a jewel." And she left.

When the king heard of this incident he was elated.

"Gopa, alone, could face my son," he thought;

"She alone is worthy of him. Gopa, who would not accept the ring that you took from your finger, Gopa, O my son, will be your fairest jewel."

And he summoned Gopa's father to the palace.

"Friend," said he, "the time has come for my son Siddhartha to marry. I believe your daughter Gopa has found favour in his eyes. Will you marry her to my son?"

Dandapani did not answer at once. He hesitated, and again the king asked him:

"Will you marry your daughter to my son?" Then Dandapani said:

"My lord, your son has been brought up in luxury; he has never been outside the palace-gates; his physical and intellectual abilities have never been proven. You know that the Sakyas only marry their daughters to men who are skilful and strong, brave and wise. How can I give my daughter to your son who, so far, has shown a taste only for indolence?"

These words disturbed King Suddhodana. He asked to see the prince. Siddhartha came immediately.

"Father," said he, "you look very sad. What has happened?"

The king did not know how to tell him what Dandapani had so bluntly expressed. He remained silent.

The prince repeated:

"Father, you look very sad. What has happened?"

"Do not ask me," replied Suddhodana.

"Father, you are sad, what has happened?"

"It is a painful subject; I would rather not speak of it."

"Explain yourself, father. It is always well to be explicit."

The king finally decided to relate the interview he had with Dandapani. When he had finished, the prince began to laugh.

"My lord," said he, "you are needlessly disturbed. Do you believe there is anyone in Kapilavastu who is my superior in strength or in intellect? Summon all who are famous for their attainments in any field whatsoever; command them to measure their skill with mine, and I shall show you what I can do."

The king recovered his serenity. He had it proclaimed throughout the city:

"That on the seventh day from this day, Prince Siddhartha will compete with all who excel in any field whatsoever."

On the day designated, all those who claimed to be skilful in the arts or in the sciences appeared at the palate. Dandapani was present, and he promised his daughter to the one, whether of noble or of humble birth, who would be victorious in the contests which were to take place.

First, a young man, who knew the rules of writing, sought to challenge the prince, but the learned Vishvamitra stepped before the assembly and said:

"Young man, such a contest would be futile. You are already defeated. The prince was still a child when he was placed in my care; I was to teach him the art of writing. But he already knew sixty-four varieties of script! He knew certain varieties that were unknown to me even by name!"

Vishvamitra's testimony was enough to give the prince a victory in the art of writing.

Then they sought to test his knowledge of numbers. It was decided that a certain Sakya named Arjuna, who had time and again solved intricate problems, would act as judge in the contest.

One young man claimed to be an excellent mathematician, and to him Siddhartha addressed a question, but the young man was unable to reply.

"And yet it was an easy question," said the prince. "But here is one that is still easier; who will answer it?"

No one answered this second question.

"It is now your turn to examine me," said the prince.

They asked him questions that were considered difficult, but he gave the answers even before they had finished stating the problem.

"Let Arjuna himself examine the prince!" came the cry from all sides.

Arjuna gave him the most intricate problems, and never once was Siddhartha at a loss for the correct solution.

They all marvelled at his knowledge of mathematics and were convinced that his intelligence had probed to the bottom of all the sciences. They then decided to challenge his athletic skill, but at jumping and at running he won with little effort, and at wrestling he had only to lay a finger upon his adversary, and he would fall to the ground.

Then they brought out the bows, and skilful archers placed their arrows in targets that were barely visible. But when it came the prince's turn to shoot, so great was his natural strength that he broke each bow as he drew it. Finally, the king sent guards to fetch a very ancient, very precious bow that was kept in the temple. No one within the memory of man had ever been able to draw or lift it.

Siddhartha took the bow in his left hand, and with one finger of his right hand he drew it to him. Then he took as target a tree so distant that he alone could see it. The arrow pierced the tree, and, burying itself in the ground, disappeared. And there, where the arrow had entered the ground, a well formed, which was called the Well of the Arrow.

Everything seemed to be over, and they led toward the victor a huge white elephant on which, in triumph, he was to ride through Kapilavastu. But a young Sakya, Devadatta, who was very proud of his strength, seized the animal by the trunk and, in fun, struck it with his fist. The elephant fell to the ground.

The prince looked reprovingly at the young man and said:

"You have done an evil thing, Devadatta."

He touched the elephant with his foot, and it stood up and paid him homage.

Then they all acclaimed his glory, and the air rang with their cheers. Suddhodana was happy, and Dandapani, weeping with joy, exclaimed:

"Gopa, my daughter Gopa, be proud to be the wife of such a man."

SIDDHARTHA'S FIRST MEDITATION

The prince grew older, and the time came for him to study with the teacher who instructed the young Sakyas in the art of writing. This teacher was called Vishvamitra.

Siddhartha was entrusted to his care. He was given, to write on, a tablet of gilded sandalwood, set round with precious stones. When he had it in his hands, he asked:

"Which script, master, would you have me learn?"

And he enumerated the sixty-four varieties of script. Then again he asked:

"Master, which of the sixty-four would you have me learn?"

Vishvamitra made no answer: he was struck dumb with astonishment. Finally, he replied:

"I see, my lord, that there is nothing I can teach you. Of the scripts you mentioned, some are known to me only by name, and others are unknown to me even by name. It is I who should sit at your feet and learn. No, my lord, there is nothing I can teach you."

He was smiling, and the prince returned his affectionate glance.

Upon leaving Vishvamitra, the prince went into the country and started walking toward a village.

On the way, he stopped to watch some peasants working in the fields, then he entered a meadow where stood a clump of trees. They attracted him, for it was noon and very hot. The prince went and sat down in the shade of a tree; there, he began to ponder, and he was soon lost in meditation.

Five itinerant hermits passed near the meadow. They saw the prince meditating, and they wondered:

"Is he a God, he who is seated there, resting? Could he be the God of riches, or the God of love?

Could he be Indra, bearer of thunder, or the shepherd Krishna?"

But they heard a voice saying to them:

"The splendour of the Gods would pale before the splendour of this Sakya who sits under the tree and ponders majestic truths!"

Whereupon they all exclaimed:

"Verily, he who sits and meditates under the tree bears the marks of omnipotence; he will doubtless become the Buddha!"

Then they sang his praises, and the first one said: "To a world consumed by an evil fire, he has come like a lake. His law will refresh the world."

The second one said: "To a world darkened by ignorance, he has come like a torch. His law will bring light into the world."

The third one said: "Over the sea of suffering, that sea so difficult to sail, he has come like a ship. His law will bring the world safely into harbour."

The fourth one said: "To those bound in chains of evil, he has come like a redeemer. His law will set the world free."

The fifth one said: "To those tormented by old age and sickness, he has come like a saviour. His law will bring deliverance from birth and death."

Three times they bowed, then continued on their way.

In the meanwhile, King Suddhodana wondered what had become of the prince, and he sent many servants out to search for him. One of them found him absorbed in meditation. The servant drew near, then suddenly stopped, overcome with admiration. For the shadows of all the trees had lengthened, except of that tree under which the prince was seated. Its shadow had not moved; it still sheltered him.

The servant ran back to the palace of the king.

"My lord," he cried, "I have seen your son; he is meditating under a tree whose shadow has not moved, whereas the shadows of all the other trees have moved and lengthened."

Suddhodana left the palace and followed the servant to where his son was seated. Weeping for joy, he said to himself:

"He is as beautiful as fire on a mountain-top. He dazzles me. He will be the light of the world, and my limbs tremble when I see him thus in meditation."

The king and his servant dared neither move nor speak. But some children passed by, drawing a little chariot after them. They were making a noise. The servant said to them, in a whisper:

"You must not make a noise."

"Why?" asked the children.

"See him who meditates under the tree? That is Prince Siddhartha. The shadow of the tree has not left him. Do not disturb him, children; do you not see that he has the brilliance of the sun?"

But the prince awoke from his meditations. He rose and approaching his father, he said to him:

"We must stop working in the fields, father; we must seek the great truths."

And he returned to Kapilavastu.

SIDDHARTHA IS EAGER TO KNOW THE GREAT TRUTHS

Siddhartha could no longer find peace. He strode through the halls of his palace like a lion stung by some poisoned dart.

He was unhappy. One day, there came to him a great longing for the open fields and the sight of green meadows. He left the palace, and as he strolled aimlessly through the country, he mused:

> *"It is indeed a pity that man, weak as he really is, and subject to sickness, with old age a certainty and death for a master, should, in his ignorance and pride, contemn the sick, the aged and the dead. If I should look with disgust upon some fellow-being who was sick or old or dead, I would be unjust, I would not be worthy of understanding the supreme law."*

And as he pondered the misery of mankind, he lost the vain illusion of strength, of youth and of life. He knew no longer joy or grief, doubt or weariness, desire or love, hatred or scorn.

Suddenly, he saw a man approaching who looked like a beggar and who was visible to him alone.

"Tell me, who are you?" the prince asked him.

"Hero," said the monk, "through fear of birth and death, I became an itinerant monk. I seek deliverance. The world is at the mercy of destruction. I think not as other men; I shun pleasures; I know nothing of passion; I look for solitude. Sometimes I live at the foot of a tree; sometimes I live in the lonely mountains or sometimes in the forest. I own nothing; I expect nothing. I wander about, living on charity, and seeking only the highest good."

He spoke. Then he ascended into the sky and disappeared. A God had taken the form of a monk in order to arouse the prince.

Siddhartha was happy. He saw where his duty lay; he decided to leave the palace and become a monk.

He returned to the city. Near the gates he passed a young woman who bowed and said to him, "She who is your bride must know supreme blessedness, O noble prince." He heard her voice, and his soul was filled with peace: the thought had come to him of supreme blessedness, of beatitude, of nirvana.

He went to the king; he bowed and said to him:

"King, grant the request I have to make. Do not oppose it, for I am determined. I would leave the palace, I would walk in the path of deliverance. We must part, father."

The king was deeply moved. With tears in his voice, he said to his son:

"Son, give up this idea. You're still too young to consider a religious calling. Our thoughts in the springtime of life are wayward and changeable. Besides, it is a grave mistake to perform austere practises in our youth. Our senses are eager for new pleasures; our firmest resolutions are forgotten when we learn the cost in effort. The body wanders in the forest of desire, only our thoughts escape. Youth lacks experience. It is for me, rather, to embrace religion. The time has come for me to leave the palace. I abdicate, O my son. Reign in my stead. Be strong and courageous; your family needs you. And first know the joys of youth, then those of later years, before you betake yourself to the woods and become a hermit."

The prince answered:

"Promise me four things, O father, and I shall not leave your house and repair to the woods."

"What are they?" asked the king.

"Promise me that my life will not end in death, that sickness will not impair my health, that age will not follow my youth, that misfortune will not destroy my prosperity."

"You are asking too much," replied the king. "Give up this idea. It is not well to act on a foolish impulse."

Solemn as Meru mountain, the prince said to his father:

"If you can not promise me these four things, do not hold me back, O father. When some one is trying to escape from a burning house, we should not hinder him. The day comes, inevitably, when we must leave this world, but what merits is there in a forced separation? A voluntary separation is far better. Death would carry me out of the world before I had reached my goal, before I had satisfied my ardour. The world is a prison: would that I could free those beings who are prisoners of desire!

The world is a deep pit wherein wander the ignorant and the blind: would that I could light the lamp of knowledge, would that I could remove the film that hides the light of wisdom! The world has raised the wrong banner, it has raised the banner of pride: would that I could pull it down, would that I could tear to pieces the banner of pride! The world is troubled, the world is in a turmoil, the world is a wheel of fire: would that I could, with the true law, bring peace to all men!"

With tears in his eyes, he returned to the palace. In the great hall Gopa's companions were laughing and singing. He paid no heed to them. Night came on, and they were silent.

They fell asleep. The prince looked at them.

Gone was their studied grace, gone the sparkle of their eyes. Their hair was dishevelled, their mouths gaped, their breasts were crushed, and their arms and legs were stiffly outstretched or clumsily twisted under them. And the prince cried:

"Dead! They are dead! I am standing in a graveyard!"

And he left, and made his way toward the royal stables.

SIDDHARTHA AT THE TEMPLE

They pleased Suddhodana at first, these words of Asita's, and he pondered them. "So my son will live, and live gloriously," he thought, but then he became anxious. For it had been said that the prince would renounce royalty; that he would lead the life of a hermit, and did that not mean that at his death Suddhodana's family would cease?

But his anxiety was short-lived, for since the birth of Siddhartha the king could undertake nothing that did not prosper. Like a great river whose waters are swollen by many tributaries, each day new riches poured into his treasury; the stables were too small to hold the horses and elephants that were presented to him, and he was constantly surrounded by a host of loyal friends. The kingdom was rich in fertile lands, and sleek, fatted cattle grazed in the meadows. Women bore their children without suffering; men lived at peace with their neighbours, and happiness and tranquillity reigned in the land of Kapilavastu.

But the joy that had come to Maya proved too sweet. It soon became unbearable. The earth knew her as a mother but seven days; then she died and ascended to the sky, to be received among the Gods.

Maya had a sister, Mahaprajapati, who in beauty and virtue was almost her equal. The prince was given into Mahaprajapati's care, and she looked after his wants as tenderly as if he were her own child. And like fire fanned by an auspicious wind, like the moon, queen of the stars in the luminous skies, like the morning sun rising over the mountains in the East, Siddhartha grew in strength and stature.

Everyone now delighted in bringing him precious gifts. They gave him toys that would amuse a child of his age: tiny animals, deer and elephants, horses, cows, birds and fish, and little chariots; and they were toys made not of wood or of clay but of gold and of precious stones. And they brought him costly materials and rare gems, pearl necklaces and jewelled bracelets.

One day, while he was playing in a garden not far from the city, Mahaprajapati thought, "It is time I taught him to wear necklaces and bracelets," and she ordered the servants to bring the jewels that had been given to him. She clasped them around his arms and his neck, but it was as if he wore none at all. The gold and the precious stones seemed dull and lifeless, so brilliant was the light he diffused. And the Goddess who lived among the flowers of that garden came to Mahaprajapati and said:

> *"If the earth were made of gold, a single ray of light emanating from this child, the world's future guide, would be enough to dull its splendour. The light of the stars and the light of the moon, yes, even the light of the sun, are dimmed by his refulgence. And would you have him wear jewels, baubles crudely fashioned by jewellers and goldsmiths? Woman, remove those necklaces, take off those bracelets. They are only fit to be worn by slaves; give them to the slaves. This child will have his thoughts; they are gems of a purer water."*

Mahaprajapati gave heed to the words of the Goddess. She unclasped the bracelets and the necklaces, and she never wearied of admiring the prince.

The time came to take Siddhartha to the temple of the Gods. By the king's command, the streets of the city and the public squares were superbly decorated; drums were sounded and bells joyously rung. While Mahaprajapati was dressing him in his richest apparel, the child asked:

"Mother, where are you taking me?"

"To the temple of the Gods, my son," she replied. The child smiled and quietly went with her to meet his father.

It was a magnificent sight. In the procession were Brahmans from the city, warriors and all the chief merchants. A host of guards followed, and the Sakyas surrounded the chariot that bore the prince and the king. In the streets the air was heavy with incense, flowers were strewn in their path, and the people waved flags and streamers as they passed.

They arrived at the temple. The king took Siddhartha by the hand and led him to the hall where stood the statues of the Gods. As the child stepped across the threshold the statues came to life, and all the Gods, Shiva, Skanda, Vishnu, Kuvera, Indra, Brahma, descended from their pedestals and fell at his feet. And they sang:

> *"Meru, king of the mountains, does not bow before a grain of wheat; the Ocean does not bow before a pool of rainwater; the Sun does not bow before a glowworm; he who will have the true knowledge does not bow before the Gods. Like the grain of wheat, like the pool of rainwater, like the glowworm is the man or the God with stubborn pride; like Meru mountain, like the Ocean, like the Sun is he who will have supreme knowledge. Let the world pay him homage, and the world will be set free!"*

3

Siddhartha Leads a Life of Pleasure

Prince Siddhartha lived happily with his wife, the princess. And the king, whose love for his son now verged on adoration, took infinite care to spare him the sight of anything that might distress him. He built three magnificent palaces for him: one for the winter, one for the summer, and the third for the rainy season; and these he was forbidden ever to leave, to wander over the broad face of the earth.

In his palaces, white as autumn clouds and bright as the celestial chariots of the Gods and Goddesses, the prince drained the cup of pleasure. He led a life of voluptuous ease; he spent languid hours listening to music played by the princess and her maidens, and when beautiful, smiling dancers appeared before him and performed to the sound of golden kettle-drums, with delight he watched them as they swayed with a grace and loveliness rare even among the happy Apsarases.

Women cast furtive glances at him: their eyes boldly offered or archly pleaded, and their drooping lashes were a promise of ineffable delight. Their games amused him, their charms held him in thrall, and he was content to remain in these palaces so full of their laughter and song. For he knew nothing of old age and sickness; he knew nothing of death.

Suddhodana rejoiced at the life his son was leading, though his own conduct he judged with the utmost severity. He strove to keep his soul serene and pure; he refrained from doing evil, and he lavished gifts on those who were virtuous. He never yielded to indolence or pleasure; he was never burned by the poison of avarice. As wild horses are made to bear the yoke, even so did he subdue his passions, and in virtue he surpassed his kinsmen and his friends. The knowledge he acquired he placed at the service of his fellow-men, and he only studied those subjects that were useful to all. He not only sought the welfare of his own people but he also wanted the whole world to be happy. He purified his body with the water from the sacred ponds, and he purified his soul with the holy water of virtue. He never uttered a word that was pleasant and yet a lie; the truths he spoke never gave offense or pain. He tried to be just, and it was by honesty, not by force, that he defeated the pride of his enemies. He did not strike, he did not even look with anger upon those who deserved the penalty of death; instead, he gave them useful advice, and then their freedom. The king was an example to all his subjects, and Kapilavastu was the happiest and most virtuous of kingdoms.

Then beautiful Gopa bore the prince a son, and he was given the name of Rahula. King Suddhodana was happy to see his family prosper, and he was as proud of the birth of his grandson as he had been of the birth of his son.

He continued in the path of virtue, he lived almost like a hermit, and his actions were saintly; yet he kept urging on his beloved son to new pleasures, so great was his fear to see him leave the palace and the city and seek the austere refuge of the holy forests.

The Three Encounters

One day, some one spoke in the presence of the prince and told how the grass in the woods had become a tender green and the birds in the trees were singing of the spring, and how, in the ponds, the great lotuses were unfolding. Nature had broken the chains that winter had forged, and, around the city, those gardens so dear to young maidens were now gaily carpeted with flowers. Then, like an elephant too long confined in his stable, the prince had an irresistible desire to leave the palace. The king learned of his son's desire, and he knew no way to oppose it.

"But," he thought, "Siddhartha must see nothing that will trouble the serenity of his soul; he must never suspect the evil there is in the world. I shall order the road cleared of beggars, of those who are sick and infirm and of all who suffer."

The city was decorated with garlands and streamers; a magnificent chariot was prepared, and the cripples, the aged and the beggars were ordered off the streets where the prince would pass.

When the time came, the king sent for his son, and there were tears in his eyes as he kissed him on the brow. His gaze lingered over him, then he said to him, "Go!" And with that word he gave him permission to leave the palace, though his heart spoke differently.

The prince's chariot was made of gold. It was drawn by four horses caparisoned in gold, and the charioteer held gold reins in his hands. Only the rich, the young and the beautiful were allowed on the streets he drove through, and they stopped to watch him as he went by. Some praised him for the kindness of his glance; others extolled his dignified bearing; still others exalted the beauty of his features; while many glorified his exuberant strength. And they all bowed before him, like banners dipped before the statue of some God. The women in the houses heard the cries in the street. They awoke or left their household tasks and ran to the windows or quickly ascended to the terraces. And gazing at him in admiration, they murmured, "Happy the wife of such a man!"

And he, at the sight of the city's splendour, at the sight of the wealth of the men and the beauty of the women, felt a new joy pour into his soul.

But the Gods were jealous of the celestial felicity enjoyed by this city of the earth. They made an old man, and, in order to trouble Siddhartha's mind, they set him down on the road the prince was travelling.

The man was leaning on a staff; he was worn out and decrepit. His veins stood out on his body, his teeth chattered, and his skin was a maze of black wrinkles. A few dirty grey hairs hung from his scalp; his eyelids had no lashes and were red-rimmed; his head and limbs were palsied.

The prince saw this being, so different from the men around him. He gazed at him with sorrowful eyes, and he asked the charioteer:

"What is this man with grey hair and body so bent? He clings to his staff with scrawny hands, his eyes are dull and his limbs falter. Is he a monster? Has nature made him thus, or is it chance?"

The charioteer should not have answered, but the Gods confused his mind, and without understanding his mistake he said:

"That which mars beauty, which ruins vigour, which causes sorrow and kills pleasure, that which weakens the memory and destroys the senses is old age. It has seized this man and broken him. He, too, was once a child, nursing at his mother's breast; he, too, once crawled upon the floor; he grew, he was young, he had strength and beauty; then he reached the twilight of his years, and now you see him, the ruin that is old age." The prince was deeply moved. He asked:

"Will that be my fate, also?"

The charioteer replied:

"My lord, youth will also leave you some day; to you, too, will come troublesome old age. Time saps our strength and steals our beauty."

The prince shuddered like a bull at the sound of thunder. He uttered a deep sigh and shook his head. His eyes wandered from the wretched man to the happy crowds, and he spoke these solemn words:

"So old age destroys memory and beauty and strength in man, and yet the world is not frantic with terror! Turn your horses around, O charioteer; let us return to our homes. How can I

delight in gardens and flowers when my eyes can only see old age, when my mind can only think of old age?"

The prince returned to his palace, but nowhere could he find peace. He wandered through the halls, murmuring, "Old age, oh, old age!" and in his heart there was no longer any joy.

He decided, nevertheless, to ride once more through the city. But the Gods made a man afflicted with a loathsome disease, and they set him down on the road Siddhartha had taken. Siddhartha saw the sick man; he stared at him, and he asked the charioteer:

"What is this man with a swollen paunch? His emaciated arms hang limp, he is deathly pale and pitiful cries escape from his lips. He gasps for breath; see, he staggers and jostles the bystanders; he is falling.... Charioteer, charioteer, what is this man?"

The charioteer answered:

"My lord, this man knows the torment of sickness, for he has the king's evil. He is weakness itself; yet he, too, was once healthy and strong!"

The prince looked at the man with pity, and he asked again:

"Is this affliction peculiar to this man, or are all creatures threatened with sickness?"

The charioteer answered:

"We, too, may be visited with a similar affliction, O prince. Sickness weighs heavily upon the world."

When he heard this painful truth, the prince began to tremble like a moonbeam reflected in the waves of the sea, and he uttered these words of bitterness and pity:

"Men see suffering and sickness, yet they never lose their self-confidence! Oh, how great must be their knowledge! They are constantly threatened with sickness, and they can still laugh and be merry! Turn your horses around, charioteer; our pleasure trip is ended; let us return to the palace. I have learned to fear sickness. My soul shuns pleasure and seems to close up like a flower deprived of light."

Wrapped in his painful thoughts, he returned to the palace. King Suddhodana noticed his son's sombre mood. He asked why the prince no longer went out driving, and the charioteer told him what had happened.

The king grieved; he already saw himself forsaken by the child he adored. He lost his usual composure and flew into a rage at the man whose duty it was to see that the streets were clear; he punished him, but so strong was his habit of being indulgent that the punishment was light. And the man was astonished at being thus upbraided, for he had seen neither the old man nor the sick man.

The king was more anxious now than ever before to keep his son from leaving the palace. He provided him with rare pleasures, but nothing, it seemed, could arouse Siddhartha. And the king thought, "I shall let him go out once more! Perhaps he will recover the joy he has lost." He gave strict orders to have all cripples and all who were ill or aged driven out of the city. He even changed the prince's charioteer, and he felt certain that this time there would be nothing to trouble Siddhartha's soul.

But the jealous Gods made a corpse. Four men carried it, and others followed behind, weeping. And the corpse, as well as the men who carried it and the men who were weeping, was visible only to the prince and to the charioteer.

And the king's son asked:

"What is he that is being carried by four men, followed by those others, wearing dark clothes and weeping?"

The charioteer should have held his peace, but it was the will of the Gods that he reply:

"My lord, he has neither intelligence nor feeling nor breath; he sleeps, without consciousness, like grass or a piece of wood; pleasure and suffering are meaningless to him now, and friend and enemy alike have deserted him."

The prince was troubled. He said, "Is this a condition peculiar to this man, or does this same end await all creatures?"

And the charioteer answered: "This same end awaits all creatures. Whether of humble or of noble birth, to every being who lives in this world, death comes inevitably."

Then Prince Siddhartha knew what death was.

In spite of his fortitude, he shuddered. He had to lean against the chariot, and his words were full of distress:

> *"So to this does destiny lead all creatures! And yet, without fear in his heart, man amuses himself in a thousand different ways! Death is about, and he takes to the world's highroads with a song on his lips! Oh, I begin to think that man's soul has become hardened! Turn your horses around, charioteer; this is no time to wander through the flower-gardens. How can a sensible man, a man who knows what death is, seek pleasure in the hour of anguish?"*

But the charioteer kept on driving toward the garden where the king had ordered him to take his son. There, at Suddhodana's command, Udayin, who was a son of the household priest and Siddhartha's friend since childhood, had assembled many beautiful maidens, skilled in the art of dancing and of song, and skilful also in the game of love.

Gopa's Dream

The cariot entered the wood. The young trees were in bloom, birds fluttered about joyously as though intoxicated by the light and atmosphere, and on the surface of the pools the lotuses had cupped their petals to drink in the cool air.

Siddhartha went unwillingly, like a young hermit, still new to his vows, who fears temptation and is taken to some celestial palace where lovely Apsarases are wont to dance. Filled with curiosity, the maidens rose and came forward as though to greet a betrothed. Their eyes were bright with admiration, and the hands they extended were like flowers. They all thought, "This is Kama himself come back to earth." But they did not speak nor even smile, so timid were they in his presence.

Udayin called to the boldest and the most beautiful, and he said to them:

"Why do you fail me today, you whom I have chosen from among many to captivate the prince, my friend? What makes you behave like shy, silent children? Your charm, your beauty, your boldness would win even a woman's heart, and you tremble before a man! You mortify me. Come, wake up! Use your charms! Make him yield to love!" One of the maidens spoke up:

"He frightens us, O master; his majestic splendour frightens us."

"Great as it is," replied Udayin, "it should not frighten you. For strange is the power of women. Let him remind you of all those who, in the past, have been at the mercy of a tender glance. Once upon a time the great hermit Vyasa, whom even the Gods were afraid to offend, was kicked by a courtesan called the Belle of Benares, and he was not displeased. The monk Manthalagotama, who was famous for his long penances, became an undertaker's assistant, in order to win the favour of the wanton Jangha, a woman of the very lowest caste. Santa artfully managed to seduce Rishyasringa, a learned man who had never known woman; and that most pious of all men, glorious Vishvamitra, one day, in the forest, yielded to the importunities of the Apsaras Ghritaki. And I could name many more who succumbed to women like you, O lovely maidens! Come, do not be afraid of the king's son. Smile at him, and he will fall in love with you."

Udayin's words encouraged the maidens. Smiling, and with exquisite grace, they gradually formed a ring around the prince. They used the most engaging wiles in order to approach Siddhartha, in order to brush past him or hold him and steal a caress. One pretended to stumble and clung to his girdle. Another drew near and mysteriously whispered in his ear, "Deign to hear my secret, O prince." Another feigned intoxication; she slowly unwound the blue veil that bound her breasts, then came and leaned against his shoulder. Another jumped down from the branch of a mango-tree and laughingly tried to stop him as he passed. Still another offered him a lotus-flower. And one sang: "Look, dear love, this tree is covered with blossoms, with blossoms whose perfume cloys the air; in the branches, rare birds trill their happy songs, as though in a golden cage. Listen to the bees, hovering over the flowers; they are roused and consumed by a burning ardour. Look at those creepers, warmly embracing the tree; the breeze ruffles them with a jealous hand. Over there, in that lovely glade, do you see the silver pool asleep? It is smiling, drowsily, like a maiden caressed by a bold moonbeam."

But the prince was not smiling; he was unhappy, for he was thinking on death.

He thought, "They do not know these maidens, that youth is fleeting, and that old age will come and strip them of their beauty! They are blind to the menace that is sickness, though it is already master of the world! They know nothing of death, of imperious death, of death that destroys everything! And that is why they can laugh, that is why they can play!"

Udayin tried to interrupt Siddhartha's thoughts.

He said, "Why are you so discourteous to these maidens? Perhaps they do not interest you? What matter! Be kind to them, even at the cost of a few lies. Spare them the shame of being spurned. How can your beauty profit you if you are ungracious? You will be like a forest without flowers."

"What good are lies, what good is flattery?" replied the prince. "I would not deceive these women. Old age and death lie in wait for me. Do not try to tempt me, Udayin; do not ask me to join in any vulgar amusement. I have seen old age, I have seen sickness, I am certain of death; nothing now can give me peace of mind. And you would have me yield to love? Of what metal is that man made who knows of death and still seeks love? A cruel, implacable guard stands at his door, and he does not even weep!"

The sun was setting. The maidens had ceased their laughter; the prince had no eyes for their garlands and their jewels. They felt their charms were of no avail, and slowly they took the road back to the city. The prince returned to the palace. King Suddhodana heard from Udayin that his son was shunning all pleasure, and that night he found no sleep.

Gopa was waiting for the prince. He avoided her. It made her anxious, and when she finally fell asleep, she had a dream:

> *The whole earth shook; the tallest mountains swayed; a savage wind blew, shattering and uprooting the trees. The sun, the moon and the stars had fallen from the sky to the earth. She, Gopa, was stripped of her clothes and of her ornaments; she it had lost her crown; she was naked. Her hair was cut. The bridal bed was broken; the prince's robes and the precious stones with which they were embroidered were scattered about. Meteors sped across the sky over a darkened city, and Meru, king of the mountains, trembled.*

Overcome with terror, Gopa awoke. She ran to her husband.

"My lord, my lord," she cried, "what will happen? I have had a terrible dream! My eyes are full of tears, and my heart is full of fear."

"Tell me your dream," the prince replied.

Gopa related all that she had seen in her sleep. The prince smiled.

"Rejoice, Gopa," said he, "rejoice. You saw the earth shake? Then one day the Gods themselves shall bow before you. You saw the moon and the sun fall from the sky? Then you shall soon defeat evil, and you shall receive infinite praise. You saw the trees uprooted? Then you shall find a way out of the forest of desire. Your hair was cut short? Then you shall free yourself from the net of passions that holds you captive. My robes and my jewels were scattered about? Then I am on the road to deliverance. Meteors were speeding across the sky over a darkened city? Then to the ignorant world, to the world that is blind, I shall bring the light of wisdom, and those who have faith in my words will know joy and felicity. Be happy, O Gopa, drive away your melancholy; you will soon be singularly honoured. Sleep, Gopa, sleep; you have dreamed a lovely dream."

Siddhartha Leaves His Father's Palace

He called his equerry, fleet Chandaka. "Bring me my horse Kanthaka, at once," said he. "I would be off, to find eternal beatitude. The deep joy I feel, the indomitable strength that now sustains my will, the assurance that I have a protector even though I am alone, all these things tell me that I am about to attain my goal. The hour has come; I am on the road to deliverance."

Chandaka knew the king's orders, but he felt some superior power urging him to disobey. He went to fetch the horse.

Kanthaka was a magnificent animal; he was strong and supple. Siddhartha stroked him quietly, then said to him in a gentle voice:

> *"Many times, O noble beast, my father rode you into battle and defeated his powerful enemies. Today, I go forth to seek supreme beatitude; lend me your help, O Kanthaka! Companions in arms or in pleasure are not hard to find, and we never want for friends when we set out to acquire wealth; but companions and friends desert us when it is the path of holiness we would take. Yet of this am I certain: he who helps another to do good or to do evil shares in that good or in that evil. Know then, O Kanthaka, that it is a virtuous impulse that moves me. Lend me your strength and your speed; the world's salvation and your own is at stake."*

The prince had spoken to Kanthaka as he would have to a friend. He now eagerly climbed into the saddle, and he looked like the sun astride an autumn cloud.

The horse was careful to make no noise, for the night was clear. No one in the palace or in Kapilavastu was awakened. Heavy iron bars protected the gates of the city, an elephant could have raised them only with great difficulty, but, to allow the prince to pass, the gates opened silently, of their own accord.

Leaving his father, his son and his people, Siddhartha went forth from the city. He felt no regret, and in a steady voice, he cried: "Until I shall have seen the end of life and of death, I shall not return to the city of Kapila."

Siddhartha the Hermit

Kanthaka bravely carried him a great distance. When the

sun finally peered between the eyelids of night, the most noble of men saw that he was near a wood where dwelt many pious hermits. Deer were asleep under the trees, and birds fluttered about fearlessly. Siddhartha felt rested, and he thought he need go no further. He dismounted and gently stroked his horse. There was happiness in his glance and in his voice as he said to Chandaka:

> *"Truly, a horse has the strength and swiftness of a God. And you, dear friend, by bearing me company, have proved to me how great is your affection and your courage. It was a noble deed and pleases me. Those who, like yourself, can combine energy and devotion are indeed rare. You have shown that you are my friend, and you expect no reward from me! Yet it is usually a selfish interest that brings men together. I assure you, you have made me very happy. Take the horse now and return to the city. I have found the forest I was seeking."*

The hero took off his jewels and handed them to Chandaka.

"Take this necklace," said he, "and go to my father. Tell him to believe in me and not give way to his grief. If I enter a hermitage, it is not because I am wanting in affection for my friends or because my enemies provoke my anger; nor is it because I seek a place among the Gods. Mine is a worthier reason: I will destroy old age and death. Therefore, do not grieve, Chanda, and do not let my father be unhappy. I left my home to be rid of unhappiness. Unhappiness is born of desire; that man is to be pitied who is a slave to his passions. When a man dies, there are always heirs to his fortune, but heirs to his virtues are rarely found, are never found. If my father says to you, 'He left for the forest before the appointed time,' you will answer that life is so uncertain that the practise of virtue is never untimely. Say this to the king, O my friend, and do your best to make him forget me. Tell him that I possess neither virtue nor merit; for a man without virtue is never loved, and he who is never loved is never mourned."

With tears in his eyes, Chandaka replied:

> *"Oh, how they will weep, those who love you! You are young, you are beautiful, the palace of the Gods should be your home;*

yet you would live in the woods and sleep on the coarse grass? I knew of your cruel resolve; I should not have gone to fetch Kanthaka; but a supernatural power urged me, deceived me, and I brought him to you. How could I have done such a thing of my own will? Sorrow will now find its way into Kapilavastu. O prince, your father loves you dearly, do not forsake him! And Mahaprajapati? What has she not done for you! She is your foster-mother; do not be ungrateful! And is there not still another woman who loves you? Do not abandon faithful Gopa! Raise your son with her help, and one day he will bring you glory!"

He wept bitterly. The hero was silent. Chanda continued:

"You are going to leave your family for ever! Oh, if you must cause them grief, spare me, at least, the anguish of imparting the sad news! What would the king say to me if he saw me return without you? What would your mother say to me? What would Gopa say? And when I appear before your father, you ask me to deny your merit and your virtue! How can I do that, my lord? I can not lie. And even if I should decide to lie, who would believe me? Who can be made to believe that the moon has fiery beams?"

He seized the hero's hand.

"Do not forsake us! Come back, oh, come back!"

Siddhartha still remained silent. Finally, he said in a solemn voice:

"We must part, Chanda. There comes a time when people who are bound by the closest ties must go their own ways. If, out of love for my family, I were not to leave, death would still separate us, in spite of everything. What am I now to my mother? What is she to me? Birds that sleep in the same tree at night scatter to the four winds at the first flush of dawn; clouds that some puff of wind has brought together by another puff of wind are again dispersed. I can no longer live in a world that is but a dream. We must part, my friend. Tell the people of Kapilavastu that I have done nothing worthy of blame, tell them to forget their affection for me; and tell them also that they will see me again, soon, the conquerer of old age and death, unless I should fail miserably and die."

Kanthaka was licking his feet. The hero gently stroked his horse and spoke to him as though to a friend:

"Do not weep. You have shown that you are a noble animal. Be patient. The time is near when your toil will be rewarded."

Then he took a sword that Chandaka was holding. The hilt was of gold and was studded with jewels; the blade was sharp. With one blow he cut off his hair, then tossed the sword into the air where it glistened like a new star. The Gods caught it and held it in great reverence.

But the hero was still wearing his gorgeous robe. He wanted a plain one, one suitable to a hermit. Whereupon a hunter appeared, wearing a coarse garment made of a reddish material. Siddhartha said to him:

"Your peaceful robe is like those worn by hermits; it offers a strange contrast to your savage bow. Give me your clothes and take mine in exchange. They will suit you better."

"Thanks to these clothes," said the hunter, "I can deceive the beasts in the forests. They do not fear me, and I can kill them at close range. But if you have need of them, my lord, I shall willingly give them to you and take yours in exchange.

Siddhartha joyfully donned the coarse, reddish-coloured clothes belonging to the hunter, and the hunter reverently accepted the hero's robe, then he disappeared into the sky. Siddhartha realized that the Gods themselves had wished to present him with his hermit's robe, and he rejoiced. Chandaka was filled with wonder.

Arrayed in his reddish-coloured robes, the saintly hero set out on the path to the hermitage. He was like the king of the mountains wrapped in clouds at dusk. And Chandaka, with a heavy heart, took the road back to Kapilavastu.

Gopa and Suddhodana Grieve

Gopa had awakened in the deep of night. A strange uneasiness possessed her. She called to her beloved, Prince

Siddhartha, but there was no answer. She rose. She ran through the halls of the palace; he was nowhere to be found. She became frightened. Her maidens were asleep. A cry escaped her lips:

"Oh, wicked, wicked! You have betrayed me! You have allowed my beloved to escape!"

The maidens awoke. They searched every room. There was no longer any doubt: the prince had left the palace. Gopa rolled on the ground; she tore her hair, and her face bore the marks of her deep despair.

"He once told me that he would go away, far away, he, the king of men! But I never thought the cruel parting would come so soon. Oh, where are you, my well-beloved? Where are you? I can not forget you, I, who am forlorn, so forlorn! Where are you? Where are you? You are so beautiful! Your beauty is unrivalled among men. Your eyes sparkle. You are good, and you are beloved, my well-beloved! Were you not happy? Oh, my dear, my beloved, where have you gone?"

Her companions tried in vain to console her.

"Hereafter, I will drink only to quench my thirst, I will eat only to still my hunger. I will sleep on the bare ground, for crown I will wear a hermit's braid, no more sweet-scented baths will I take, I will mortify my flesh. The gardens are bare of flowers and of fruit; the faded garlands are heavy with dust. The palace is deserted. No longer will it ring with the happy songs of yesterday."

Mahaprajapati learned from one of her maidens of Siddhartha's flight. She went to Gopa. The two women wept in each other's arms.

King Suddhodana heard the lamentation. He asked the reason. A servant went to inquire and returned with this answer:

"My lord, the prince can not be found anywhere in the palace."

"Close the gates of the city," cried the king, "and search for my son in the streets, in the gardens, in the houses."

He was obeyed, but the prince was nowhere to be found. The king broke down.

"My son, my only child!" he sobbed, and fell into a swoon. He was soon brought to, and he ordered:

"That horsemen be dispatched in all directions, and that they bring me back my son!"

In the meanwhile, Chandaka and the horse Kanthaka were slowly returning from the hermitage. As they approached the city, they both hung their heads in dejection. Some horsemen espied them.

"It is Chandaka! It is Kanthaka!" they cried, and they galloped their horses. They saw that Chandaka was carrying the prince's jewels. They asked, anxiously:

"Was the prince murdered?"

"No, no," Chandaka quickly replied. "He entrusted me with his jewels that I might return them to his family. He has donned a hermit's robe, and he has entered a forest where dwell some holy men."

"Do you think," said the horsemen, "that if we went to him, we could persuade him to return with us?"

"Your words would be futile. He is obdurate. He said, 'I shall not return to Kapilavastu until I have conquered old age and death.' And what he has said, he will do."

Chandaka followed the horsemen to the palace. The king summoned him at once.

"My son! My son! Where has he gone, Chandaka?"

The equerry told him what the prince had done. The king grieved, yet he could not help admiring his son's greatness.

Gopa and Mahaprajapati entered; they had heard of Chandaka's return. They questioned him, and they learned of Siddhartha's high resolve.

"O you who were my joy," said Gopa through her tears, "you whose voice was so sweet, you who had such strength and such grace, such knowledge and such virtue! When you spoke to me, I thought I was listening to some lovely song, and when I leaned over you, I inhaled the perfume of all the flowers.

Now I am far away from you, and I weep. What shall become of me, now, for he is gone, he who was my guide? I shall know poverty, for I have lost my treasure. He was my eyes; I can no longer see the light; I am blind. Oh, when will he return, he who was my joy?"

Mahaprajapati saw the jewels Chandaka had brought back with him. She stood looking at them a great while. She was weeping. Then, taking the jewels, she left the palace.

Still weeping, she walked through the garden until she carne to a pool. Once again, she looked at the jewels, then threw them into the water.

Kanthaka had returned to the stables. The other horses were happy at his return and neighed in a friendly manner. But he did not hear them; he did not see them. He was very sad. He whinnied pitifully once or twice, and, suddenly, fell dead.

THE BUDDHA ANNOUNCES HIS DEATH

Said the Tathagata to Ananda: "In former years, Ananda, Mara, the Evil One, approached the holy Buddha three times to tempt him. And now, Ananda, Mara, the Evil One, came again today to the place where I was, and, standing beside me, addressed me in the same words as he did when I was resting under the shepherd's Nigrodha tree on the bank of the Neranjara River: 'Be greeted, thou Holy One. Thou has attained the highest bliss and it is time for thee to enter into the final Nirvana.'- And when Mara had thus spoken, Ananda, I answered him and said: 'Make thyself happy, O wicked one; the final extinction of the Tathagata shall take place before long."

The venerable Ananda addressed the Blessed One and said: "Vouchsafe, Lord, to remain with us, O Blessed One I for the good and the happiness of the great multitudes, out of pity for the world, for the good and the gain of mankind!" Said the Blessed One: "Enough now, Ananda, beseech not the Tathagata!"

And again, a second time, the venerable Ananda besought the Blessed One in the same words. He received from the

Blessed One the same reply. And again, the third time, the venerable Ananda besought the Blessed One to live longer; and the Blessed One said: "Has thou faith, Ananda?" Said Ananda: "I have, my Lord!"

The Blessed One, seeing the quivering eyelids of Ananda, read the deep grief in the heart of his beloved disciple, and he asked again: "Has thou, indeed, faith, Ananda?" And Ananda said: "I have faith, my Lord."

Then the Blessed One continued: "If thou has faith, Ananda in the wisdom of the Tathagata, why, then, Ananda, does thou trouble the Tathagata even until the third time? Have I not formerly declared to you that it is in the very nature of all compound things that they must be dissolved again? We must separate ourselves from all things near and dear to us, and must leave them. How then, Ananda, can it be possible for me to remain, since everything that is born, or brought into being, and organized, contains within itself the inherent necessity of dissolution? How, then, can it be possible that this body of mine should not be dissolved? No such condition can exist! And this mortal existence, O Ananda, has been relinquished, cast away, renounced, rejected, and abandoned by the Tathagata."

And the Blessed One said to Ananda: "Go now, Ananda, and assemble in the Service Hall such of the brethren as reside in the neighbourhood of Vesali."

Then the Blessed One proceeded to the Service Hall, and sat down there on the mat spread out for him. And when he was seated, the Blessed One addressed the brethren, and said: "O brethren, ye to whom the truth has been made known, having thoroughly made yourselves masters of it, practice it, meditate upon it, and spread it abroad, in order that pure religion may last long and be perpetuated, in order that it may continue for the good and happiness of the great multitudes, out of pity for the world, and to the good and gain of all living beings! Star-gazing and astrology, forecasting lucky or unfortunate events by signs, prognosticating good or evil, all these are things forbidden. He who lets his heart go loose without restraint shall not attain Nirvana; therefore, must we hold the heart in check, and retire from worldly excitements and seek tranquility of mind. Eat your food to satisfy your hunger, and drink to satisfy your thirst. Satisfy the necessities of life like the butterfly that sips the flower, without destroying its fragrance or its texture.

It is through not understanding and grasping the four truths, O brethren, that we have gone astray so long and wandered in this weary path of transmigrations, both you and I, until we have found the truth. Practice the earnest meditations I have taught you. Continue in the great struggle against sin. Walk steadily in the roads of saintship. Be strong in moral powers. Let the organs of your spiritual sense be quick. When the seven kinds of wisdom enlighten your mind, you will find the noble, eightfold path that leads to Nirvana.

"Behold, O brethren, the final extinction of the Tathagata will take place before long. I now exhort you, saying: All component things must grow old and be dissolved again. Seek ye for that which is permanent, and work out your salvation with diligence."

CHUNDA, THE SMITH

The Blessed One went to Pava. When Chunda, the worker in metals, heard that the Blessed One had come to Pava and was staying in his mango grove, he came to the Buddha and respectfully invited him and the brethren to take their meal at his house. And Chunda prepared rice-cakes and a dish of dried boar's meat.

When the Blessed One had eaten the food prepared by Chunda, the worker in metals, there fell upon him a dire sickness, and sharp pain came upon him even unto death. But the Blessed One, mindful and self-possessed, bore it without complaint. And the Blessed One addressed the venerable Ananda, and said: "Come, Ananda, let us go on to Kusinara."

On his way the Blessed One grew tired, and he went aside from the road to rest at the foot of a tree, and said: "Fold the robe, I pray thee, Ananda, and spread it out for me. I am weary,

Ananda, and must rest awhile!" "Be it so, Lord!" said the venerable Ananda; and he spread out the robe folded fourfold. The Blessed One seated himself, and when he was seated he addressed the venerable Ananda, and said: "Fetch me some water, I pray thee, Ananda. I am thirsty, Ananda, and would drink."

When he had thus spoken, the venerable Ananda said to the Blessed One: "But just now, Lord, five hundred carts have gone across the brook and have stirred the water; but a river, O Lord, is not far off. Its water is clear and pleasant, cool and transparent, and it is easy to get down to it, the Blessed One may both drink water and cool his limbs."

A second time the Blessed One addressed the venerable Ananda, saying: "Fetch me some water, I pray thee, Ananda, I am thirsty, Ananda, and would drink."

And a second time the venerable Ananda said: "Let us go to the river."

Then the third time the Blessed One addressed the venerable Ananda, and said: "Fetch me some water, I pray thee, Ananda, I am thirsty, Ananda and would drink." "Be it so, Lord!" said the venerable Ananda in assent to the Blessed One; and, taking a bowl, he went down to the streamlet. And lo! the streamlet, which, stirred up by wheels, had become muddy, when the venerable Ananda came up to it, flowed clear and bright and free from all turbidity. And he thought: "How wonderful, how marvellous is the great might and power of the Tathagata!"

Ananda brought the water in the bowl to the Lord, saying: "Let the Blessed One take the bowl. Let the Happy One drink the water. Let the Teacher of men and gods quench his thirst. Then the Blessed One drank of the water.

Now, at that time a man of low caste, named Pukkusa, a young Malla, a disciple of Alara Kalama, was passing along the high road from Kusinara to Pava. Pukkusa, the young Malla, saw the Blessed One seated at the foot of a tree. On seeing him he went up to the place where the Blessed One was, and when he had come there, he saluted the Blessed One and took his seat respectfully on one side. Then the Blessed One instructed, edified, and gladdened Kukkusa, the young Malla, with religious discourse.

Aroused and gladdened by the words of the Blessed One, Pukkusa, the young Malla, addressed a certain man who happened to pass by, and said: "Fetch me, I pray thee, my good man, two robes of cloth of gold, burnished and ready for wear."

"Be it so, sir!" said that man in assent to Pukkusa, the young Malla; and he brought two robes of cloth of gold, burnished and ready for wear.

The Malla Pukkusa presented the two robes of cloth of gold, burnished and ready for wear, to the Blessed One, saying: "Lord, these two robes of burnished cloth of gold are ready for wear. May the Blessed One show me favour and accept them at my hands!"

The Blessed One said: "Pukkusa, robe me in one, and Ananda in the other one." And the Tathagata's body appeared shining like a flame, and he was beautiful above all expression.

The venerable Ananda said to the Blessed One: "How wonderful a thing is it, Lord, and how marvellous, that the colour of the skin of the Blessed One should be so clear, so exceedingly bright! When I placed this robe of burnished cloth of gold on the body of the Blessed One, lo! it seemed as if it had lost its splendour!"

The Blessed One said: "There are two occasions on which a Tathagata's appearance becomes clear and exceeding bright. In the night, Ananda, in which a Tathagata attains to the supreme and perfect insight, and in the night in which he passes finally away in that utter passing away which leaves nothing whatever of his earthly existence to remain.

And the Blessed One addressed the venerable Ananda, and said: "Now it may happen, Ananda, that some one should stir up remorse in Chunda, the smith, by saying: 'It is evil to thee, Chunda, and loss to thee, that the Tathagata died, having eaten his last meal from thy provision.' Any such remorse, Ananda, in Chunda, the smith, should be checked by saying:

'It is good to thee, Chunda, and gain to thee, that the Tathagata died, having eaten his last meal from thy provision. From the very mouth of the Blessed One, O Chunda, have I heard, from his own mouth have I received this saying, "These two offerings of food are of equal fruit and of much greater profit than any other: the offerings of food which a Tathagata accepts when he has attained perfect enlightenment and when he passes away by the utter passing away in which nothing whatever of his earthly existence remains behind-these two offerings of food are of equal fruit and of equal profit, and of much greater fruit and much greater profit than any other.

There has been laid up by Chunda, the smith, a karma redounding to length of life, redounding to good birth, redounding to good fortune, redounding to good fame, redounding to the inheritance of heaven and of great power."' In this way, Ananda, should be checked any remorse in Chunda, the smith."

Then the Blessed One, perceiving that death was near, uttered these words: "He who gives away shall have real gain. He who subdues himself shall be free, he shall cease to be a slave of passions. The righteous man casts off evil; and by rooting out lust, bitterness, and illusion, do we reach Nirvana."

ENTERING INTO NIRVANA

Then the Mallas, with their young men and maidens and their wives, being grieved, and sad, and afflicted at heart, went to the Upavattana, the sala grove of the Mallas, and wanted to see the Blessed One, in order to partake of the bliss that devolves upon those who are in the presence of the Holy One.

The Blessed One addressed them and said: "Seeking the way, ye must exert yourselves and strive with diligence. It is not enough to have seen me Walk as I have commanded you; free yourselves from the tangled net of sorrow. Walk in the path with steadfast aim. A sick man may be cured by the healing power of medicine and will be rid of all his ailments without beholding the physician. He who does not do what I command sees me in vain. This brings no profit; while he who lives far off from where I am and yet walks righteously is ever near me. A man may dwell beside me, and yet, being disobedient, be far away from me. Yet he who obeys the Dharma will always enjoy the bliss of the Tathagata's presence."

Then the mendicant Subhadda went to the sala grove of the Mallas and said to the venerable Ananda: "I have heard from fellow mendicants of mine, who were deep stricken in years and teachers of great experience: 'Sometimes and full seldom do Tathagatas appear in the world, the holy Buddhas.' Now it is said that today in the last watch of the night, the final passing away of the samana Gautama will take place. My mind is full of uncertainty, yet have I faith in the samana Gautama and trust he will be able so to present the truth that I may become rid of my doubts. O that I might be allowed to see the samana Gautama!"

When he had thus spoken the venerable Ananda said to the mendicant Subhadda: "Enough! friend Subhadda. Trouble not the Tathagata. The Blessed One is weary." Now the Blessed One overheard this conversation of the venerable Ananda with the mendicant Subhadda. And the Blessed One called the venerable Ananda, and said: "Ananda! Do not keep out Subhadda. Subhadda may be allowed to see the Tathagata. Whatever Subhadda will ask of me, he will ask from a desire for knowledge, and not to annoy me, and whatever I may say in answer to his questions, that he will quickly understand."

Then the venerable Ananda said: "Step in, friend Subhadda; for the Blessed One gives thee leave."

When the Blessed One had instructed Subhadda, and aroused and gladdened him with words of wisdom and comfort, Subhadda said to the Blessed One: "Glorious Lord, glorious Lord! Most excellent are the words of thy mouth, most excellent! They set up that which has been overturned, they reveal that which has been hidden. They point out the right road to the wanderer who has gone astray. They bring a lamp into the darkness so that those who have eyes to see can see. Thus,

Lord, the truth has been made known to me by the Blessed One and I take my refuge in the Blessed One, in the Truth, and in the Order. May the Blessed One accept me as a disciple and true believer, from this day forth as long as life endures."

And Subhadda, the mendicant, said to the venerable Ananda: "Great is thy gain, friend Ananda, great is thy good fortune, that for so many years thou has been sprinkled with the sprinkling of discipleship in this brotherhood at the hands of the Master himself!"

Now the Blessed One addressed the venerable Ananda, and said: "It may be, Ananda, that in some of you the thought may arise The word of the Master is ended, we have no teacher more!' But it is not thus, Ananda, that you should regard it. It is true that no more shall I receive a body, for all future sorrow has now forever passed away. But though this body will be dissolved, the Tathagata remains. The truth and the rules of the order which I have set forth and laid down for you all, let them, after I am gone, be a teacher unto you. When I am gone, Ananda, let the order, if it should so wish, abolish all the lesser and minor precepts."

Then the Blessed One addressed the brethren, and said: "There may be some doubt or misgiving in the mind of a brother as to the Buddha, or the truth, or the path. Do not have to reproach yourselves afterwards with the thought, 'We did not inquire of the Blessed One when we were face to face with him.' Therefore inquire now, O brethren, inquire freely."

The brethren remained silent. Then the venerable Ananda said to the Blessed One: "Verily, I believe that in this whole assembly of the brethren there is not one brother who has any doubt or misgiving as to the Buddha, or the truth, or the path!"

Said the Blessed One: "It is out of the fullness of faith that thou has spoken, Ananda! But Ananda, the Tathagata knows for certain that in this whole assembly of the brethren there is not one brother who has any doubt or misgiving as to the Buddha, or the truth, or the path! For even the most backward, Ananda, of all these brethren has become converted, and is assured of final salvation."

Then the Blessed One addressed the brethren and said: "If ye now know the Dharma the cause of all suffering, and the path of salvation, O disciples, will ye then say: 'We respect the Master, and out of reverence for the Master do we thus speak?'" The brethren replied: "That we shall not, O Lord."

And the Holy One continued: "Of those beings who live in ignorance, shut up and confined, as it were, in an egg, I have first broken the egg-shell of ignorance and alone in the universe obtained the most exalted, universal Buddhahood. Thus, O disciples, I am the eldest, the noblest of beings.

"But what ye speak, O disciples, is it not even that which ye have yourselves known, yourselves seen, yourselves realized?" Ananda and the brethren said: "It is, O Lord."

Once more the Blessed One began to speak: "Behold now, brethren, said he, I exhort you, saying, 'Decay is inherent in all component things, but the truth will remain forever Work out your salvation with diligence!" This was the last word of the Tathagata. Then the Tathagata fell into a deep meditation, and having passed through the four jhanas, entered Nirvana. When the Blessed One entered Nirvana there arose, at his passing out of existence, a mighty earthquake, terrible and awe-inspiring: and the thunders of heaven burst forth, and of those of the brethren who were not yet free from passions some stretched out their arms and wept, and some fell headlong on the ground, in anguish at the thought: "Too soon has the Blessed One died! Too soon has the Happy One passed away from existence! Too soon has the Light of the world gone out!"

Then the venerable Anuruddha exhorted the brethren and said: "Enough, my brethren! Weep not, neither lament! Has not the Blessed One formerly declared this to us, that it is in the very nature of all things near and dear unto us, that we must separate from them and leave them, since everything that is born, brought into being, and organized, contains within itself the inherent necessity of dissolution? How then can it be possible that the body of the Tathagata should not be dissolved? No such condition can exist! Those who are free from passion will bear the loss, calm and self-possessed, mindful of the truth he has taught us."

The venerable Anuruddha and the venerable Ananda spent the rest of the night in religious discourse. Then the venerable Anuruddha said to the venerable Ananda: "Go now, brother Ananda, and inform the Mallas of Kusinara saying, 'The Blessed One has passed away: do, then, whatsoever seems fit!'" And when the Mallas had heard this saying they were grieved, and sad, and afflicted at heart.

Then the Mallas of Kusinara gave orders to their attendants, saying, "Gather together perfumes and garlands, and all the music in Kusinara!" And the Mallas of Kusinara took the perfumes and garlands, and all the musical instruments, and five hundred garments, and went to the sala grove where the body of the Blessed One lay.

There they passed the day in paying honour and reverence to the remains of the Blessed One, with hymns, and music, and with garlands and perfumes, and in making canopies of their garments, and preparing decorative wreaths to hang thereon. And they burned the remains of the Blessed One as they would do to the body of a king of kings.

When the funeral pyre was lit, the sun and moon withdrew their shining, the peaceful streams on every side were torrent-swollen, the earth quaked, and the sturdy forests shook like aspen leaves, whilst flowers and leaves fell untimely to the ground, like scattered rain, so that all Kusinara became strewn knee-deep with mandara flowers raining down from heaven.

When the burning ceremonies were over, Devaputta said to the multitudes that were assembled round the pyre: "Behold, O brethren, the earthly remains of the Blessed One have been dissolved, but the truth which he has taught us lives in our minds and cleanses us from all error.

Let us, then, go out into the world, as compassionate and merciful as our great master, and preach to all living beings the four noble truths and the eightfold path of righteousness, so that all mankind may attain to a final salvation, taking refuge in the Buddha, the Dharma, and the Sangha." When the Blessed One had entered into Nirvana and the Mallas had burned the body with such ceremonies as would indicate that he was the great king of kings, ambassadors came from all the empires that at the time had embraced his doctrine, to claim a share of the relics; and the relics were divided into eight parts and eight dagobas were erected for their preservation.

One dagoba was erected by the Mallas, and seven others by the seven kings of those countries whose people had taken refuge in the Buddha.

METTEYYA

The Blessed One proceeded with a great company of the brethren to the sala grove of the Mallas, the Upavattana of Kusinara on the further side of the river Hirannavati, and when he had arrived he addressed the venerable Ananda, and said: "Make ready for me, I pray you, Ananda, the couch with its head to the north, between the twin sala trees. I am weary, Ananda, and wish to lie down."

"Be it so, Lord!" said the venerable Ananda, and he spread a couch with its head to the north, between the twin sala trees. And the Blessed One laid himself down, and he was mindful and self-possessed.

Now, at that time the twin sala trees were full of bloom with flowers out of season; and heavenly songs came wafted from the skies, out of reverence for the successor of the Buddhas of old. And Ananda was filled with wonder that the Blessed One was thus honoured. But the Blessed One said: "Not by such events, Ananda, is the Tathagata rightly honoured, held sacred, or revered. But the devout man, who continually fulfills the greater and lesser duties, walking according to the precepts, it is who rightly honours, holds sacred, and reveres the Tathagata with the worthiest homage. Therefore, O Ananda, be ye constant in the fulfilment of the greater and of the lesser duties, and walk according to the precepts; thus, Ananda, will ye honour the Master."

Then the venerable Ananda went into the vihara, and stood leaning against the doorpost, weeping at the thought: "Alas! I remain still but a learner, one who has yet to work out his own perfection. And the Master is about to pass away from me-who is so kind!"

Now, the Blessed One called the brethren, and said: "Where, O brethren, is Ananda?" One of the brethren went and called Ananda. And Ananda came and said to the Blessed One: "Deep darkness reigned for want of wisdom; the world of sentient creatures was groping for want of light; then the Tathagata lit up the lamp of wisdom, and now it will be extinguished again, ere he has brought it out."

The Blessed One said to the venerable Ananda, as he sat there by his side: "Enough, Ananda! Let not thy self be troubled; do not weep! Have I not already, on former occasions, told you that it is in the very nature of all things most near and dear unto us that we must separate from them and leave them? The foolish man conceives the idea of 'self,' the wise man sees there is no ground on which to build the idea of 'self,' thus he has a right conception of the world and well concludes that all compounds amassed by sorrow will be dissolved again, but the truth will remain. Why should I preserve this body of flesh, when the body of the excellent law will endure? I am resolved; having accomplished my purpose and attended to the work set me, I look for rest! For a long time, Ananda, thou has been very near to me by thoughts and acts of such love as is beyond all measure. Thou has done well, Ananda! Be earnest in effort and thou too shalt soon be free from evils, from sensuality, from selfishness, from delusion, and from ignorance!"

Ananda, suppressing his tears, said to the Blessed One: "Who shall teach us when thou art gone?"

And the Blessed One replied: "I am not the first Buddha who came upon earth, nor shall I be the last. In due time another Buddha will arise in the world, a Holy One, a supremely enlightened One, endowed with wisdom in conduct, auspicious, knowing the universe, an incomparable leader of men, a master of angels and mortals. He will reveal to you the same eternal truths which I have taught you. He will preach his religion, glorious in its origin, glorious at the climax, and glorious at the goal, in the spirit and in the letter. He will proclaim a religious life, wholly perfect and pure; such as I now proclaim."

Ananda said: "How shall we know him?" The Blessed One said: "He will be known as Metteyya, which means 'he whose name is kindness.'"

THE PATH OF LIFE

Let us suppose that a great prophet appeared on earth, one who was in equal degrees a lover of his kind and a dreamer of spiritual dreams. Let us suppose that this prophet had drunk at the pure fountain of Indian thought, that he had accepted and assimilated the ideas which found expression in the Upanishads, the idea of the reality of the soul, of the development of the individual soul through a chain of earth-lives, of the consummation of this process of development in the union of the individual with the Universal Soul and its consequent admission into a life of unimaginable peace and bliss. Let us further suppose that, when his heart and mind had become saturated with these ideas, he became possessed with the desire to communicate them to his fellow-men. Let us imagine him looking down, from the standpoint of his exalted faith, on the toiling, suffering masses of mankind.

Let us picture to ourselves the sorrow that must have pierced his heart when he saw how profoundly ignorant were the masses of the great truth which he had made his own; how entirely they were absorbed in the pursuit of what was material, trivial, perishable, unreal; how they were living, without knowing it, in a world of shadows and illusions; how even religion, which must once have had an inward meaning, had become for them a round of ceremonies and a network of formula; how dense, in fine, and how deadly were the mists that overhung their lives, and how seldom could those mists be parted by any breath of spiritual freedom, or pierced by any ray of spiritual hope and joy. Let us suppose that he then looked forward into the future, and saw his fellow men returning to earth again and again, and leading lives as hollow, as purposeless, and as joyless as the lives which they were leading then; the process of their soul-growth being so slow, owing to their fundamental ignorance of reality, that for a long sequence of earth-lives no appreciable progress could be made. Would not the sympathetic sorrow which the vision of the present had awaked in him, be intensified by his vision of the future; and would not the longing to help his fellow men, to enlighten them, to lead them into the path of light and life, become at last an absorbing passion which left no room in his heart for any other desire?

But how could he give men the knowledge that they needed? It was ignorance of reality that had darkened and debased their lives. It was knowledge which they were waiting for, knowledge of what was real and what was true. How could he give them this most rare and most precious of all gifts? How could he transform their sense of reality, and quicken and purify their perception of truth? Philosophical knowledge of the truth of things is, for obvious reasons, beyond the reach of the masses. The average man has no turn for metaphysical speculation, and the worse service that one can render him is to tempt him to indulge in it; for in the atmosphere of verbal controversy reality becomes an abstraction, truth becomes a formula, while love, which is the real unsealer of all spiritual secrets, inevitably withers and dies.

The intuitive apprehension of the truth of things is equally, and for equally obvious reasons, beyond the reach of the masses. The "psychical" faculties, which generate that rare but vividly real type of knowledge, though potentially present in all men, are developed in an exceedingly small minority; and the premature attempt to develop them would end in hysteria being mistaken for inspiration, and hallucination for divine truth.

The emotional apprehension of the truth of things may seem to be within the reach of ordinary men. In reality it also is reserved for a chosen few; for it is only in the genuinely poetic nature that it can maintain its equable heat and pristine purity.

In lower natures it burns itself away in the pitchy flames of undisciplined sentiment, and dies out at last into formalism, dogmatism, and other "bodies of death." Moreover, the teacher who appeals to the spiritual emotion of his disciples, and who thereby enters into emotional relations with them, and through them with their disciples and spiritual descendants, runs one serious risk.

The chances are that, sooner or later, those who come under his influence, without having known him in the flesh, and who are therefore free to construct imaginary pictures of his life and person, will transfer to his personality the devotion which he wished them to give to his ideas, and will end by regarding his inevitable limitations, or rather the limitations of their own imagination—for by this time the teacher will have become a legendary hero—as the very boundaries of reality.

There remains what I have elsewhere called the real apprehension of ultimate truth. This, and this alone, is within the reach of all men. The actual expansion of the soul, in response to the forces in Nature that are making for its development, will give men, little by little, the knowledge that they need; for, as the soul expands, as it increases in wisdom and stature, its consciousness will enlarge its horizon, its vision will become clearer and deeper, and its sense of proportion will be transformed. When the knowledge of reality has been finally won, the attractive forces of earth, which will then be felt to be wholly illusory, will have ceased to act, and the end of the soul's pilgrimage will be at hand. The best service, then, that a man can render to his fellow men is to persuade them to enter the path of soul-growth. Or rather—for they entered it long ago—to follow it, no longer blindly and instinctively, but deliberately and of their own free will; and, by thus consciously cooperating with the expansive forces of Nature, to shorten the path of soul-growth, and to hasten the advent of its glorious goal.

That our prophet, looking at things from the standpoint of his own higher knowledge, should desire to render this service to his fellow men, may be taken for granted. But how should he persuade men that escape from the cycle of earth-lives was intrinsically desirable, that the path of soul-growth was the path of real life, that the goal to which it would lead them was worthy of their highest aspiration and their most strenuous endeavour? If their ignorance of reality was as dense as it seemed to be, to what faculty should he appeal and on what ground of admitted truth should he take his stand?

The relation between knowledge and action, in the sphere of moral life, presents a problem which is insoluble, except on one hypothesis. Our difficulty is that for right action we need right knowledge; that for right knowledge we need inward enlightenment; that for inward enlightenment we need the transforming influence of a life of right action. There is but one way of escape from this seemingly vicious circle. Apply the law of development to the inward life of the soul; and it will become clear that the sense of reality, like every other sense and power, exists in embryo in each individual man.

It is to this embryonic sense of reality that our prophet would make his appeal. In doing so, he would provide both for the development of that sense, and for the concurrent development in the soul of his disciple of the germ of his own teaching. For the sense of reality, like every other sense and power, grows by being exercised; and if it is to be exercised, it must be appealed to and called upon to exert itself. It follows that, in appealing to a man's sense of reality, one helps it to grow; and it follows that, in helping the sense to grow, one trains it to understand and respond to the appeal that is made to it. We may conjecture, then, that the teacher who wished to lead men to the knowledge of reality would begin by assuming that the sense of reality was latent in every heart. He would say to them, "Does this earth-life really satisfy you? Cannot you see for yourselves that in the last resort it is hollow and unreal? Do the prizes for which you strive content you when you have won them?

Do they not crumble into dust as you grasp them? Everything that earth can give you—health, wealth, pleasure, power, success, fame—proves to be either transient or illusory. Health lasts a few years, and is then undermined by disease and decay. Wealth has neither meaning nor value except so far as it enables you to buy pleasure, power, success, and fame. Pleasure palls upon you, and at last ceases to please. Or, if it does continue to please, age and disease forbid you to enjoy it. Power brings with it a weight of care and responsibility. Success has its counterpart in failure, for:

'Things won are done: joy's soul lies in the doing.'

Fame is 'Enjoyed no sooner but despised straight.'

Look down the vista of the years. If you continue to desire the things of earth, you will return to earth, drawn by the influences that now attract you, again and again. Does this prospect content you? Has your experience of earth been so happy that you wish to renew it again and again? Is it not true that the earth-life brings real happiness to those only who have found inward peace? And is it not true that inward peace, though it can transfigure earth and make it spiritual and beautiful, is won by detachment from earth, not by devotion to it? This inward peace, in enjoying which you drink the only draught of real happiness that the earth-life can offer you, is a faint foretaste of what is in store for the soul when all its wanderings are over. Beyond all earth-lives a goal awaits you—a goal which crowns and completes the process of the soul's evolution—the goal of deep, perfect, inexhaustible bliss. This reward will be yours when you have broken the last of the ties by which earth attracts you, and in doing so have escaped, once and for ever, from the 'whirlpool of rebirth.'"

If there was anything in the heart of man which could respond to this appeal, the seed of the prophet's teaching would have been safely sown. His philosophy would have taught him that his appeal would not be made in vain. The germ of divine wisdom is implicit in the germ of soul-life; and the teacher who took for granted that men could see for themselves the inner truth of things, would find that the insight with which he credited them would evolve itself, little by little, in response to his appeal.

But, be it carefully observed, he would make his appeal to the people as simple and direct as possible. He would not attempt to base it on metaphysical or theological grounds. He would not employ arguments which appeal to the intellectual faculties only, for he would know that the people have no capacity for abstract speculation, and he would infer from this that the more cogent a metaphysical or a theological argument might seem to be, when addressed to popular thought, the more certain it would be to delude and mislead. The reticence which he would thus impose upon himself might carry him very far, but he would respect all its obligations. He would make no attempt to lead the undeveloped minds of his hearers into the presence of what was ultimate, either in themselves or in the world at large. He would say nothing to them about the "Ego," nothing about God. He would put no truth before them which was not in some measure self-evident.

To say that life, as we know it, is full of pain, sorrow, and disappointment; that its pleasures are transitory and delusive; that its prizes are intrinsically worthless; that the inward peace which moral goodness generates is the only real happiness; and that to escape into a world of inward peace is, therefore, the highest imaginable bliss;—to advance such arguments as these is to appeal to an inward sense which exists potentially in all men. But to go beyond the limits of those simple yet profound conceptions, would be to lead men into a region of doubt, bewilderment, and wordy strife.

Having won from men some measure of assent to the self-evident truths which he had set before them, the teacher would proceed to draw for them the practical inferences from his premises. He would tell them that there was a path, by following which they would become gradually detached from earth and its shadows and delusions, and brought within sight of their spiritual goal; and he would then teach them how to enter that path and walk in it.

The path of deliverance is the path of soul-growth. As the soul grows, and its perceptive faculties widen and deepen, the unreality of the earth-life will become gradually apparent; and when this has been fully realized, the last chain that binds the soul to earth will snap of its own accord, and deliverance will be won. The one thing needful, then, the one thing which every man ought to do and which any man can do, is so to live as to make his soul grow. How is this to be done? We need not go far for an answer to this question. In the first place, all the influences which directly thwart the growth of the soul must be subdued and disarmed.

The lusts and passions of the animal self; the desires and ambitions, the moods and impulses, that are generated by petty egoism; the tendencies, whatever they may be, that make for the contraction of the life of the soul, for the restriction of its vital energies to the plane of the lower self,—all these must, for obvious reasons, be kept under due control. To allow the soul to identify itself with any of the lower selves which egoism seeks to magnify, would be fatal to its spiritual progress. Also, since it is of the essence of the new scheme of life to entrust to each man in turn the duty of ordering his own goings, it is clear that if any carnal or semi-carnal desire or passion were allowed to seize the helm of the will, the voyaging soul would make early shipwreck.

This is the negative side of soul-growth. The positive side is of even greater importance. If the soul is to grow, it must go out of itself into some sphere of being which seems for the moment to lie beyond its own. Now there are many avenues of escape from the ordinary self; and each of these helps, in its own way, to foster the growth of the soul. But there is one and one only which is open to all men,—the avenue of sympathy, of living or beginning to live in the lives of other persons and other things.

In teaching men to live in the lives of others, our moralist would be content to lead them on from strength to strength, and would make no attempt to initiate them, while they were still in pupilage, into the esoteric mystery of an all-embracing, all-consuming love. He would take for granted that the germ of sympathy was in every heart, and that the germ would evolve itself, under the stress of the natural forces that make for the expansion of the soul, when once the adverse influences that hindered its outgrowth had been removed or, at least, reduced to inaction. What hinders the outgrowth of sympathy is not the lust of cruelty (for that is a rare and artificial by-product of human development), but the reckless egoism which prompts the strong, in the general struggle for existence, to trample down the weak.

The impulse—half fear, half anger—which makes a man strike in self-defence; the "instinct to live" which makes him ready to sacrifice life in other beings in order that he may preserve it in himself; the desire for material comfort and well-being, which makes him reckless of the comfort and well-being of others, these tendencies are not in themselves incompatible with sympathy, though they may, if uncontrolled, develop into darker and deadlier passions, and generate an egoism more callous and more self-seeking than that from which they spring. But the scheme of life which we are considering has provided for all the animal and semi-animal passions being placed under due control; and he who had laid this teaching to heart would be ready to receive the further lesson, that he ought to refrain from wanton unkindness, first to his fellow-men, and then to all other living things.

In other words, though he would be left free to take whatever steps might prove to be necessary for the protection and preservation of his life, he would be taught that no wound was to be wantonly inflicted, no life to be recklessly destroyed; and that, speaking generally, each man in turn was to make his pilgrimage on earth as free as might be possible from harm and offence to others. Under the influence of this teaching, gentleness, kindness, and tolerance would gradually impregnate the atmosphere of man's daily life; and in that atmosphere the germ of sympathy would make strong and steady growth.

To trace the stages in the growth of that soul-expanding germ would be beside my present purpose. That the destiny of sympathy is to transform itself into the passion of spiritual love, can scarcely be doubted. It is of the essence of the individual life to seek to outgrow itself, to seek to mingle itself with other lives on its way to that Universal life which is its own true self; and when once the individual life has begun to lose itself in the lives of others, a process has been initiated, of which absorption into the Universal life—itself the highest imaginable development of love—is the natural and necessary consummation.

But one who was addressing himself to the rank and file of mankind, and was therefore taking thought for the earlier stages of soul-growth, would be careful to disabuse the minds of his disciples of the idea that there was any short cut to spiritual perfection. The critic who looks at things from the standpoint of the "enthusiasm of humanity," may possibly condemn the gospel of sympathy as a cold and pallid substitute for the gospel of love; but the moralist who had taken upon himself to lead the average man into the path of life, would not allow this criticism to deflect him from his purpose.

Knowing that in the earlier stages of soul-growth self-control was the one thing needful, and that until the self-seeking desires had been mastered the outgrowth of the soul-expanding desires was not to be looked for; and knowing further that sympathy, which has much in common with self-control, and follows naturally from it, would gradually prepare the way for the outgrowth of spiritual love and the desires that are akin to it, or rather would itself, in the natural course of things, develop into these;—knowing this, the idealistic moralist would be content that men should aim in the first instance at the skyline which was visible to them, and that the heights which this hid from view should unfold themselves, little by little, as the soul surmounted the foothills of its life. Herein he would show his practical wisdom and make good his claim to be a teacher of mankind. The premature development of the "enthusiasm of humanity" and other spiritual passions might well have fatal consequences; for experience has amply proved that the lower desires and impulses are all too ready to masquerade as the higher,—lust, for example, as love, race-hatred as patriotism, religious intolerance as spiritual devotion, egoism as self-respect, censoriousness and uncharitableness as moral zeal. The truth is that in ordinary men the passion of love necessarily directs itself towards what is individual and quasi-concrete, whereas sympathy, just because it is a colder and paler sentiment, has an immeasurably wider and more abstract range. There are indeed exceptional natures which can sublimate personal into impersonal love; but, speaking generally, if the impersonal passion of universal love is to be our goal, the safer path to it,—at any rate in the earlier stages of man's development,—will be that of the impersonal sentiment of sympathy rather than the personal passion of love.

The master principle, that deliverance from the illusions of earth is to be won by self-control and sympathy, would be embodied in a simple "Law."

It is in this form, and no other, that the new philosophy of life would have to be presented to the rank and file of mankind. It may be possible for ordinary men to see for themselves that escape from the "whirlpool of rebirth" into the calm haven of inward peace and spiritual bliss, is a desirable end; but the teacher who should try to explain to them that this end was to be compassed by the practice of self-control and the cultivation of sympathy, would find that his words had missed their mark. The average man has no turn for abstract thinking; and to ask him to trace the logical connection between this or that moral principle and the paramount end of life, is to set him a task beyond his power. What is needed for his edification is to give him a few simple moral rules, and to tell him that these, if faithfully followed, will lead him to the goal that he desires to reach.

But the rules that are given him must be simple and few. In other words, they must be the axiomata media of morality, the broad rules of life which mediate between the master principles of moral action and those meticulous details into which the mind that values rules for their own sake is so ready to descend. The force and authority of each rule must be self-evident. The teacher must be able to say to his disciples: "Cannot you see for yourselves that this course of action is better than that,—that continence (let us say) is better than incontinence, sobriety than intemperance, kindness than cruelty, gentleness than violence?"

In making this appeal to his disciples he would at once exercise and cultivate their spiritual intelligence and their power of moral choice. When we say that the force and authority of the axiomata media of morality are self-evident, we imply that they stand very near to the moral principles which are behind them, so near that, in yielding to their attractive force, the soul is brought into subconscious contact with the truth and beauty of the teacher's philosophy of life. We imply, in other words, that the simple rules of a sane morality are in themselves a source of inward illumination, and that the soul which disregards them sins, in some sort, "against light and knowledge" and misuses its power of choice.

To this proposition there are corollaries which are of profound importance. The growth of the soul, and its consequent absorption into itself of forces and influences which seem to be external to its life, are necessarily accompanied by the diminution of outward pressure and the consequent growth of freedom; and it stands to reason that, when the individual has becomc one with the Universal Self, so that all forces and all influences are gathered at last within the compass of its conscious life, absolute freedom will have been won.

It follows that freedom is the very counterpart of spiritual life. Now freedom is of two kinds,—freedom to know and freedom to do; and these two are in the last resort one. The teacher who would lead men into the path of life must assume at the outset that man is free, potentially if not actually,—free both to discern good from evil and to make his choice between the two; and he must so shape his teaching that this dual faculty shall be constantly exercised, and to that extent encouraged to grow.

It is because the teacher who limits himself, when framing his Law, to a few axiomata media and refuses to go further into detail, makes ample provision, first for the recognition and then for the culture of spiritual freedom,—it is for this, if for no other reason, that he must take rank as the wisest of Lawgivers. The superiority of a simple to an elaborate Code of

Law, in respect of the services that they respectively render to the cause of spiritual freedom, may be looked at from another point of view. The connection between the broader rules of conduct and the goal by which obedience to those rules is at last to be rewarded, though possibly not directly traceable by the man of average insight and intelligence, is always felt by him to be natural and real.

In an elaborate Code of Law, on the other hand, nine-tenths of the rules that men are directed to obey are so unreasonable and so unattractive that the man who obeys them can neither discern their moral significance, nor see that there is any natural connection between his obedience and his promised goal.

The consequence is that he gets to regard both the law and its reward as wholly alien from his own inward life. He is to obey such and such rules of conduct because he is told to obey them, and for no other reason; and if, and so far as, he is obedient to them, he is to reap such and such rewards, not because there is any natural connection between his conduct and its recompense, but because the irresponsible despot who framed the Code of Law chose, for reasons of his own, to attach certain prizes to obedience, and certain penalties to rebellion.

When such a conception of life and duty has fully established itself, spiritual freedom has been mortally wounded, and the soul has entered the valley of the shadow of death.

Against this danger the teacher who regarded soul-growth as both the way and the end of "salvation," would be ever on his guard. Not only would he make his moral rules as few, as simple, and as broad as possible, but he would also impress upon his disciples that by obeying those rules, by following the path, which they marked out for them, they would, in the natural course of things, arrive in due season at the promised goal of inward peace and bliss;—a goal which is so vitally connected with the way of living that leads up to it, that those who seek it enjoy it in some measure before they reach it, its foreglow—"the peace which passes all understanding"—falling in ever deepening splendour on each successive stage in the path of life.

He would therefore warn his disciples against whatever scheme of conduct might tend to substitute a mechanical for a spiritual, a supernatural for a natural, conception of life and duty.

Thus he would teach them that "sacrifices and burnt offerings" could profit them nothing; that ceremonial observances had no intrinsic meaning or value; that obedience to rules, for the mere sake of obedience, far from strengthening their souls, would entangle them at last in the clinging meshes of the infinitesimal. He would teach them, further, that actions produce their natural and necessary consequences, and that the most vital of these is the reaction of what is done on the soul of the doer.

Is the soul really growing? Are the earth-ties being strengthened or weakened? These are the questions which men must learn to ask themselves, and to answer. It is by the strictly natural process of growth, and in no other way, that the soul is to be "saved alive"; and the idealistic teacher would urge his disciples to repudiate the authority of his own law, if it set any other path or any other ideal than that of soul-growth before them.

Above all—and this is perhaps "the conclusion of the whole matter"—the teacher who preached the gospel of soul-growth would impress upon his disciples that each of them must work out his salvation for himself; that he must take the conduct of his life into his own hands; that he must enlist his will-power on the side of those natural forces which are ever making for the expansion of his life; that his will-power was in fact the last and the highest of those natural forces; that its outgrowth had come, gradually and naturally, with the outgrowth of his soul; that whatever tended to arrest its growth tended also, and in an equal degree, to arrest the growth of his soul; that in this, as in other matters, the end of life must control the way, and the way foreshadow the end; that in this, as in other matters, a man must achieve his ideal by applying it to the solution of his practical problems, and giving expression to it in the daily round of his life.

CONCLUSION

When the Blessed One had passed away into Nirvana, the disciples came together and consulted what to do in order to keep the Dharma pure and uncorrupted by heresies.

Upali rose, saying: "Our great Master used to say to the brethren: 'O bhikkhus! after my final entrance into Nirvana you must reverence and obey the law. Regard the law as your master. The law is like unto a light that shines in the darkness, pointing out the way; it is also like unto a precious jewel to gain which you must shun no trouble, and be ready to bring any sacrifice; even, should it be needed, your own lives. Obey the Dharma which I have revealed to you; follow it carefully and if as in no way different from myself.' Such were the words of the Blessed One. The law, accordingly, which the Buddha has left us as a precious inheritance has now become the visible body of the Tathagata. Let us, therefore, revere it and keep it sacred. For what is the use of erecting dagobas for relics, if we neglect the spirit of the Master's teachings?"

Then Anuruddha arose and said: "Let us bear in mind, O brethren, that Gautama Siddhattha has revealed the truth to us. He was the Holy One and the Perfect One and the Blessed One, because the eternal truth had taken abode in him. The Tathagata taught us that the truth existed before he was born into this world, and will exist after he has entered into Nirvana. The Tathagata said: 'The truth is omnipresent and eternal, endowed with excellencies innumerable, above all human nature, and ineffable in its holiness.'

"Now let us bear in mind that not this or that law which is revealed to us in the Dhanna is the Buddha, but the entire truth, the truth which is eternal, omnipresent, immutable, and most excellent. Many regulations of the Sangha are temporary; they were prescribed because they suited the occasion and were needed for some transient emergency. The truth, however, is not temporary. The truth is not arbitrary nor a matter of opinion, but can be investigated, and he who earnestly searches for the truth will find it. The truth is hidden to the blind, but he who has the mental eye sees the truth. The truth is Buddha's essence, and the truth will remain the ultimate standard. Let us, then, revere the truth; let us inquire into the truth and state it, and let us obey the truth. For the truth is Buddha our Master, our Teacher."

And Kassapa rose and said: "Truly thou has spoken well, O brother Anuruddha. Neither is there any conflict of opinion on the meaning of our religion. For the Blessed One possesses three personalities and each of them is of equal importance to us. There is the Dharma Kaya. There is the Nirmana Kaya. There is the Sambhoga Kaya. Buddha is the all-excellent truth, eternal, omnipresent, and immutable: this is the Sambhoga Kaya which is in a state of perfect bliss. Buddha is the all-loving teacher assuming the shape of the beings whom he teaches: this is the Nirmana Kaya, his apparitional body. Buddha is the all-blessed dispensation of religion; he is the spirit of the Sangha and the meaning of the commands left us in his sacred word, the Dharma: this is the Dharma Kaya, the body of the most excellent law.

"If Buddha had not appeared to us as Gautama Sakyamuni, how could we have the sacred traditions of his doctrine? And if the generations to come did not have the sacred traditions preserved in the Sangha, how could they know anything of the great Sakyamuni? And neither we nor others would know anything about the most excellent truth which is eternal, omnipresent, and immutable. Let us then keep sacred and revere the traditions; let us keep sacred the memory of Gautama Sakyamuni, so that people may find the truth."

Then the brethren decided to convene a synod to lay down the doctrines of the Blessed One, to collate the sacred writings, and to establish a canon which should serve as a source of instruction for future generations.

4

The Silence of Buddha

IT is the silence of Buddha which has misled so many of his commentators. The teacher who, while pointing out to us the ultimate issues of life, keeps silence as to its ultimate realities and ultimate principles, must be prepared for his philosophy—the philosophy that is at the heart of his silence—to be misunderstood. It is not merely that he gives us no clue to the labyrinth of his deeper thoughts, and so leaves each of us free to explore that labyrinth for himself. There is another and a graver danger to which he exposes the faith of his heart. Of those who take a speculative interest in his ideas, few will be content to regard his silence as purely agnostic. The majority will see in it either the negation or the confirmation of their own philosophical prejudices. The positive dogmatist, who has made up his mind that the ultimate realities of existence are such and such, will regard it as a challenge and a defiance, and will apply to it the epithets which he reserves for denial of his own creed. The negative dogmatist will insist that it is a polite concession to the weakness of the "orthodox," and that behind it is a conception of life as fundamentally negative as his own. In either case the silence of the Master will be construed as equivalent to denial and revolt.

This is the fate which has befallen Buddha. Because he said nothing about God he is held—by the "orthodox" as well as by the "unbeliever"—to have "denied the divine." Because he said little about the "Self," and because that little was mainly negative, 1 he is held to have denied the Ego. And he is credited with all the consequences of these tremendous denials. He who on principle kept silence about what is, ultimate is supposed to have elaborated a complete system of negatively ultimate thought.

There is nothing in the history of human thought more dramatic or more significant than the silence of Buddha. Let us try to fathom its depths. That there is a deep spiritual meaning, that there was a deep spiritual conviction, at the heart of it can scarcely be doubted. It was not from indifference that Buddha, of all men, became and remained to the end an apparent agnostic. And, apart from indifference, though there may be silence about "great matters," there can be no agnosticism (in the sense of metaphysical neutrality) in the thinker's inner life. A state of perfect mental equilibrium is incompatible with living interest in the deeper problems of existence. The silence of Buddha seems to have been the deliberate fulfilment of a self-imposed vow. At any rate there was a strong purpose behind it; and that purpose must have been the outcome, not of philosophical indifference, but of some master theory of things.

The more closely I study the stories in which Buddha answers the overcurious with silence and gives his reasons for doing so, and the more freely I surrender myself to the subtle influence of their atmosphere, the stronger does my conviction become that Buddha kept silence, when metaphysical questions were discussed, not because he had nothing to say about great matters, but because he had far too much, because he was overwhelmed by the flood of his own mighty thoughts, and because the channels of expression which the riddle-mongers of his day invited him to use were both too narrow and too shallow to give his soul relief. As it is on the plane of spiritual emotion, so it is on the plane of spiritual thought. "Silence," says one of Shakespeare's characters,

"is the perfectest herald of joy:
I were but little happy if I could say how much."

The babbling river, as another poet reminds us, is overwhelmed and silenced by the flow of the tide-wave from the unfathomed sea. This simile has the beauty of truth. The mind that is visited by world-encompassing waves of thought (or of emotion) has more to say than words can express, or than other minds can receive. There are, indeed, some gifted souls for whom the channel of poetry provides an overflow (rather than an outflow) for their flooding thoughts. For the rest of us (as Buddha saw clearly) there is but one available outlet,—that of action, conduct, life; and life will have a stronger purpose and a larger scope when silence is behind it than when its motive force is a flux of words. So eloquent and so significant is Buddha's own silence, that it seems at last, when one becomes familiar with it, to give a clearer insight into the secrets of his soul than any formulated confession of words could ever have done.

Let us now hear the reasons which Buddha himself (or those who spoke in his name) gave for his silence. Let us study the three stories which Dr. Oldenberg has selected as indicative of his attitude towards the questions with which the thinkers of his day perplexed themselves. The first runs thus:

"Then the wandering monk Vacchagotta went to where the Exalted One was staying. When he had come near him, he saluted him. When saluting him, he had interchanged friendly words with him, he sat down beside him. Sitting beside him the wandering monk Vacchagotta spake to the Exalted One, saying: 'How does the matter stand, venerable Gautama, is there the Ego?'

"When he said this, the Exalted One was silent.

"'How then, venerable Gautama, is there not the Ego?'

"And still the Exalted One maintained silence. Then the wandering monk Vacchagotta rose from his seat and went away.

"But the venerable ananda, when the wandering monk Vacchagotta had gone to a distance, soon said to the Exalted One:

"'Wherefore, sire, has the Exalted One not given an answer to the questions put by the wandering monk Vacchagotta?'

"'If I, ananda, when the wandering monk Vacchagotta asked me: "Is there the Ego?" had answered: "The Ego is," then that, ananda, would have confirmed the doctrine of the Samanas and Brahmanas who believe in permanence. If I, ananda, when the wandering monk Vacchagotta asked me: "Is there not the Ego?" had answered: "The Ego is not," then that, ananda, would have confirmed the doctrine of the Samanas and Brahmanas who believe in annihilation. If I, ananda, when the wandering monk Vacchagotta asked me: "Is there the Ego?" had answered: "The Ego is," would that have served my end, ananda, by producing in him the knowledge: all existences are non-Ego?'

"'That it would not, sire.'

"'But if I, ananda, when the wandering monk Vacchagotta asked me: "Is there not the Ego?" had answered: "The Ego is not," then that, ananda, would only have caused the wandering monk Vacchagotta to be thrown from one bewilderment into another: "My Ego, did it not exist before? but now it exists no longer!""'

In this story Buddha gives two reasons for refusing to answer Vacchagotta's question. He is asked to answer Yes or No. Whichever answer he may give, some school of metaphysicians is sure to claim him as its own. And whichever answer he may give, he is sure to bewilder Vacchagotta.

That Buddha had no patience with the metaphysicians is made clear by this and by other stories. He had many quarrels with them. He objected to them for playing with words, with the result that on the one hand they drew people away from the main business of life and on the other hand profaned by the inadequacy of their symbols the deep mysteries which they professed to explore. He objected to the misconception of knowledge, of truth, of reality, which underlay their shallow dualism, and made it possible for them to assume that all the problems of existence could be brought to the issue of a simple Yes or a simple No. Above all, he deplored the loss of temper which the very futility of their wordy wrangling rendered inevitable,—the loss of charity, the loss of serenity, the loss of self-control, the loss of all the qualities which he had called upon men to cultivate. "The theory that the world is eternal, the theory that the world is infinite, the theory that the soul and the body are identical"—of each of these and of all kindred theories he says the same thing—"this theory is a jungle, a wilderness, a puppet show, a writhing and a fetter, and is coupled with misery, ruin, despair and agony and does not tend to aversion, absence of passion, cessation, quiescence, knowledge, supreme wisdom and Nirvana."

But we shall the better understand his antipathy to the metaphysicians if we consider the second of his reasons for remaining silent,—his fear of either misleading or bewildering Vacchagotta. Dr. Oldenberg thinks that in giving this reason he came very near to saying that there was no Ego, and that it was only regard for Vacchagotta's susceptibilities which kept him silent. This criticism is, I think, based on a misconception of Buddha's mental attitude. Buddha saw clearly enough that the answer to Vacchagotta's question, as to all similar questions, was "Yes and No,"—"Yes" from this point of view, "No" from that. The words that are ascribed to him—words which may well have been his—suggest that some such thoughts as these were passing through his mind: "The Ego is real beyond all reality, but I cannot hope to make Vacchagotta understand this. If I tell him that the Ego is, he will assume that I mean by the word what he does, and so be led astray. If, foreseeing this, I tell him that the body is not the Ego, the sensations are not the Ego, the consciousness is not the Ego, and so forth,—if, in my desire to bring home to him the transcendent reality of the Ego, I refuse to allow him to identify it with any of those things which he has been accustomed to regard as real,—he will come to the conclusion that there is no Ego, that the word is an empty name.

If, on the other hand, I tell him that, as he understands the word, there is no Ego, that the sense of individuality, of separateness, which seems to him to be of the essence of the sense of self, is delusive (separateness being the very negation of true selfhood), he will be equally bewildered. In either case he will feel that he has been living in a dream. What can I do, then, but keep silent? Had Buddha shared Dr. Paul Carus' fundamental antipathy to the Ego—to the whole idea of selfhood—he would, I think, without hesitation have answered the monk's question with an uncompromising No; for metaphysical atomism, like every other development of materialism, is very easy to explain, the strength of materialism lying in this, that it is the precise system of thought which the average man, who had forgotten his mother's teaching and silenced the questionings of his heart, would—if he took to thinking—construct for himself. Had Buddha believed in the Ego, as the pious Christian believes in it, as a something (to use Dr. Rhys Davids' words) "which flies out away from the body" and retains its individuality for all time, he would have answered the monk's question with an unqualified "Yes"; for he would have known that the monk's conception of the Ego coincided with, or at any rate approximated to, his own.

That he said neither "Yes" or "No" suggests that he neither believed in the Ego, as the pious Christian believes in it, nor disbelieved in it, as the votary of the "religion of science" disbelieves in it; and leaves us free to conjecture that his conception of the Ego, whatever form it may have taken, transcended the range of ordinary thought and would not suffer itself to be translated into intelligible speech.

The second story has been thus epitomized for us by Dr. Oldenberg:

> *"The venerable Malukya comes to the Master, and expresses his astonishment that the Master's discourse leaves a series of the very most important and deepest questions unanswered. Is the world eternal or is it limited by bounds of time? Does the Perfect Buddha live on beyond death? Does the Perfect One not live on beyond death? It pleases me not, says the monk, that all this shall remain unanswered and I do not think it right; therefore I am come to the Master to interrogate him about these doubts. May it please Buddha to answer them if he can. 'But when anyone does not understand a matter and does not know it, then a straightforward man says: I do not understand that, I do not know that.'*

"We see: the question of the Nirvana is brought before Buddha by that monk as directly and definitely as could ever be possible. And what answers Buddha? He says in his Socratic fashion, not without a touch of irony, 'What have I said to thee before now, Malukyaputta? Have I said, Come, Malukyaputta, and be my disciple; I shall teach thee whether the world is everlasting or not everlasting, whether the world is finite or infinite, whether the vital faculty is identical with the body or separate from it, whether the Perfect One lives on after death or does not live on, or whether the Perfect One lives on and at the same time does not live on after death, or whether he neither lives on nor does not live on?'

"'That thou hast not said, Sire.'

"'Or hast thou,' Buddha goes on, 'said to me: I shall be thy disciple, declare unto me, whether the world is everlasting or not everlasting, and so on?'

"This also must Malukya answer in the negative.

"'If a man,' Buddha proceeds, 'were struck by a poisoned arrow, and his friends and relatives called in a skilful physician, what if the wounded man said: "I shall not allow my wound to be treated until I know who the man is by whom I have been wounded, whether he is a noble, a Brahman, a Vaicya, a Cudra"—or if he said: "I shall not allow my wound to be treated until I know what they call the man who has wounded me, and of what family he is, whether he is tall or small or of middle stature, and how his weapon was made with which he has struck me." What would the end of the case be? The man would die of his wound.'

"Why has Buddha not taught his disciples, whether the world is finite or infinite, whether the saint lives on beyond death or not? Because the knowledge of these things does not conduct to progress in holiness, because it does not contribute to peace and enlightenment. What contributes to peace and enlightenment, Buddha has taught his own: the truth of suffering, the truth of the origin of suffering, the truth of the path to the cessation of suffering. 'Therefore, Malukyaputta, whatsoever has not been revealed by me, let that remain unrevealed, and what has been revealed, let it be revealed.'"

In this story Buddha claims to have taught his disciples all that they need to know and can be made to understand. More than this he cannot and will not teach them. He may know more about the deeper realities of existence than he chooses to reveal. Malukya suggests that he should make open confession of his ignorance, but he makes no response to this. His reason for keeping silent is that, if men are to wait till Malukya's questions have been adequately answered, they will have to wait for ever, and meanwhile the main concerns of life—the pursuit of peace and enlightenment, the practice of self-control, the cultivation of sympathy—will be forgotten and neglected. The average man may either ask the "Doctors" to answer those great questions for him, or he may try to answer them for himself. The result will be the same in either case. The questions will never be answered; the Path will never be entered; and, what is worse, the evil passions which are generated by verbal controversy will poison the springs of spiritual life.

When we read this dialogue we seem to have travelled far from the Indian idea that knowledge of reality is the first condition of "salvation." But, in truth, we have never really quitted it. The metaphysical path to knowledge was one which Buddha looked upon with distrust and aversion; but knowledge itself—the knowledge which has its counterpart in inward enlightenment, the knowledge of reality which makes for peace and deliverance—was the very goal to which the Path was intended to lead.

The truth of things, as Buddha conceived of it, could not be set forth in a series of formulas, for (to go no further) the laws of language would make that impossible; but it could be lived up to and lived in to: and so he bade men control their passions and desires, and cultivate kindness and goodwill, that the consequent growth of their souls might be rewarded by the expansion of their consciousness and the deepening of their insight, till it became possible for them to know (in the truest sense of the word) the fleeting from the abiding, the phantasmal from the real. The propositions which Malukya challenged Buddha to answer had but little meaning for him. This we may take for granted. But he might conceivably have waived them aside, and tried to disclose to his disciples the inner faith of his own heart. That he made no attempt to do so does not prove that there was no master theory of things behind his formal teaching. When we read the words "whatsoever has not been revealed by me let that remain unrevealed," we cannot but feel that what "remained unrevealed" was something well worth revealing. What the silence of Buddha does prove, or at least suggest, is that the creed of his heart was too deep for words,—that the realities which it sought to encompass and co-ordinate far transcended the normal range of human thought.

What the first story left us free to conjecture, the second has suggested to us as a plausible hypothesis,—namely, that Buddha's silence was the outcome, not of the hollowness of his creed, but of the very abundance of his spiritual faith. The third story falls into line with the first and second, but brings us nearer to the same conclusion.

"King Pasenadi of Kosala, we are told, on one occasion on a journey between his two chief towns, Saketa and Savatthi, fell in with the nun Khema, a female disciple of Buddha, renowned for her wisdom. The King paid his respects to her, and inquired of her concerning the sacred doctrine.

"'Venerable lady,' asked the King, 'does the Perfect One exist after death?'

"'The Exalted One, O great King, has not declared: the Perfect One exists after death.'

"'Then does the Perfect One not exist after death, venerable lady?'

"'This also, O great King, the Exalted One has not declared: the Perfect One does not exist after death.'

"'Thus, venerable lady, the Perfect One does exist after death, and at the same time does not exist after death?—thus, venerable lady, the Perfect One neither exists after death, nor does he not exist?'

"The answer is still the same: the Exalted One has not revealed it....

"The King is astonished. 'What is the reason, venerable lady, what is the ground, on which the Exalted One has not revealed this?'

"'Permit me,' answers the nun, 'now to ask thee a question, O great King, and do thou answer me as the case seems to thee to stand. How thinks thou, O great King, hast thou an accountant, or a mint-master, or a treasurer, who could count the sands of the Ganges, who could say: there are there so many grains of sand, or so many hundreds, or thousands, or hundreds of thousands of grains of sand?'

"'No, venerable lady, I have not.'

"'Or hast thou an accountant, a mint-master, or a treasurer, who could measure the water in the great ocean, who could say: there are therein so many measures of water, or so many hundreds, or thousands, or hundreds of thousands of measures of water?'

"'No, venerable lady, I have not.'

"'And why not? The great ocean is deep, immeasurable, unfathomable. So also, O great King, if the existence of the Perfect One be measured by the predicates of corporeal form: these predicates of the corporeal form are abolished in the Perfect One, their root is severed, they are hewn away like a palm tree and laid aside, so that they cannot germinate again in the future. Released, O great King, is the Perfect One from this, that his being should be gauged by the measure of the corporeal world: he is deep, immeasurable, unfathomable as the great ocean. "The Perfect One exists after death," this is not apposite; "the Perfect One does not exist after death," this also is not apposite; "the Perfect One at once exists and does not exist after death," this also is not apposite; "the Perfect One neither does nor does not exist after death," this also is not apposite.'

"But Pasenadi, the King of Kosala, received the nun Khema's discourse with satisfaction and approbation, rose from his seat, bowed reverently before Khema, the nun, turned and went away."

Supreme reality—the ideal object of all high thinking, of all knowledge, of all wisdom—is here symbolized by the Perfect One's existence. And that existence, we are told, is "deep, unfathomable, immeasurable as the great ocean." "When such a reason," says Dr. Oldenberg, "is assigned for the waiving of the question as to whether the Perfect One lives for ever, is not this very giving of a reason itself an answer? And is not this answer a Yes? No being in the ordinary sense, but still assuredly not a non-being; a sublime positive, of which thought has no idea, for which language has no expression, which beams out to meet the cravings of the thirsty for immortality in that same splendour of which the apostle says: 'Eye hath not seen, nor ear heard, neither have entered into the heart of man, the things which God hath prepared for them that love Him.'"

The nun Khema had caught the spirit of her Master's teaching. The explanation that she gave of his teaching harmonizes so well with those which he himself is reported to have given, when challenged with probing questions by Vacchagotta and Malukya, that we must needs regard it as at least provisionally true. Buddha kept silent because his heart was overfull, because he had too much to say.

What other explanations of his silence can be given?

Three, and three only, suggest themselves to my mind.

The first is that he was a pure and consistent agnostic, an indifferentist not only in the presence of the wrangling dogmatists, but also in the depths of his own soul. Had he been this, had he been what no man is who feels and thinks deeply, he would have told his disciples that he regarded all the statements and all the solutions of the ultimate problems with equal indifference, and in telling them this would have explained and justified his silence.

The second is that his own attitude towards great matters was one of helpless bewilderment. Had it been this, had the light of his clear and authoritative teaching been the reflection of an impenetrable fog of doubt, he would have openly said so, for such a confession would have added force and weight to his contention that men must win deliverance, not by trying to guess metaphysical riddles, but by walking in the Path.

Thus the bare fact of Buddha's silence makes the first and the second explanations of it untenable.

The third is that he was a negative dogmatist, who refrained, for fear of scandalizing his disciples and paralyzing their spiritual energies, from openly formulating his sweeping negations. This is the hypothesis which Dr. Rhys Davids, Dr. Paul Carus, and others are disposed to accept. I have already given my reasons for rejecting the first part of it. I will now consider the second. Had Buddha been a negative dogmatist, would he have refrained from formulating his nihilistic creed? I think not. So sincere was he and so deeply in earnest, that he would have kept nothing back from his disciples—this we may assume at the outset—which it would have been possible for him to communicate to them.

Now it happens that a creed whose formulæ are all negations is, of all creeds, the easiest to expound; and the fact that Buddha made no attempt to expound his creed is therefore a convincing proof that the faith of his heart was not the "religion of science." When he expounded his scheme of life, he gave such reasons as he could for inviting men to adopt it. That he kept other reasons in reserve can scarcely be doubted. Had these occult reasons admitted of being stated, he would surely have stated them. That he would have played the opportunist in a matter of more than life and death, that he would have kept silence about the master problems of human thought when it was possible and even easy for him to set forth his solution of them, is to my mind incredible.

The question which confronts us admits of being discussed on other than a priori grounds. There are stories which bear on it. Just before he died Buddha is reported to have said, "I have preached the truth without making any distinction between exoteric and esoteric doctrine; for in respect of the truth, ananda, the Tathagata has no such thing as the closed fist of a teacher who keeps some things back." The inference which Dr. Rhys Davids draws from these words—that there is nothing esoteric in Buddhism—is not warranted by the premises, and is inconsistent with Dr. Rhys Davids' own contention that, in his reply to the two young Brahmins who asked him to show them the way to union with God, Buddha "adopted the opportunist position" and gave his sanction to beliefs which in his heart of hearts he disowned. There is always, in the nature of things, something esoteric in the faith of a man who has thought deeply and sincerely.

There are many thoughts which he cannot communicate—the intervening barriers are insuperable—to the rank and file of mankind. There are some thoughts which he cannot communicate even to those who are in close sympathy with his general attitude towards the deepest of all problems. There are a few thoughts which he is compelled to keep back even from those whose inner life is very near and dear to his own. And, behind and beyond all these, there are movements of his own inner being which will probably some day shape themselves into thoughts, but which meanwhile remain—unformulated and unformulable—below the threshold of his own conscious life. When Buddha told ananda that he had kept nothing back from his disciples, he was doubtless contrasting in his mind his own methods with those of the Brahmanic teachers of his day,—teachers who kept everything back from their disciples, who sought to regulate the lives of the people down to the minutest details of conduct, yet gave no reason for what they prescribed, and so crushed down the spiritual life of India under the deadly burden of an apparently meaningless ceremonialism. And he doubtless meant that he had told his disciples everything which it was possible for him to disclose to them. More than that he did not mean: or the stories of his silence are all untrue.

But whatever his words to ananda may have meant, it is certain that he who spoke them was not an opportunist: it is certain that, if he had been in possession of a creed as clear, as intelligible, and as easy to formulate as the (so-called) "religion of science," he would have disclosed it to all who came to him for guidance. Dr. Rhys Davids makes no attempt to harmonize the ultra-candour of the man who claimed to have kept nothing back from his disciples, with the shiftiness of the man who kept back from the two young Brahmins, while he responded to their demand for spiritual guidance, his disbelief in the fundamental dogma of their creed.

But the attempt deserves to be made. There is surely a mean between the complacent opportunism which allows a man to simulate complete sympathy with beliefs which he has long outgrown, and the aggressive candour which makes him blurt out, or try to blurt out, whatever is in his mind, with the result that he misleads and deceives his neighbour in the sacred name of Truth. "Ilyades choses," says Joubert, *"que l'homme ne peut connaitre que vaguement: les grands esprits se contentent d'en avoir des notions vagues; mais cela ne suffit point aux esprits vulgaires. Il faut, pour leur repos, qu'ils se forgent ou qu'on leur offre des idees fixes et determinees sur les objets meme où toute precision est erreur. Ces esprits communs n'ont point d'ailes; ils ne peuvent se soutenir dans rien de ce qui n'est que de l'espace; il leur faut des points d'appui, des fables, des mensonges, des idoles.*

Mentez leur donc, et ne les trompez pas." It is certainly better to "lie" to men than to "deceive" them. But Buddha did not lie to the "esprits vulgaires" of his day. He kept silence in their presence.

Having rejected as untenable three plausible explanations of Buddha's silence, we are left face to face with the only theory which takes account both of the fact of his silence and of the reasons which he gave for it,—the theory that he had a creed of his own, a creed which went to the root of all great matters, but which, in some sort, bound him to silence. Such a creed was, as it happens, already in existence. The deeply spiritual philosophy which had inspired the authors of the Upanishads was, in its essence, esoteric.

The conception of God—the Supreme Reality—as, on the one hand, the soul or inner life of the Universe, and, on the other hand, the true self of each individual man, is one in the presence of which thought becomes an impertinence and speech a profanation. The feelings which arise in the soul in response—if there happens to be any response—to an idea which is at once overpoweringly vast and elusively subtle, do not suffer themselves to be systematized or formulated, but pass in an instant, in the first pulsation of their mighty movement, far beyond the limits of any tabulated creed. This the sages of India instinctively felt, and feeling this they "let their words be few." Even in the Upanishads, which were composed, not for the world at large but for an inner circle of sages and recluses, the language used is that of paradox and negation. That in which all their thinking centred—the Divine in man—was not to them an object of scientific curiosity, a being whose nature could be exhaustively analyzed or whose attributes could be set forth in a series of formulae.

They habitually spoke of him as "That." They shrank from applying any name to him which might suggest either that he was a member of a class, or that he had a distinct individuality of his own.

If they predicated anything of him, they at once predicated its opposite. He is swifter than the mind, yet he moves not: he is far and near: he is at once innermost and outermost: and so forth. The moment of apprehension, as thought strives to grasp him, is also the moment of discomfiture and recoil. Speech, thought, sight, hearing,—each of these in turn is made possible by him, and therefore each in turn fails to reach him. He is beyond sight, beyond speech, beyond mind, beyond the known, beyond the unknown.

He is veiled from thought by the excess of his own inward light. Dwelling at the heart of man, as the "unbeholden essence" of all things,—gathering into his infinite inwardness all the outermost boundaries of the Universe,—he is at once too subtle to be grasped by any effort of mental analysis, and too vast to be encompassed by any flight of imaginative thought. "He thinks of it, for whom it passes thought; who thinks of it doth never know it."

Men who had to use such language as this within the narrow limits of an esoteric circle, had no choice but to become silent when those limits were passed. For "those who understand," the language of paradox and negation has a meaning; but paradoxes bewilder the uninitiated, and the language of negation is apt to be mistaken for the language of denial and revolt. This, then, was the tremendous problem that confronted the sages of the Upanishads. Possessed with a spiritual idea, so deeply, so inexhaustibly true that, if it could but be assimilated by the heart of man, it would in the fullness of time "redeem the world,"—they were debarred, on the one hand by the fundamental laws of thought and language, on the other hand by the very depth and truth of their cherished idea, from revealing it—as an idea—to mankind. How, then, were they to bring it home to the hearts and lives of their fellow-men? The ceremonial solution of the problem, which they adopted as a counsel of despair, proved to be no solution; and the problem remained unsolved till Buddha himself solved it—whether consciously or unconsciously, is the question that now confronts us—by transferring it to the plane of practical life.

That Buddha's ethical scheme was a practical interpretation, an exposition in terms of human conduct and human life, of the paramount idea of the Upanishads, I have already attempted to show. Was the coincidence—at every vital point—between the scheme and the idea an accident, or was it deliberately planned? That the latter is by many degrees the more reasonable hypothesis, is too obvious to need demonstration. If we hesitate to adopt it, the reason is that Buddha, though he worked out the idea, as a principle of action, with consistent thoroughness and consummate skill, not only made no attempt to expound it, but even turned back, on the threshold of their inquiry, all who sought to go behind the scheme to the philosophy that it embodied. But this difficulty will vanish when we remind ourselves that if Buddha, who made it his life's work to preach the gospel of deliverance to all men, had accepted the paramount idea of the Upanishads and made it his own, he would have been bound by the very strength and depth of his faith in it to wall it round with inviolable silence.

Link by link, the chain of proof has been forged which connects the inmost soul of Buddha with the spiritual idealism of ancient India. It is true that, in such a matter as this, demonstration is not to be looked for; but it is also true that each new link adds strength and elasticity to the chain as a whole. The theory that Buddha was at heart a spiritual idealist has received confirmation from many quarters. The last of the arguments that support it—the last and not the least weighty—is that it, and it alone, accounts for and justifies his silence.

THE MATERIALISM OF BUDDHA

Let us assume that, far from denying the Ego, Buddha believed in it, in his heart of hearts,—believed in it with the depth and subtlety of belief which are characteristic of Indian idealism,—believed in it as the "unbeholden essence" of all things, as the all-generating, all-sustaining life which individualizes itself in every human breast, yet is what it really is at the heart of the Universe, and nowhere else.

What would be the attitude of one who so conceived of the Ego towards the popular belief—popular, one may safely conjecture, in Buddha's day as in ours—in the intrinsic reality of the individualized Ego, or individual soul? That the Ego is not real, in the fullest sense of the word, till it has become one with the Universal Soul, is the postulate on which all his philosophy, both as a whole and under each of its aspects, would be hinged. On its way to the goal of union with the Divine, the individual soul must needs pass through many stages of unreality.

So long as it retains its sense of isolation, its mistaken sense of I-ness, it is, comparatively speaking, unreal. What is real in it is its potential universality. What is unreal is what it regards as of its very essence,—its individuality, its sense of separateness from all other things. Had Buddha looked at the problem of selfhood from the standpoint of Indian idealism, he would have seen that the popular belief in the intrinsic value of the individual Soul is fundamentally false, not on the plane of metaphysical speculation only, but on every plane of human life; and he would have set himself to combat it in each of its many forms.

Of the many forms that it takes I need not speak at length. The materialism of him who identifies his soul (his "self") with his body, or who conceives of it as the "totality" of his own sensations, perceptions, or other states of consciousness; the semi-materialism of him who (like the pious Christian) regards the soul as "something which flies out away from the body at death," or as one of many parts or organs of a complex being; the sentimental clinging to individuality; the metaphysical clinging to individuality;—these may be mentioned as typical forms of that reluctance to regard the Universal Soul as the only true self, which is so characteristic of popular thought in all the stages of its development, and against which Buddha, if I have not misread his philosophy, must have waged a relentless war.

If I am asked why Buddha, who eschewed metaphysical controversy, should have thought it necessary to combat a belief which seems to be primarily metaphysical, my answer is that the belief is not primarily metaphysical, that on the contrary it is the reflection in consciousness of a deep-seated instinct which has vital ethical consequences—the instinct to affirm the ordinary self, to accept it, minister to it, magnify it, rest in it—in a word, the egoistic instinct, the hidden root of every form of spiritual evil, and the first and last of moral defects.

As the suppression of egoism was the very end and aim of Buddha's scheme of life, and as in this matter the distinction between theory on the one hand and sentiment, desire, and impulse on the other, is hard to draw and easy to efface, it was but natural that Buddha should wage war against the egoistic instinct even when it disguised itself as a semi-philosophical theory. But he waged that war, as he did everything else that he took in hand, within the limits prescribed by his own "sweet reasonableness" and exalted common-sense. Leaving it to the metaphysical experts to wrangle over the more abstract aspects of the problem of selfhood, he contented himself with combating on quasi-popular grounds the popular delusion that the individual Ego is real, permanent, self-contained.

Let us assume this much; and we shall see a new meaning in each of the many passages on which Western criticism has based its theory that denial of the Ego was the cardinal article of Buddha's creed. We shall see that, whenever he seems to be denying existence to the Ego as such, what he is really doing is to deny reality to the individual Ego, to the ordinary surface self.

Let us first consider a dialogue in which the principal speaker is the venerable Sariputta, but in which the arguments advanced may well have been devised by Buddha himself, coinciding as they do with arguments which he is reported to have used in one of his early discourses. A monk, named Yamaka, had convinced himself, as many modern interpreters of Buddhism have done, that the "doctrine taught by the Blessed One "amounted to this, "that on the dissolution of the body the monk who has lost all depravity is annihilated, perishes, and does not exist after death." His fellow-monks urged him to abandon what they regarded as a "wicked heresy," but to no purpose. At last they besought the venerable Sariputta to "draw near" to Yamaka and try to convert him to a truer view of the Blessed One's teaching.

"And the venerable Sariputta consented by his silence. Then the venerable Sariputta in the evening of the day arose from meditation, and drew near to where the venerable Yamaka was; and having drawn near he greeted the venerable Yamaka, and having passed the compliments of friendship and civility, he sat down respectfully on one side. And seated respectfully at one side, the venerable Sariputta spoke to the venerable Yamaka as follows: 'Is the report true, brother Yamaka, that the following wicked heresy has sprung up in your mind: Thus do I understand the doctrine taught by the Blessed One, that on the dissolution of the body the monk who has lost all depravity is annihilated, perishes, and does not exist after death?'

"'Even so, brother, do I understand the doctrine taught by the Blessed One, that on the dissolution of the body the monk who has lost all depravity is annihilated, perishes, and does not exist after death.'

"'What think you, brother Yamaka? Is form permanent, or transitory?"

"'It is transitory, brother.'

"'And that which is transitory—is it evil, or is it good?'

"'It is evil, brother.'

"'And that which is transitory, evil, and liable to change—is it possible to say of it: This is mine—this am I—this is my Ego?'

"'Nay, verily, brother.'

"'Is sensation... perception... the predispositions... consciousness, permanent, or transitory?'

"'It is transitory, brother.'

"'And that which is transitory—is it evil, or is it good?'

"'It is evil, brother.'

"'And that which is transitory, evil, and liable to change—is it possible to say of it: This is mine; this am I; this is my Ego?'

"'Nay, verily, brother Yamaka.'

"'Accordingly, brother Yamaka, as respects all form whatsoever—as respects all sensation whatsoever—as respects all perception whatsoever—as respects all predispositions whatsoever—as respects all consciousness whatsoever, past, future or present, be it subjective or existing outside, gross or subtle, mean or exalted, far or near, the correct view in the light of the highest knowledge is as follows: This is not mine; this am I not; this is not my Ego.

"'Perceiving this, brother Yamaka, the learned and noble disciple conceives an aversion for form, conceives an aversion for sensation, conceives an aversion for perception, conceives an aversion for the predispositions, conceives an aversion for consciousness. And in conceiving this aversion he becomes divested of passion, and by the absence of passion he becomes free, and when he is free he becomes aware that he is free; and he knows that rebirth is exhausted, that he has lived the holy life, that he has done what it behaved him to do, and that he is no more for the world.

"'What think you, brother Yamaka? Do you consider form as the Saint?'

"'Nay, verily, brother.'

"'Do you consider sensation... perception... the predispositions... consciousness as the Saint?'

"'Nay, verily, brother.'

"'What think you, brother Yamaka? Do you consider the Saint as comprised in form?'

"'Nay, verily, brother.'

"'Do you consider the Saint as distinct from form?'

"'Nay, verily, brother.'

"'Do you consider the Saint as comprised in sensation?... as distinct from sensation?... as comprised in perception?... as distinct from perception?... as comprised in the predispositions?... as distinct from the predispositions?... as comprised in consciousness?... as distinct from consciousness?'

"'Nay, verily, brother.'

"'What think you, brother Yamaka? Are form, sensation, perception, the predispositions and consciousness united the Saint?'

"'Nay, verily, brother.'

"'What think you, brother Yamaka? Do you consider the Saint as a something having no form, sensation, perception, predispositions or consciousness?'

"'Nay, verily, brother.'

"'Considering now, brother Yamaka, that you fail to make out and establish the existence of the Saint in the present life, is it reasonable for you to say: Thus do I understand the doctrine taught by the Blessed One, that on the dissolution of the body the monk who has lost all depravity is annihilated, perishes, and does not exist after death?" "'Brother Sariputta, it was because of my ignorance that I held this wicked heresy; but now that I have listened to the doctrinal instruction of the venerable Sariputta, I have abandoned that wicked heresy and acquired the true doctrine.'"

Mr H. C. Warren, from whose translation of the dialogue in his learned work, "Buddhism in Translation," I have made this extract, heads each page in the dialogue with the significant words, "There is no Ego." That is how he interprets the teaching of Sariputta. But surely what Sariputta intended to teach was the exact opposite of this. The monk Yamaka believed that at the death of the "Saint"—at the moment when his cycle of earth-lives had come to an end—he ceased to be. This belief, we are expressly told, was regarded as a "wicked heresy"; and Sariputta disabused Yamaka's mind of it by showing him that it was as difficult for him to "make out and establish" the existence of the "Saint" in the present life as in the life beyond death (and beyond rebirth). He reminds him, in words which, according to tradition, had been used by Buddha himself, that the Ego is not to be identified with form, with sensation, with perception, with the "predispositions," with consciousness, since each of these is transitory and therefore evil, and "of that which is transitory, evil and liable to change it is not possible to say 'This is mine; this am I; this is my Ego.'" "The ignorant unconverted man... considers form in the light of an Ego, considers sensation... perception... the predispositions... consciousness in the light of an Ego," and therefore clings to those apparent "selves" though they are all transitory and evil. "The learned and noble disciple does not consider form, sensation, etc., in the light of an Ego," and he therefore detaches himself from each of those delusive "selves." Not a word is said, in any part of the discourse, in disproof of the existence of the Ego. The point of the argument is that each of the apparent Egos—the Ego of form, the Ego of sensation, and the rest—is unreal; and that the man who regards the Ego of the "Saint" as non-existent after death, because it will then be finally detached from form, sensation, etc., is bound by the logic of his own delusion to regard the Ego of the "Saint" as non-existent while on earth, since, if the "Saint" has indeed won deliverance, he will have finally detached himself, even while on earth, from each of those phantom Egos, and in doing so will have found his true self.

From this point it is possible to advance to two conclusions. As disbelief in the after-death existence of the "Saint" is a "wicked heresy," it stands to reason that it is also a "wicked heresy" to regard the "Saint"—the true Ego—as non-existent now. This is the first conclusion, which the Western critic who seeks to father upon Buddha his own denial of the Ego will do well to bear in mind. The second seems to have been tacitly drawn by both Sariputta and Yamaka, and to have carried conviction to the latter's mind. As it is obviously absurd to say that the "Saint" is non-existent now, it stands to reason that it is also absurd to say—as Yamaka had said—that the "Saint" will cease to be after death. The whole discourse is directed nominally against Yamaka's "wicked heresy," but really against the erroneous belief that the individual Ego, the Ego which is associated with form, with sensation, and the rest, is the true Ego,—a belief which had generated in Yamaka's mind the "wicked heresy" that "on the dissolution of the body" the Saint "is annihilated, perishes, and does not exist." Indeed it is no exaggeration to say that in this discourse disbelief in the reality of the Ego—the true Ego which transcends the limits of the transitory, and therefore passes beyond the reach of thought and language—is authoritatively condemned.

Dr. Rhys Davids lays great stress on a discourse in which various attempts to conceive of the existence of the Ego after death are condemned as heresies. Here, as in the dialogue which has just been considered, the Ego is that of the man who has won deliverance while still living on earth, and whose cycle of earth-lives is therefore coming to an end. The prying attempt to follow the liberated Ego into the life beyond death, into the unimaginable bliss of Nirvana, is repelled as impertinent and delusive, and every form that it takes is condemned as a "heresy." The discourse ends with these words: "Mendicants [Monks], that which binds the Teacher [the Saint, the Perfect One] to existence is cut off; but his body still remains. While his body shall remain he will be seen by gods and men, but after the dissolution of the body, neither gods nor men will see him." "Would it be possible," asks Dr. Rhys Davids, "in a more complete and categorical manner to deny that there is any soul—anything of any kind, which continues to exist, in any manner, after death?"

This criticism (so characteristically Western) is as wide of the mark as is Mr Warren's headline comment on the dialogue between Sariputta and Yamaka. What the preacher is trying to enforce is what Sariputta had impressed upon Yamaka, that the Ego of the "Saint"—the true Ego, for the "Saint" is one who has found his true self does not exist after death in any form or mode which is comprehensible by human thought. Far from denying the existence of the Ego, the preacher is insisting on its transcendent reality. "Neither gods nor men" will see the "Saint" after death, not because he will then be non-existent, but because his being will have out-soared all the categories of human thought.

In these and other such discourses Buddha falls into line with the thinkers of the Upanishads, who described by a series of negations what they regarded as the true Ego,—the Divine in man. The coincidences between his teaching and theirs are so significant that the only way to account for them is to assume that his faith—the deepest faith of his heart—was in its essence identical with theirs.

If the account that he gave of the Ego was purely negative, if he abstained from positive statements (even in that paradoxical form which was dear to the thinkers of the Upanishads), the reason was that he wished men to find out for themselves, by following the Path of soul-expansion, what the Ego really is. He said to them, in thought if not in words: "The Ego is not this thing or that; it is not any of the things with which you are used to identify it. If you wish to know what it is, enter the Path and follow it to the end. Your question will then be answered, for it will have transformed itself into a burning thirst for the ideal and the divine; and in the bliss of Nirvana that thirst will be eternally slaked and eternally renewed."

Dr. Rhys Davids is confirmed in his belief that Buddha denied the Ego, by the fact that the "heresy of individuality" is one of the three "Fetters" which have to be broken on the very threshold of the new life. But here, as elsewhere, Buddha is denying the reality, not of the Ego as such, but of the individual Ego; in other words, he is condemning by implication the blindness of him who regards the limitations which his individuality imposes upon him as the essential conditions of his existence.

So, too, when he names among the fetters which have to be broken in the later stages of the Eightfold Path, the desire for life in the worlds of form, and the desire for life in the formless worlds, he is thinking, not of the desire for life as such but of the desire for separate life, for the continuance of individuality,—the hydra-headed desire which is ever tending to counteract the centripetal energy of love.

There is one set of discourses on which those who regard Buddha as a negative dogmatist lay great stress,—the so-called Milinda dialogues, or conversations between the Greek King, Menanda, of Baktria, and Nagasena, the Buddhist teacher. Nagasena seems to have been an acute controversialist who loved argument for its own sake almost as much as Buddha disliked it, and who, had he lived in Europe in the Middle Ages, would probably have nailed theological or metaphysical theses to church-doors.

That he had caught the deeper spirit of the Master's teaching is, to say the least, improbable; but that his discourses present to us an interpretation of that teaching, which had gained currency in his day, can scarcely be doubted. I have elsewhere allowed, for argument's sake, that he may have had an academic antipathy to the Ego. If he had, his discourses do less than justice to their theme. The arguments by which a merely academic belief (or disbelief) is sustained are in the nature of things ineffective. The spiritual atmosphere of his age, the words that he finds himself compelled to use, even his own subconscious convictions—are all against the thinker. In the well known Chariot dialogue, Nagasena is supposed to have proved conclusively that "there is no Ego." I cannot see that he has done this, and I am by no means sure that he has attempted to do it. What he has proved is that, just as the name chariot belongs to the vehicle as a whole and not to any of its parts, so the name Nagasena belongs to the living being as a whole and not to any of his organs or faculties.

If the dialogue is directed against anything, it is directed against the vulgar belief that the Soul is a quasi-material something (like the babe of vapour in mediaeval art) which can be separated from the rest of the man, just as a wheel can be separated from the rest of the chariot; or again that the soul is one among many faculties which go to make up the whole man. The flame simile, which is also supposed to be directed against the soul-theory of the Brahmanic philosophy, is one which that theory, far from rejecting, would accept as singularly apt. For just as fire uses up fuel, and in doing so manifests itself as flame (that is, as burning fuel), so the Soul, in its journey through the earth-life, continually uses up physical matter, and in doing so manifests itself as a living body (that is, as physical matter fused and vitalized by the Soul-fire). When the Soul retires from the physical plane, the body, deprived of its vitalizing influence, disintegrates into dust, just as fuel, when its fire is extinct, turns to ashes; but the Soul itself (if we may follow its progress through the intervening stages of existence) continues to use up matter, though, as the matter used is now impalpable, the Soul-flame becomes invisible till the time comes for it to feed again on the fuel of physical nature,—in other words, to appear again on earth.

Even when Nagasena's hostility to the Ego is unmistakable, his belief in re-incarnation causes his arguments to miscarry. He may flatter himself that he has disproved the identity between A (who is living now) and B (the future inheritor of his Karma); but, as a believer in re-incarnation, he must needs take pains to prove that B will justly be held responsible for what A has done or left undone; and in his attempt to make good this point he has to admit (or rather insist) that the relation between A and B is exactly analogous to that between a "young girl" and the same girl "when grownup and marriageable."

Dr. Rhys Davids has truly said that Buddha's "whole training was Brahmanism; and that he probably deemed himself to be the most correct exponent of the spirit as distinct from the letter of the ancient faith." If this is a true statement of Buddha's attitude towards Brahmanism, it surely behoves the student of Buddhism to seek initiation into the deeper mysteries of the "ancient faith," before he attempts to interpret the creed of one who, while breaking with the letter of that faith, "deemed himself to be the most correct exponent of its spirit."

This, however, is what the Western critic, with his instinctive contempt for alien modes of thought, is extremely reluctant to do. What he does, in nine cases out of ten, is to carry with him to the study of Buddhism the prejudices and prepossessions of Western thought—foremost among which is the assumption that nothing exists, in the order of nature, except what is perceptible by man's bodily senses—and to insist that the teaching of Buddha shall conform to these, and be measured by their standards. Hence arise misconceptions and misunderstandings which might have been avoided.

If Buddhism seems to our Western minds to abound in errors and anomalies, the reason is that we insist on looking at it through a distorting medium. One who had steeped himself in the spirit of the Brahmanic philosophy before he began his study of Buddhism, would see that wherever Buddha seems to be denying existence to the Ego, what he is really doing is to deny reality to the apparent Ego or superficial Self, so that he may thereby clear the way for the exposition, not in words but in the unwritten language of conduct, character, and life, of the profound conception which is the very quintessence of the "ancient faith,"—the conception "that Brahma and the Self—the true Self—are one."

THE ATHEISM OF BUDDHA

The Christian critics of Buddhism call Buddha an atheist, nominally because he said nothing about God, really because his conception of God differs from their own.

I have already attempted to show that the silence of Buddha about God—the Supreme Reality—was quite compatible with a sublimely spiritual conception of God and a deeply spiritual faith in him. I have shown that such a conception and such a faith were in the air that Buddha breathed, and that, if he had accepted them and made them his own, the very reverence which they would have generated would have bound him to silence in the presence of his audience,—the rank and file of mankind. I have shown that his own ethical teaching was the practical exposition of this unformulated theology,—the revelation of it, not as a theology but as a scheme of life, to those who would have been bewildered by it, and who would therefore have misunderstood and misapplied it, had any attempt been made to expound it to them in words, I have inferred from this that Buddha did believe in God, not as the West believes in him, but as the Far East, at the highest level of its imaginative thinking, has ever believed in him,—as the Supreme Reality which is at the heart of the Universe, and which is at once the life and soul of Nature and the true self of Man.

But the fact remains that Buddha, though he preached the gospel of deliverance, said nothing about God. To us, with the Jehovah-virus in our veins, to us who for many centuries have been content to believe that the Universe is under the direct rule of that national deity whose sayings and doings are recorded in the Hebrew Scriptures, it seems the height of impiety to keep silence about God. It is well for us to remind ourselves that in the Far East, in the days of India's spiritual greatness, it was deemed the height of impiety to talk freely about God. We call the silence of the East atheistic.

The sages of India, though they would have thought it discourteous to say so, would have regarded our loquacity as profane. To unveil to the mind of the average man ideas which are in the nature of things so large, so deep, and so subtle that, without mental power of a very high order, it is impossible to grasp their initial—let alone their final—meaning, is to expose the most sacred of all truths to the risk (the certainty, one might almost say) of being misinterpreted and misused. From such a risk the sages of India shrank as from blasphemy against the Divine. It may be difficult for us to enter into this feeling, but it is well that we should know that it did (and does) exist.

The silence of the Far East has another aspect, and one which is equally repugnant to the "orthodox" thought of the West. In itself, in the eloquence of its dumbness, it is an abiding protest, not merely against the profane loquacity of Western dogmatism, but also against its deadly despotism. To tell men that they must, under pain of eternal damnation, believe such and such things about God—or rather accept as divinely true such and such theological formulae, whether they see any meaning in them or not—is to quench in their breasts that spark of spiritual freedom which is also the germ of spiritual life. It is true that the symbolical presentation of religious truth, which official Brahmanism adopted in preference to the doctrinal, may develop, as it certainly did in India, into a ceremonial despotism as oppressive as any that the creeds of the West have ever exerted. But Buddha's own silence was agnostic, in the deeper sense of the word, to the very core. We could imagine him saying to his disciples: "I have given you my reasons for urging you to enter the Path. If those reasons commend themselves to you, enter the Path and see to what goal it will lead you.

But do not ask me to explain my own explanation. Do not ask me for deeper reasons than those which I have given you. Do not ask me to tell you what I, for one, believe about the greatest of all great matters. The words that make sense to me would ring as nonsense in your ears. The thoughts that bring light to me would dazzle you to the verge of blindness. And I should but deepen your perplexity if I tried to give you the guidance that you seek. But the Path itself will enlighten you if you will trust yourself to it; and when you have followed it far enough you will be wise with a wisdom beyond that of the wisest sage." The idea which underlies the whole of Buddha's teaching—underlying what he said and also what he left unsaid—the idea that knowledge of divine truth must be evolved from within, instead of being imposed from without, is the direct negation of that idea of a supernatural revelation, which underlies all the creeds of the West.

After all, it is not so much the silence of Buddha that the West regards as atheistic, as the creed which that silence hints at and seems, in a sense, to shadow forth,—a creed which seals the lips of those who see deepest into the heart of its hidden truth. The orthodox Christian, who believes that to give assent to a series of formulae is to enter into possession of divine truth, and who therefore regards intolerance as a virtue and self-assertion as a sacred duty, feels instinctively that a creed which will not suffer itself to be formulated, and which therefore makes no attempt to impose its yoke upon human thought, is the hereditary enemy of his faith. His instinct has not misled him. Between the "Higher Pantheism" of India and the Supernaturalism of the Western World there is, in the region of ideas, a truceless war. Had Buddha tried to expound the creed of his heart, it would assuredly have been branded as atheistic by those who now apply that epithet to his silence.

"Such divinity," said the late Canon Liddon, "as Pantheism can ascribe to Christ is, in point of fact, no divinity at all. God is Nature, and Nature is God; everything indeed is Divine, but also nothing is Divine; and Christ shares this phantom divinity with the universe,—nay with the agencies of moral evil itself. In truth, our God does not exist in the apprehension of Pantheistic thinkers; since, when such truths as creation and personality are denied, the very idea of God is fundamentally sapped, and... the broad practical result is in reality neither more nor less than Atheism."

The writer of this passage proves nothing by his arguments but his fundamental inability to understand a creed which belongs to a plane of thought on which his mind has never learned to move: and, having misrepresented that creed beyond recognition, he brands it with a title which he regards as in the highest degree opprobrious and offensive. "Men become personal," says Dr. Newman, "when logic fails; it is their mode of appealing to their own primary elements of thought and their own illative sense, against the principles and the judgment of another." When A calls B an atheist, he does not necessarily mean that B denies the existence of God. What he does mean is that B's conception of God differs fundamentally from his own, and that he cannot by any effort of thought place himself at B's point of view.

On the whole, then, I incline to the opinion that Christianity calls the teaching of Buddha atheistic, chiefly because it suspects that behind his scheme of life and at the heart of his silence dwells a rival conception of God. If this is so, Christianity has misplaced its censure; for if trust is of the essence of faith, there is no conception of God to which the term atheistic is so strangely inappropriate as to that which sealed the lips of Buddha. Curiosity and doubt are the foster-mothers of theology; but he who has once convinced himself, as Buddha must have done, that light and love are at the heart of the Universe, ceases to be curious about God.

In the glow of his radiant and all-embracing optimism the petty theories by which man seeks to justify to himself the ways of God and his own timid faith in God, are seen to be worthless and vain. The sceptics who pride themselves on their "orthodoxy" are startled and alarmed by his silence. But out of its depths comes forth, whenever one listens for it, a message, not of atheistic denial but of whole-hearted trust in God,—trust so full, so firmly rooted, and so sure of itself, that silence alone can measure its strength and its serenity.

"And I say to mankind, Be not curious about God,

For I who am curious about each am not curious about God,

(No array of terms can say how much I am at peace about God and about death)."

5

Teaching of Buddha

SAMSARA AND NIRVANA

Look about and contemplate life! Everything is transient and nothing endures. There is birth and death, growth and decay; there is combination and separation. The glory of the world is like a flower: it stands in full bloom in the morning and fades in the heat of the day.

Wherever you look, there is a rushing and a struggling, and an eager pursuit of pleasure. There is a panic flight from pain and death, and hot are the flames of burning desires. The world is Vanity Fair, full of changes and transformations. All is Samsara, the turning Wheel of Existence.

Is there nothing permanent in the world? Is there in the universal turmoil no resting-place where our troubled heart can find peace? Is there nothing everlasting? Oh, that we could have cessation of anxiety, that our burning desires would be extinguished! When shall the mind become tranquil and composed?

The Buddha, our Lord, was grieved at the ills of life. He saw the vanity of worldly happiness and sought salvation in the one thing that will not fade or perish, but will abide for ever and ever.

You who long for life, learn that immortality is hidden in transiency. You who wish for happiness without the sting of regret, lead a life of righteousness. You who yearn for riches, receive treasures that are eternal. Truth is wealth, and a life of truth is happiness. All compounds will be dissolved again, but the varieties which determine all combinations and separations as laws of nature endure for ever and aye. Bodies fall to dust, but the truths of the mind will not be destroyed.

Truth knows neither birth nor death; it has no beginning and no end. Welcome the truth. The truth is the immortal part of mind. Establish the truth in your mind, for the truth is the image of the eternal; it portrays the immutable; it reveals the everlasting; the truth gives unto mortals the boon of immortality.

The Buddha has proclaimed the truth; let the truth of the Buddha dwell in your hearts. Extinguish in yourselves every desire that antagonizes the Buddha, and in the perfection of your spiritual growth you will become like unto him. That of your heart which cannot or will not develop into Buddha must perish, for it is mere illusion and unreal; it is the source of your error; it is the cause of your misery.

You attain to immortality by filling your minds with truth. Therefore, become like unto vessels fit to receive the Master's words. Cleanse yourselves of evil and sanctify your lives. There is no other way of reaching truth.

Learn to distinguish between Self and Truth. Self is the cause of selfishness and the source of evil; truth cleaves to no self; it is universal and leads to justice and righteousness. Self, that which seems to those who love their self as their being, is not the eternal, the everlasting, the imperishable. Seek not self, but seek the truth.

If we liberate our souls from our petty selves, wish no ill to others, and become clear as a crystal diamond reflecting the light of truth, what a radiant picture will appear in us mirroring things as they are, without the admixture of burning desires, without the distortion of erroneous illusion, without the agitation of clinging and unrest.

Yet you love self and will not abandon self-love. So be it, but then, verily, you should learn to distinguish between the false self and the true self. The ego with all its egotism is the false self. It is an unreal illusion and a perishable combination. He only who identifies his self with the truth will attain Nirvana; and he who has entered Nirvana has attained Buddhahood; he has acquired the highest good; he has become eternal and immortal.

All compound things shall be dissolved again, worlds will break to pieces and our individualities will be scattered; but the words of Buddha will remain for ever.

The extinction of self is salvation; the annihilation of self is the condition of enlightenment; the blotting out of self is Nirvana.

Happy is he who has ceased to live for pleasure and rests in the truth. Verily his composure and tranquility of mind are the highest bliss.

Let us take our refuge in the Buddha, for he has found the everlasting in the transient. Let us take our refuge in that which is the immutable in the changes of existence. Let us take our refuge in the truth that is established through the enlightenment of the Buddha. Let us take our refuge in the community of those who seek the truth and endeavour to live in the truth.

ANATHAPINDIKA, THE MAN OF WEALTH

At this time there was Anathapindika, a man of unmeasured wealth, visiting Rajagaha. Being of a charitable disposition, he was called "the supporter of orphans and the friend of the poor." Hearing that the Buddha had come into the world and was stopping in the bamboo grove near the city, he set out on that very night to meet the Blessed One.

And the Blessed One saw at once the sterling quality of Anathapindika's heart and greeted him with words of religious comfort. And they sat down together, and Anathapindika listened to the sweetness of the truth preached by the Blessed One. And the Buddha said: "The restless, busy nature of the world, this, I declare, is at the root of pain. Attain that composure of mind which is resting in the peace of immortality. Self is but a heap of composite qualities, and its world is empty like a fantasy.

"Who is it that shapes our lives? Is it Isvara, a personal creator? If Isvara be the maker, all living things should have silently to submit to their maker's power. They would be like vessels formed by the potter's hand; and if it were so, how would it be possible to practice virtue? If the world had been made by Isvara there should be no such thing as sorrow, or calamity, or evil; for both pure and impure deeds must come from him. If not, there would be another cause beside him, and he would not be self-existent. Thus, thou sees, the thought of Isvara is overthrown.

"Again, it is said that the Absolute has created us. But that which is absolute cannot be a cause. All things around us come from a cause as the plant comes from the seed; but how can the Absolute be the cause of all things alike? If it pervades them, then, certainly, it does not make them.

"Again, it is said that Self is the maker. But if self is the maker, why did it not make things pleasing? The causes of sorrow and joy are real and touchable. How can they have been made by self?

"Again, if we adopt the argument that there is no maker, our fate is such as it is, and there is no causation, what use would there be in shaping our lives and adjusting means to an end? Therefore, we argue that all things that exist are not without cause. However, neither Isvara, nor the absolute, nor the self nor causeless chance, is the maker, but our deeds produce results both good and evil according to the law of causation.

"Let us, then, abandon the heresy of worshipping Isvara and of praying to him; let us no longer lose ourselves in vain speculations or profitless subtleties; let us surrender self and all selfishness, and as all things are fixed by causation, let us practice good so that good may result from our actions."

And Anathapindika said: "I see that thou art the Buddha, the Blessed One the Tathagata, and I wish to open to the my whole mind. Having listened to my words advise me what I shall do. My life is full of work, and having acquired great wealth, I am surrounded with cares. Yet I enjoy my work, and apply myself to it with all diligence. Many people are in my employ and depend upon the success of my enterprises.

"Now, I have heard thy disciples praise the bliss of the hermit and denounce the unrest of the world. 'The Holy One,' they say, 'has given up his kingdom and his inheritance, and has found the path of righteousness, thus setting an example to all the world how to attain Nirvana.' My heart yearns to do what is right and to be a blessing unto my fellows. Let me then ask thee, Must I give up my wealth, my home, and my business enterprises, and, like thyself, go into homelessness in order to attain the bliss of a religious life?"

And the Buddha replied: "The bliss of a religious life is attainable by every one who walks in the noble eightfold path. He that cleaves to wealth had better cast it away than allow his heart to be poisoned by it; but he who does not cleave to wealth, and possessing riches, uses them rightly, will be a blessing unto his fellows. It is not life and wealth and power that enslave men, but the cleaving to life and wealth and power. The bhikkhu who retires from the world in order to lead a life of leisure will have no gain, for a life of indolence is an abomination, and lack of energy is to be despised. The Dharma of the Tathagata does not require a man to go into homelessness or to resign the world, unless he feels called upon to do so; but the Dharma of the Tathagata requires every man to free himself from the illusion of self, to cleanse his heart, to give up his thirst for pleasure, and lead a life of righteousness.

And whatever men do, whether they remain in the world as artisans, merchants, and officers of the king, or retire from the world and devote themselves to a life of religious meditation, let them put their whole heart into their task; let them be diligent and energetic, and, if they are like the lotus, which, although it grows in the water, yet remains untouched by the water, if they struggle in life without cherishing envy or hatred, if they live in the world not a life of self but a life of truth, then surely joy, peace, and bliss will dwell in their minds."

THE FIRST CONVERTS

The Blessed One tarried in solitude seven times seven days, enjoying the bliss of emancipation. At that time Tapussa and Bhallika, two merchants, came travelling on the road near by, and when they saw the great samana, majestic and full of peace, they approached him respectfully and offered him rice cakes and honey.

This was the first food that the Enlightened One ate after he attained Buddhahood.

And the Buddha addressed them and pointed out to them the way of salvation. The two merchants, seeing the holiness of the conqueror of Mara, bowed down in reverence and said: "We take our refuge, Lord, in the Blessed One and in the Dharma." Tapussa and Bhallika were the first that became followers of the Buddha and they were lay disciples.

THE BRAHMA'S REQUEST

The Blessed One having attained Buddhahood while resting under the shepherd's Nigrodha tree on the banks of the river Neranjara, pronounced this solemn utterance:

"How sure his pathway in this wood,
Who follows truth's unchanging call!
How blessed, to be kind and good,
And practice self-restraint in all!
How light, from passion to be free,
And sensual joys to let go by!
And yet his greatest bliss will be
When he has quelled the pride of 'I'.

"I have recognized the deepest truth, which is sublime and peace-giving' but difficult to understand; for most men move in a sphere of worldly interests and find their delight in worldly desires. The worldling will not understand the doctrine, for to him there is happiness in selfhood only, and the bliss that lies in a complete surrender to truth is unintelligible to him. He will call resignation what to the enlightened mind is the purest joy. He will see annihilation where the perfected one finds immortality. He will regard as death what the conqueror of self knows to be life everlasting. The truth remains hidden from him who is in the bondage of hate and desire. Nirvana remains incomprehensible and mysterious to the vulgar whose minds are beclouded with worldly interests. Should I preach the doctrine and mankind not comprehend it, it would bring me only fatigue and trouble."

Mara, the Evil One, on hearing the words of the Blessed Buddha, approached and said: "Be greeted, thou Holy One. Thou has attained the highest bliss and it is time for thee to enter into the final Nirvana."

Then Brahma Sahampati descended from the heavens and, having worshipped the Blessed One, said: "Alas! the world must perish, should the Holy One, the Tathagata, decide not to teach the Dharma. Be merciful to those that struggle; have compassion upon the sufferers; pity the creatures who are hopelessly entangled in the snares of sorrow. There are some beings that are almost free from the dust of worldliness. If they hear not the doctrine preached, they will be lost. But if they hear it, they will believe and be saved."

The Blessed One, full of compassion, looked with the eye of a Buddha upon all sentient creatures, and he saw among them beings whose minds were but scarcely covered by the dust of worldliness, who were of good disposition and easy to instruct. He saw some who were conscious of the dangers of lust and wrong doing. And the Blessed One said to Brahma Sahampati: "Wide open be the door of immortality to all who have ears to hear. May they receive the Dharma with faith."

Then the Blessed One turned to Mara, saying: "I shall not pass into the final Nirvana, O Evil One, until there be not only brethren and sisters of an Order, but also lay disciples of both sexes, who shall have become true hearers, wise, well trained, ready and learned, versed in the scriptures, fulfilling all the greater and lesser duties, correct in life, walking according to the precepts-until they, having thus themselves learned the doctrine, shall be able to give information to others concerning it, preach it, make it known, establish it, open it, minutely explain it, and make it clear-until they, when others start vain doctrines, shall be able to vanquish and refute them, and so to spread the wonder-working truth abroad. I shall not die until the pure religion of truth shall have become successful, prosperous, widespread, and popular in all its full extent-until, in a word, it shall have been well proclaimed among men!"

Then Brahma Sahampati understood that the Blessed One had granted his request and would preach the doctrine.

FOUNDING THE KINGDOM

Upaka Sees the Buddha

Now the Blessed One thought: "To whom shall I preach the doctrine first? My old teachers are dead. They would have received the good news with joy. But my five disciples are still alive. I shall go to them, and to them shall I first proclaim the gospel of deliverance."

At that time the five bhikkhus dwelt in the Deer Park at Benares, and the Blessed One rose and journeyed to their abode, not thinking of their unkindness in having left him at a time when he was most in need of their sympathy and help, but mindful only of the services which they had ministered unto him, and pitying them for the austerities which they practiced in vain.

Upaka, a young Brahman and a Jain, a former acquaintance of Siddhattha, saw the Blessed One while he journeyed to Benares, and, amazed at the majesty and sublime joyfulness of his appearance, said to him: "Thy countenance, my friend, is serene; thine eyes are bright and indicate purity and blessedness."

The holy Buddha replied: "I have obtained deliverance by the extinction of self. My body is chastened, my mind is free from desire, and the deepest truth has taken abode in my heart. I have obtained Nirvana, and this is the reason that my countenance is serene and my eyes are bright. I now desire to found the kingdom of truth upon earth, to give light to those who are enshrouded in darkness and to open the gate of deathlessness."

Upaka replied: "Thou professest then, friend, to be Jina, the conqueror of the world, the absolute one and the holy one.

The Blessed One said: "Jinas are all those who have conquered self and the passions of self; those alone are victorious who control their minds and abstain from evil. Therefore, Upaka, I am the Jina."

Upaka shook his head. "Venerable Gautama, he said, "thy way lies yonder," and taking another road he went away.

THE SERMON AT BENARES

On seeing their old teacher approach, the five Bhikkus agreed among themselves not to salute him, nor to address him as a master, but by his name only. "For," so they said, "he has broken his vow and has abandoned holiness. He is no bhikkhu, but Gautama, and Gautama has become a man who lives in abundance and indulges in the pleasures of worldliness." But when the Blessed One approached in a dignified manner, they involuntarily rose from their seats and greeted him in spite of their resolution. Still they called him by his name and addressed him as "friend Gautama."

When they had thus received the Blessed One, he said: "Do not call the Tathagata by his name nor address him as 'friend,' for he is the Buddha, the Holy One. The Buddha looks with a kind heart equally on all living beings, and they therefore call him 'Father.' To disrespect a father is wrong; to despise him, is wicked. The Tathagata, the Buddha continued, does not seek salvation in austerities, but neither does he for that reason indulge in worldly pleasures, nor live in abundance. The

Tathagata has found the middle path. "There are two extremes, O bhikkhus, which the man who has given up the world ought not to follow-the habitual practice, on the one hand, of self-indulgence which is unworthy, vain and fit only for the worldly-minded and the habitual practice, on the other hand, of self-mortification, which is painful, useless and unprofitable.

"Neither abstinence from fish and flesh, nor going naked, nor shaving the head, nor wearing matted hair, nor dressing in a rough garment, nor covering oneself with dirt, nor sacrificing to Agni, will cleanse a man who is not free from delusions. Reading the Vedas, making offerings to priests, or sacrifices to the gods, self-mortification by heat or cold and many such penances performed for the sake of immortality, these do not cleanse the man who is not free from delusions. Anger, drunkenness, obstinacy, bigotry, deception, envy, self-praise, disparaging others, superciliousness and evil intentions constitute uncleanness; not verily the eating of flesh.

"A middle path, O bhikkhus avoiding the two extremes, has been discovered by the Tathagata-a path which opens the eyes, and bestows understanding, which leads to peace of mind, to the higher wisdom, to full enlightenment, to Nirvana! What is that middle path, O bhikkhus, avoiding these two extremes, discovered by the Tathagata-that path which opens the eyes, and bestows understanding, which leads to peace of mind, to the higher wisdom, to full enlightenment, to Nirvana? Let me teach you, O bhikkhus, the middle path, which keeps aloof from both extremes. By suffering, the emaciated devotee produces confusion and sickly thoughts in his mind. Mortification is not conducive even to worldly knowledge; how much less to a triumph over the senses!

"He who fills his lamp with water will not dispel the darkness, and he who tries to light a fire with rotten wood will fail. And how can any one be free from self by leading a wretched life, if he does not succeed in quenching the fires of lust, if he still hankers after either worldly or heavenly pleasures? But he in whom self has become extinct is free from lust; he will desire neither worldly nor heavenly pleasures, and the satisfaction of his natural wants will not defile him. However, let him be moderate, let him eat and drink according to the need of the body.

"Sensuality is enervating; the self-indulgent man is a slave to his passions, and pleasure-seeking is degrading and vulgar. But to satisfy the necessities of life is not evil. To keep the body in good health is a duty, for otherwise we shall not be able to trim the lamp of wisdom, and keep our minds strong and clear. Water surrounds the lotus flower, but does not wet its petals. This is the middle path, O bhikkhus, that keeps aloof from both extremes." And the Blessed One spoke kindly to his disciples, pitying them for their errors, and pointing out the uselessness of their endeavours, and the ice of ill-will that chilled their hearts melted away under the gentle warmth of the Master's persuasion.

Now the Blessed One set the wheel of the most excellent law rolling, and he began to preach to the five bhikkhus, opening to them the gate of immortality, and showing them the bliss of Nirvana.

The Buddha said: "The spokes of the wheel are the rules of pure conduct: justice is the uniformity of their length; wisdom is the tire; modesty and thoughtfulness are the hub in which the immovable axle of truth is fixed. He who recognizes the existence of suffering, its cause, its remedy, and its cessation has fathomed the four noble truths. He will walk in the right path.

"Right views will be the torch to light his way. Right aspirations will be his guide. Right speech will be his dwelling-place on the road. His gait will be straight, for it is right behaviour. His refreshments will be the right way of earning his livelihood. Right efforts will be his steps: right thoughts his breath; and right contemplation will give him the peace that follows in his footprints.

"Now, this, O bhikkhus, is the noble truth concerning suffering: Birth is attended with pain, decay is painful, disease is painful, death is painful. Union with the unpleasant is painful, painful is separation from the pleasant; and any craving that is unsatisfied, that too is painful. In brief, bodily conditions which spring from attachment are painful. This, then, O bhikkhus, is the noble truth concerning suffering.

"Now this, O bhikkhus, is the noble truth concerning the origin of suffering: Verily, it is that craving which causes the renewal of existence, accompanied by sensual delight, seeking satisfaction now here, now there, the craving for the gratification of the passions, the craving for a future life, and the craving for happiness in this life. This, then, O bhikkhus, is the noble truth concerning the origin of suffering.

"Now this, O bhikkhus, is the noble truth concerning the destruction of suffering: Verily, it is the destruction, in which no passion remains, of this very thirst; it is the laying aside of, the being free from, the dwelling no longer upon this thirst. This, then, O bhikkhus, is the noble truth concerning the destruction of suffering.

"Now, this, O bhikkhus, is the noble truth concerning the way which leads to the destruction of sorrow. Verily, it is this noble eightfold path; that is to say: Right views; right aspirations; right speech; right behaviour; right livelihood; right effort; right thoughts; and right contemplation. This, then, O bhikkhus, is the noble truth concerning the destruction of sorrow.

"By the practice of loving-kindness I have attained liberation of heart, and thus I am assured that I shall never return in renewed births. I have even now attained Nirvana."

When the Blessed One had thus set the royal chariot wheel of truth rolling onward, a rapture thrilled through all the universes. The devas left their heavenly abodes to listen to the sweetness of the truth; the saints that had parted from life crowded around the great teacher to receive the glad tidings; even the animals of the earth felt the bliss that rested upon the words of the Tathagata: and all the creatures of the host of sentient beings, gods, men, and beasts, hearing the message of deliverance, received and understood it in their own language.

And when the doctrine was propounded, the venerable Kondanna, the oldest one among the five bhikkhus, discerned the truth with his mental eye, and he said: "Truly, O Buddha, our Lord, thou has found the truth!" Then the other bhikkhus too, joined him and exclaimed: "Truly, thou art the Buddha, thou has found the truth."

And the devas and saints and all the good spirits of the departed generations that had listened to the sermon of the Tathagata, joyfully received the doctrine and shouted: "Truly, the Blessed One has founded the kingdom of righteousness. The Blessed One has moved the earth; he has set the wheel of Truth rolling, which by no one in the universe, be he god or man, can ever be turned back. The kingdom of Truth will be preached upon earth; it will spread; and righteousness, goodwill, and peace will reign among mankind."

TRUTH, THE SAVIOUR

THE things of the world and its inhabitants are subject to change. They are combinations of elements that existed before, and all living creatures are what their past actions made them; for the law of cause and effect is uniform and without exception.

But in the changing things there is a constancy of law, and when the law is seen there is truth. The truth lies hidden in Samsara as the permanent in its changes.

Truth desires to appear; truth longs to become conscious; truth strives to know itself.

There is truth in the stone, for the stone is here; and no power in the world, no god, no man, no demon, can destroy its existence. But the stone has no consciousness. There is truth in the plant and its life can expand; the plant grows and blossoms and bears fruit. Its beauty is marvellous, but it has no consciousness. There is truth in the animal; it moves about and perceives its surroundings; it distinguishes and learns to choose. There is consciousness, but it is not yet the consciousness of Truth. It is a consciousness of self only.

The consciousness of self dims the eyes of the mind and hides the truth. It is the origin of error, it is the source of illusion, it is the germ of evil. Self begets selfishness. There is no evil but what flows from self. There is no wrong but what is done by the assertion of self.

Self is the beginning of all hatred, of iniquity and slander, of impudence and indecency, of theft and robbery, of oppression and bloodshed. Self is Mara, the tempter, the evildoer, the creator of mischief. Self entices with pleasures. Self promises a fairy's paradise. Self is the veil of Maya, the enchanter. But the pleasures of self are unreal, its paradisian labyrinth is the road to misery, and its fading beauty kindles the flames of desires that never can be satisfied.

Who shall deliver us from the power of self? Who shall save us from misery? Who shall restore us to a life of blessedness?

There is misery in the world of Samsara; there is much misery and pain. But greater than all the misery is the bliss of truth.

Truth gives peace to the yearning mind; it conquers error; it quenches the flames of desires; it leads to Nirvana. Blessed is he who has found the peace of Nirvana. He is at rest in the struggles and tribulations of life; he is above all changes; he is above birth and death; he remains unaffected by the evils of life.

Blessed is he who has found enlightenment. He conquers, although he may be wounded; he is glorious and happy, although he may suffer; he is strong, although he may break down under the burden of his work; he is immortal, although he will die. The essence of his being is purity and goodness.

Blessed is he who has attained the sacred state of Buddhahood, for he is fit to work out the salvation of his fellow beings. The truth has taken its abode in him. Perfect wisdom illumines his understanding, and righteousness ensouls the purpose of all his actions. The truth is a living power for good, indestructible and invincible! Work the truth out in your mind, and spread it among mankind, for truth alone is the saviour from evil and misery. The Buddha has found the truth and the truth has been proclaimed by the Buddha! Blessed be the Buddha!

THE ENLIGHTENMENT

There was in Kapilavatthu a Sakya king, strong of purpose and reverenced by all men, a descendant of the Okkakas, who call themselves Gautama, and his name was Suddhodana or Pure-Rice. His wife Mayadevi was beautiful as the water-lily and pure in mind as the lotus. As the Queen of Heaven, she lived on earth, untainted by desire, and immaculate.

The king, her husband, honoured her in her holiness, and the spirit of truth, glorious and strong in his wisdom like unto a white elephant, descended upon her. When she knew that the hour of motherhood was near, she asked the king to send her home to her parents; and Suddhodana, anxious about his wife and the child she would bear him, willingly granted her request.

At Lumbini there is a beautiful grove, and when Mayadevi passed through it the trees were one mass of fragrant flowers and many birds were warbling in their branches. The Queen, wishing to stroll through the shady walks, left her golden palanquin, and, when she reached the giant sala tree in the midst of the grove, felt that her hour had come. She took hold of a branch. Her attendants hung a curtain about her and retired. When the pain of travail came upon her, four pure-minded angels of the great Brahma held out a golden net to receive the babe, who came forth from her right side like the rising sun bright and perfect.

The Brahma-angels took the child and placing him before the mother said: "Rejoice, O queen, a mighty son has been born unto thee."

At her couch stood an aged woman imploring the heavens to bless the child. All the worlds were flooded with light. The blind received their sight by longing to see the coming glory of the Lord; the deaf and dumb spoke with one another of the good omens indicating the birth of the Buddha to be. The crooked became straight; the lame walked. All prisoners were freed from their chains and the fires of all the hells were extinguished.

No clouds gathered in the skies and the polluted streams became clear, whilst celestial music rang through the air and the angels rejoiced with gladness. With no selfish or partial joy but for the sake of the law they rejoiced, for creation engulfed in the ocean of pain was now to obtain release. The cries of beasts were hushed; all malevolent beings received a loving heart, and peace reigned on earth. Mara, the evil one, alone was grieved and rejoiced not.

The Naga kings, earnestly desiring to show their reverence for most excellent law, as they had paid honour to former Buddhas, now went to greet the Bodhisattva. They scattered before him mandara flowers, rejoicing with heartfelt joy to pay their religious homage.

The royal father, pondering the meaning of these signs, was now full of joy and now sore distressed. The queen mother, beholding her child and the commotion which his birth created, felt in her timorous heart the pangs of doubt.

Now there was at that time in a grove near Lumbini Asita, a rishi, leading the life of a hermit. He was a Brahman of dignified mien, famed not only for wisdom and scholarship, but also for his skill in the interpretation of signs. And the king invited him to see the royal babe.

The seer, beholding the prince, wept and sighed deeply. And when the king saw the tears of Asita he became alarmed and asked: "Why has the sight of my son caused thee grief and pain?"

But Asita's heart rejoiced, and, knowing the king's mind to be perplexed, he addressed him, saying: "The king, like the moon when full, should feel great joy, for he has begotten a wondrously noble son. I do not worship Brahma, but I worship this child; and the gods in the temples will descend from their places of honour to adore him. Banish all anxiety and doubt. The spiritual omens manifested indicate that the child now born will bring deliverance to the whole world.

"Recollecting that I myself am old, on that account I could not hold my tears; for now my end is coming on and I shall not see the glory of this babe. For this son of thine will rule the world. The wheel of empire will come to him. He will either be a king of kings to govern all the lands of the earth, or verily will become a Buddha. He is born for the sake of everything that lives. His pure teaching will be like the shore that receives the shipwrecked. His power of meditation will be like a cool lake; and all creatures parched with the drought of lust may freely drink thereof. On the fire of covetousness he will cause the cloud of his mercy to rise, so that the rain of the law may extinguish it. The heavy gates of despondency will he open, and give deliverance to all creatures ensnared in the self-entwined meshes of folly and ignorance. The king of the law has come forth to rescue from bondage all the poor, the miserable, the helpless."

When the royal parents heard Asita's words they rejoiced in their hearts and named their new-born infant Siddhattha, that is he who has accomplished his purpose."

And the queen said to her sister, Pajapati: "A mother who has borne a future Buddha will never give birth to another child. I shall soon leave this world, my husband, the king, and Siddhattha, my child. When I am gone, be thou a mother to him." And Pajapati wept and promised. When the queen had departed from the living, Pajapati took the boy Siddhattha and reared him. And as the light of the moon increases little by little, so the royal child grew from day to day in mind and in body; and truthfulness and love resided in his heart. When a year had passed Suddhodana the king made Pajapati his queen and there was never a better stepmother than she.

THE TIES OF LIFE

When Siddhattha had grown to youth, his father desired to see him married, and he sent to all his kinsfolk, commanding them to bring their princesses that the prince might select one of them as his wife.

But the kinsfolk replied and said: "The prince is young and delicate; nor has he learned any of the sciences. He would not be able to maintain our daughter, and should there be war he would be unable to cope with the enemy."

The prince was not boisterous, but pensive in his nature. He loved to stay under the great jambu-tree in the garden of his father, and, observing the ways of the world, gave himself up to meditation. And the prince said to his father: "Invite our kinsfolk that they may see me and put my strength to the test." And his father did as his son bade him.

When the kinsfolk came, and the people of the city Kapilavatthu had assembled to test the prowess and scholarship of the prince, he proved himself manly in all the exercises both of the body and of the mind, and there was no rival among the youths and men of India who could surpass him in any test, bodily or mental. He replied to all the questions of the sages; but when he questioned them, even the wisest among them were silenced.

Then Siddhattha chose himself a wife. He selected his cousin Yasodhara, the gentle daughter of the king of Koli. In their wedlock was born a son whom they named Rahula which means "fetter" or "tie," and King Suddhodana, glad that an heir was born to his son, said: "The prince having begotten a son, will love him as I love the prince. This will be a strong tie to bind Siddhattha's heart to the interests of the world, and the kingdom of the Sakyas will remain under the scepter of my descendants."

With no selfish aim, but regarding his child and the people at large, Siddhattha, the prince, attended to his religious duties, bathing his body in the holy Ganges and cleansing his heart in the waters of the law. Even as men desire to give happiness to their children, so did he long to give peace to the world.

THE THREE WOES

The palace which the king had given to the prince was resplendent with all the luxuries of India; for the king was anxious to see his son happy. All sorrowful sights, all misery, and all knowledge of misery were kept away from Siddhattha, for the king desired that no troubles should come nigh him; he should not know that there was evil in the world.

But as the chained elephant longs for the wilds of the jungles, so the prince was eager to see the world, and he asked his father, the king, for permission to do so. And Suddhodana ordered a jewel-fronted chariot with four stately horses to be held ready, and commanded the roads to be adorned where his son would pass.

The houses of the city were decorated with curtains and banners, and spectators arranged themselves on either side, eagerly gazing at the heir to the throne. Thus Siddhattha rode with Channa, his charioteer, through the streets of the city, and into a country watered by rivulets and covered with pleasant trees.

There by the wayside they met an old man with bent frame, wrinkled face and sorrowful brow, and the prince asked the charioteer: "Who is this? His head is white, his eyes are bleared, and his body is withered. He can barely support himself on his staff."

The charioteer, much embarrassed, hardly dared speak the truth. He said: "These are the symptoms of old age. This same man was once a suckling child, and as a youth full of sportive life; but now, as years have passed away, his beauty is gone and the strength of his life is wasted."

Siddhattha was greatly affected by the words of the charioteer, and he sighed because of the pain of old age. "What joy or pleasure can men take," he thought to himself, when they know they must soon wither and pine away!"

And lo! while they were passing on, a sick man appeared on the way-side, gasping for breath, his body disfigured, convulsed and groaning with pain. The prince asked his charioteer: "What kind of man is this?" And the charioteer replied and said: "This man is sick. The four elements of his body are confused and out of order. We are all subject to such conditions: the poor and the rich, the ignorant and the wise, all creatures that have bodies are liable to the same calamity."

And Siddhattha was still more moved. All pleasures appeared stale to him, and he loathed the joys of life.

The charioteer sped the horses on to escape the dreary sight, when suddenly they were stopped in their fiery course. Four persons passed by, carrying a corpse; and the prince, shuddering at the sight of a lifeless body, asked the charioteer: "What is this they carry? There are streamers and flower garlands; but the men that follow are overwhelmed with grief!"

The charioteer replied: "This is a dead man: his body is stark; his life is gone; his thoughts are still; his family and the friends who loved him now carry the corpse to the grave." And the prince was full of awe and terror: "Is this the only dead man, he asked, or does the world contain other instances?"

With a heavy heart the charioteer replied: "All over the world it is the same. He who begins life must end it. There is no escape from death."

With bated breath and stammering accents the prince exclaimed: "O worldly men! How fatal is your delusion! Inevitably your body will crumble to dust, yet carelessly, unheedingly, ye live on." The charioteer observing the deep impression these sad sights had made on the prince, turned his horses and drove back to the city.

When they passed by the palace of the nobility, Kisa Gotami, a young princess and niece of the king, saw Siddhattha in his manliness and beauty, and, observing the thoughtfulness of his countenance, said: "Happy the father that begot thee, happy the mother that nursed thee, happy the wife that calls husband this lord so glorious."

The prince hearing this greeting, said: "Happy are they that have found deliverance. Longing for peace of mind, I shall seek the bliss of Nirvana."

Then asked Kisa Gotami: "How is Nirvana attained?" The prince paused, and to him whose mind was estranged from wrong the answer came: "When the fire of lust is gone out, then Nirvana is gained; when the fires of hatred and delusion are gone out, then Nirvana is gained; when the troubles of mind, arising from blind credulity, and all other evils have ceased, then Nirvana is gained!"

Siddhattha handed her his precious pearl necklace as a reward for the wisdom she had inspired in him, and having returned home looked with disdain upon the treasures of his palace.

His wife welcomed him and entreated him to tell her the cause of his grief. He said: "I see everywhere the impression of change; therefore, my heart is heavy. Men grow old, sicken, and die. That is enough to take away the zest of life."

The king, his father, hearing that the prince had become estranged from pleasure, was greatly overcome with sorrow and like a sword it pierced his heart.

THE BODHISATTVAS RENUNCIATION

It was night. The prince found no rest on his soft pillow; he arose and went out into the garden. "Alas!" he cried "all the world is full of darkness and ignorance; there is no one who knows how to cure the ills of existence." And he groaned with pain. Siddhattha sat down beneath the great jambu-tree and gave himself to thought, pondering on life and death and the evils of decay. Concentrating his mind he became free from confusion. All low desires vanished from his heart and perfect tranquility came over him.

In this state of ecstasy he saw with his mental eye all the misery and sorrow of the world; he saw the pains of pleasure and the inevitable certainty of death that hovers over every being; yet men are not awakened to the truth. And a deep compassion seized his heart.

While the prince was pondering on the problem of evil, he beheld with his mind's eye under the jambu tree a lofty figure endowed with majesty, calm and dignified. "When comes thou, and who may thou be asked the prince.

In reply the vision said: "I am a samana. Troubled at the thought of old age, disease, and death I have left my home to seek the path of salvation. All things hasten to decay; only the truth abides forever. Everything changes, and there is no permanency; yet the words of the Buddhas are immutable. I long for the happiness that does not decay; the treasure that will never perish; the life that knows of no beginning and no end. Therefore, I have destroyed all worldly thought. I have retired into an unfrequented dell to live in solitude; and, begging for food, I devote myself to the one thing needful.

Siddhattha asked: "Can peace be gained in this world of unrest? I am struck with the emptiness of pleasure and have become disgusted with lust. All oppresses me, and existence itself seems intolerable."

The samana replied: "Where heat is, there is also a possibility of cold; creatures subject to pain possess the faculty of pleasure; the origin of evil indicates that good can be developed. For these things are correlatives. Thus where there is much suffering, there will be much bliss, if thou but open thine eyes to behold it. Just as a man who has fallen into a heap of filth ought to seek the great pond of water covered with lotuses, which is near by: even so seek thou for the great deathless lake of Nirvana to wash off the defilement of wrong. If the lake is not sought, it is not the fault of the lake. Even so when there is a blessed road leading the man held fast by wrong to the salvation of Nirvana, if the road is not walked upon, it is not the fault of the road, but of the person. And when a man who is oppressed with sickness, there being a physician who can heal him, does not avail himself of the physician's help, that is not the fault of the physician. Even so when a man oppressed by the malady of wrong-doing does not seek the spiritual guide of enlightenment, that is no fault of the evil-destroying guide."

The prince listened to the noble words of his visitor and said: "Thou bringest good tidings, for now I know that my purpose will be accomplished. My father advises me to enjoy life and to undertake worldly duties, such as will bring honour to me and to our house. He tells me that I am too young still, that my pulse beats too full to lead a religious life."

The venerable figure shook his head and replied: "Thou should know that for seeking a religious life no time can be inopportune." A thrill of joy passed through Siddhattha's heart. "Now is the time to seek religion," he said; "now is the time to sever all ties that would prevent me from attaining perfect enlightenment; now is the time to wander into homelessness and, leading a mendicant's life, to find the path of deliverance."

The celestial messenger heard the resolution of Siddhattha with approval. "Now, indeed he added, is the time to seek religion. Go, Siddhattha, and accomplish thy purpose. For thou art Bodhisatta, the Buddha-elect; thou art destined to enlighten the world. Thou art the Tathagata, the great master, for thou wilt fulfill all righteousness and be Dharmaraja, the king of truth. Thou art Bhagavat, the Blessed One, for thou art called upon to become the saviour and redeemer of the world. Fulfill thou the perfection of truth.

Though the thunderbolt descend upon thy head, yield thou never to the allurements that beguile men from the path of truth. As the sun at all seasons pursues his own course, nor ever goes on another, even so if thou forsake not the straight path of righteousness, thou shalt become a Buddha. Persevere in thy quest and thou shalt find what thou seekest. Pursue thy aim unswervingly and thou shalt gain the prize. Struggle earnestly and thou shalt conquer. The benediction of all deities, of all saints of all that seek light is upon thee, and heavenly wisdom guides thy steps. Thou shalt be the Buddha, our Master, and our Lord; thou shalt enlighten the world and save mankind from perdition.

Having thus spoken, the vision vanished, and Siddhattha's heart was filled with peace. He said to himself: "I have awakened to the truth and I am resolved to accomplish my purpose. I will sever all the ties that bind me to the world, and I will go out from my home to seek the way of salvation. The Buddhas are beings whose words cannot fail: there is no departure from truth in their speech. For as the fall of a stone thrown into the air, as the death of a mortal, as the sunrise at dawn, as the lion's roar when he leaves his lair, as the delivery of a woman with child, as all these things are sure and certain-even so the word of the Buddhas is sure and cannot fail. Verily I shall become a Buddha." The prince returned to the bedroom of his wife to take a last farewell glance at those whom he dearly loved above all the treasures of the earth. He longed to take the infant once more into his arms and kiss him with a parting kiss. But the child lay in the arms of his mother, and the prince could not lift him without awakening both. There Siddhattha stood gazing at his beautiful wife and his beloved son, and his heart grieved. The pain of parting overcame him powerfully. Although his mind was determined, so that nothing, be it good or evil, could shake his resolution, the tears flowed freely from his eyes, and it was beyond his power to check their stream. But the prince tore himself away with a manly heart, suppressing his feelings but not extinguishing his memory.

The Bodhisattva mounted his noble steed Kanthaka, and when he left the palace, Mara stood in the gate and stopped him: "Depart not, O my Lord," exclaimed Mara. "In seven days from now the wheel of empire will appear, and will make thee sovereign over the four continents and the two thousand adjacent islands. Therefore, stay, my Lord."

The Bodhisattva replied: "Well do I know that the wheel of empire will appear to me; but it is not sovereignty that I desire. I will become a Buddha and make all the world shout for joy."

Thus Siddhattha, the prince, renounced power and worldly pleasures, gave up his kingdom, severed all ties, and went into homelessness. He rode out into the silent night, accompanied only by his faithful charioteer Channa. Darkness lay upon the earth, but the stars shone brightly in the heavens.

THE BUDDHA EXPOSES THE IMPOSTERS

From Vaisali, the Master went to Cravasti, to Jeta's park. One day, King Prasenajit came to see him. "My Lord," said the king, "six hermits have recently arrived in Cravasti. They do not believe in your law. They maintain that your knowledge is not equal to theirs, and they have tried to astonish me by performing numerous prodigies. I believe their statements to be untrue, but it would be well, my Lord, if you were to confound their audacity. The world's salvation depends upon your glory. So appear before these cheats and impostors and silence them."

"King," replied the Buddha, "order a great hall to be built near the city. Have it finished in seven days. I shall proceed there. Arrange to have the evil hermits present, and you will then see who performs the greatest prodigies, they or I."

Prasenajit ordered the hall to be built.

While awaiting the day of the trial, the lying hermits sought to delude the Master's faithful followers, and those who refused to listen to their evil words incurred their bitter enmity. Now, the Master had no truer friend in Cravasti than Prince Kala, a brother of Prasenajit. Kala had shown his utter contempt for the hermits, and they decided to take their revenge.

Kala was a very handsome man. One day, as he was walking through the royal gardens, he met one of Prasenajit's wives, and she playfully threw him a garland of flowers. The hermits heard of the incident, and they told the king that his brother had tried to seduce one of his wives. The king flew into a great rage, and without giving Kala a chance to justify himself, he had his hands and feet cut off.

Poor Kala suffered pitifully. His friends stood around his couch, weeping. One of the evil hermits happened to pass by.

"Come, show your power," they said to him. "You know that Kala is innocent. Make him well again!"

"He believes in the son of the Sakyas," replied the hermit. "It behooves the Sakyas' son to make him well again."

Then Kala began to sing:

"How can the Master of the worlds fail to see my misery? Let us worship the Lord who no longer knows desire; let us adore the Blessed One who takes pity on all creatures."

Ananda suddenly appeared before him.

"Kala," said he, "the Master has taught me the words that will heal your wounds."

He recited a few verses, and the prince immediately recovered the use of his limbs.

"Henceforth," he exclaimed, "I shall serve the Master! However humble the tasks which he may assign to me, I shall perform them with joy, to please him."

And he followed Ananda to Jeta's park. The Master received him graciously and admitted him to the community.

The day arrived on which the Master was to compete with the hermits. Early in the morning, King Prasenajit went to the hall he had built for this occasion. The six hermits were already there. They exchanged glances and smiled.

"King," said one of them, "we are the first to arrive at the place of meeting."

"Do you suppose the one we are expecting will really come?" said another.

"Hermits," said the king, "do not scoff at him. You know how he sent one of his disciples to cure my brother whom I had unjustly punished. He will come. He may even be here, in our midst, without our knowing it."

As the king finished speaking, a luminous cloud filled the hall. It became lighter and lighter; it melted into the daylight, and the Buddha appeared, arrayed in golden splendour. Behind him stood Ananda and Kala. Ananda held a red flower in his hand, Kala a yellow flower, and never, in all the gardens of Cravasti, had any one seen two such flowers as these.

Prasenajit showed his profound admiration. The evil hermits ceased their laughter.

The Blessed One spoke:

"The glowworm shines for all to see, as long as the sun stays hidden, but when the blazing star appears, the poor worm quenches his feeble light. The impostors spoke loudly as long as the Buddha was silent, but now that the Buddha speaks, they weep with fear and are silent."

The hermits were alarmed. They saw the king viewing them with a scornful eye, and they hung their heads in shame.

Suddenly, the roof of the hall disappeared, and on the dome of the sky, stretching from the east to the west, the Master traced a course over which he proceeded to travel. At the sight of this prodigy, his most insolent rival fled in terror. The hermit imagined he was being pursued by a howling pack of hounds, and he never stopped running until he came to the edge of a pool. There, he tied a stone to his neck and threw himself into the water. A fisherman found his body the following day.

In the meanwhile, the Master had created a being in his own image, and, with him, he was now walking in the celestial path. And his great voice was heard, saying:

"O my disciples, I am about to ascend to the abode of the Gods and the Goddesses. Maya, my mother, has summoned me; I must instruct her in the law. I shall remain with her three months. But, each day, I shall descend to earth, and Sariputra, alone, will know where to find me; he will rule the community according to my instructions. And while I am absent from the sky, I shall leave with my mother, to instruct her, this being whom I have created in mine own image."

Suprabha

At the end of three months, the Master descended to earth and took the road to Cravasti. As he was approaching Jeta's park, he met a young girl. She was the servant of a wealthy inhabitant of the city who happened to be working in the fields that day. She was taking him a bowl of rice for his meal. At the sight of the Buddha, she felt strangely happy.

"It is the Master, the Blessed One," she thought. "My eyes behold him; my hands could almost touch him, he is so near. Oh, what a holy joy it would be to give him alms! But I have nothing of my own."

She sighed. Her glance fell on the bowl of rice.

"This rice... My master's meal... No master can reduce to slavery one who is already a slave. Mine could strike me, but what of that! He could put me in chains, but I would bear them lightly. I shall give the rice to the Blessed One."

She presented the bowl to the Buddha. He accepted it and continued on his way to Jeta's park. The young girl, her eyes shining with happiness, went to look for her master.

"Where is my rice?" he asked, as soon as he saw her.

"I gave it to the Buddha as an alms. Punish me if you will, I shall not weep; I am too happy for what I have done."

He did not punish her. He bowed' his head and said:

"No, I shall not punish you. I am asleep and your eyes are open. Go; you are no longer a slave."

The young girl made a deep obeisance.

"With your permission then," said she, "I shall go to Jeta's park, and I shall ask the Blessed One to instruct me in the law."

"Go," said the man.

She went to Jeta's park; she sat at the Buddha's feet, and she became one of the most saintly women in the community.

Among those who sought instruction from the Blessed One at the same time as this young slave was Suprabha, the daughter of a prominent citizen of Cravasti. Suprabha was very beautiful. To see her was to fall in love with her, and she was courted by all the distinguished young men of the city. This caused her father no little concern. "To which one shall I give her in marriage?" he would repeatedly ask himself; "those whom I refuse will become my bitter enemies."

And for hours at a time, he would remain deep in thought.

One day, Suprabha said to him:

"You seem to be troubled, dear father. What is the reason?"

"Daughter," he replied, "you alone are the cause of my anxiety. There are so many in Cravasti who wish to marry you!"

"You are afraid to make a choice from among my suitors," said Suprabha. "Poor men! If they but knew my thoughts! Do not be anxious, father! Tell them to assemble, and, according to the ancient custom, I shall go among them, and I myself shall choose a husband from their number."

"I shall do as you wish, daughter."

Suprabha's father went to King Prasenajit and received permission to have a herald proclaim throughout the city:

"That seven days from this day, there will be held an assembly of all the young men who wish to marry Suprabha. The young girl herself will select a husband from among their number."

On the seventh day, a host of suitors gathered in the magnificent garden belonging to Suprabha's father. She appeared, riding in a chariot. She was holding a yellow banner on which was painted the picture of the Blessed One. She was singing his praises. They all looked at her in amazement, and they wondered, "What will she say to us?" She finally addressed the young men.

"I can not love any of you," said she, "but do not think that I spurn you. Love is not my aim in life; I want to take refuge with the Buddha. I shall go to the park where he dwells, and he will instruct me in the law."

Mournfully, the young men withdrew, and Suprabha went to Jeta's park. She heard the Blessed One speak; she was admitted to the community, and she became a most devoted nun.

One day, as she was leaving the sacred gardens, she was recognized by one of her former suitors who happened to be passing with several friends.

"We must carry off this woman," said he. "I loved her once; I still love her. She shall be mine."

His friends agreed to help him. Before Suprabha was aware of it, she was surrounded, and they suddenly rushed upon her. But as they were about to seize her, she directed her thought toward the Buddha, and, immediately, she rose in the air. A crowd gathered; Suprabha soared above them for a while, then, flying with the grace and majesty of a swan, she returned to her sacred dwelling.

And their cries followed her:

"O saintly one, you make manifest the power of the faithful;

Ȯ saint, you render manifest the power of the Buddha. It would be unjust to condemn you to the earthly pleasures of love, O saintly one, O saint."

Virupa

King Prasenajit had a daughter named Virupa. She had reached a marriageable age. Unfortunately, she was extremely ugly; no prince or warrior would have her for a wife, and even the merchants looked at her askance.

But presently a wealthy stranger came to live in Cravasti. His name was Ganga. The king thought, "Ganga has never seen my daughter. Perhaps he will not refuse to marry her." And he summoned him to the palace.

Ganga was highly flattered by Prasenajit's offer. He was of humble birth, and although, as a merchant, he had amassed a great fortune, he had never dreamed of marrying a princess. He therefore accepted the proposal.

"Then come to the palace this very evening," said the king, "and take my daughter home with you."

He obeyed. The night was dark, and the wedding took place without Ganga having seen his betrothed. Then Virupa accompanied her husband to his home.

Ganga saw his wife the next day. Her ugliness frightened him. He wanted to turn her out of the house, but he did not dare; he feared the king's vengeance. He kept her at home, but she was virtually a prisoner; she was not allowed to go out, for any reason whatsoever.

She was very unhappy. In vain she gave her husband constant proof of her affection; he only showed his aversion and his contempt for her. He never looked at her. He hardly spoke to her. And Virupa felt lonely and forlorn.

One day, Ganga was invited to a feast given by some of his friends. "Whoever comes without wife," he was warned, "will be fined five hundred pieces of gold."

Ganga decided to attend; it would relieve the monotony of his existence. But he did not want to show Virupa to his friends;

he was afraid of being ridiculed. "I shall pay the five hundred pieces of gold," he thought, "and they will not make fun of me."

That day, Virupa was sadder than usual. She knew where her husband had gone, and she wept. She said to herself:

"What good is a life as dreary as mine? I never have any pleasure. My master loathes me. And I can not blame him; I am ugly; every one has told me so. I have brought joy to no one. Oh, I loathe myself. Death would be better than this life I lead; death would be sweet. I shall kill myself."

She took a rope and hung herself.

At that same moment, in Jeta's park, the Master was wondering, "Who is suffering today in Cravasti? Whom can I save from misery? To what unfortunate being can I lend a helping hand?"

By his power of divination, he learned of Virupa's distress. He flew to Ganga's house; he entered. Virupa was still alive. The Master loosened the rope she had fastened about her neck. She breathed deeply and looked around. She recognized the Master. She fell at his feet and made him a pious offering. Then he said:

"Look at yourself in a mirror, Virupa."

She obeyed. She uttered a cry of joy and astonishment. She was as beautiful as a daughter of the Gods. Again she wanted to worship the Buddha, but he had disappeared.

In the meanwhile, Ganga had not been spared the banter of his friends.

"Why did you come without your wife?" they asked him. "Are you afraid to let us see her? She must be very beautiful. You jealous husband!"

Ganga was at a loss for an answer. The feast bored him. One of his friends handed him a cup of intoxicating wine.

"Drink, Ganga," said he. "We laugh, and you are almost in tears. Come, laugh with us. Drink; this wine will teach you to laugh."

Ganga took the cup. He drank. He became livelier. He drank again. Presently, he was drunk. And he kept on drinking until, finally, he fell into a heavy sleep.

"Let us hurry over to his house, while he is asleep," said his friends. "We shall see his wife, and we shall find out why he keeps her out of sight."

They entered Ganga's home. Virupa had the mirror in her hand; she was looking at herself. Her eyes were bright with happiness. All the guests admired her, and they went away, quietly, saying, "We now understand Ganga's jealousy."

Ganga was still sleeping. They awoke him and said:

> *"Great is your felicity, friend. What did you do that was so pleasing to the Gods, to deserve a wife of such rare beauty?"*

"This is too much!" cried Ganga. "What have I ever done to you that you should insult me so cruelly?"

And he abruptly left them. He was raging with anger and mortification. He flung open the door of his house; he strode through the halls, muttering imprecations; but, suddenly, the curses died upon his lips. He turned pale with astonishment. Before him was standing a woman of incomparable beauty. She was smiling. He slowly came to his senses; then he, too, smiled, and he asked:

> *"O you who appear before me like some radiant Goddess new-risen from her bed of flowers, O well-beloved, who made you so beautiful?"*

Virupa told him the story. From that day, she and her husband knew true happiness, and they both sought every opportunity to evince their faith in the Buddha and show him their gratitude.

Sinca's Deceit

In the meanwhile, the evil hermits, whose imposture the Buddha had exposed, were being treated with contempt by the populace, and each day their desire for vengeance grew more intense. They had established themselves near Jeta's park, and night and day they spied upon the Buddha and his disciples. But all in vain; they saw nothing that gave them the slightest excuse for slandering the community.

At last, one of the hermits said to his companions: *"We have long been observing the conduct of these monks. Their virtue can not be denied. Still, we must turn the minds of the people against them, and I think I have found a way. I know a young girl of great charm. Her name is Sinca. She is very clever at practising deceit. She will not refuse to help us, and soon the glory of this Sakya will vanish."*

The hermits sent word to Sinca. She came. "Why did you send for me?" she asked.

"Do you know the monk from Kapilavastu, the one who is worshipped as the Buddha?"

"No, but I know of his great fame. I have been told of the many prodigies he has performed."

"This man is our bitterest enemy, Sinca. He treats us shamefully and would destroy our power. Now, you believe in us; come, take our part. She who will have conquered the conqueror may well be proud; she will be famous among women, and the world will ring with her praises."

Sinca was carried away by the hermit's words. She assured him that the Buddha would soon be disgraced and his name hated throughout the earth.

Each day, now, she went to Jeta's park, at a time when those who had been listening to the Master preach were beginning to leave. She was dressed in flaming red, and she carried flowers in her arms. And if, by chance, some one asked her, "Where are you going?" she would reply, "What business is it of yours?" When she came to the park, she waited until she was quite alone; then, instead of entering the Buddha's domain, she set out for the dwelling of the evil hermits. There, she spent the night, but at dawn she returned to the gates of the park, and when she was sure to be seen by the early risers on their way to their devotions, she would leave and return home. And to those who asked, "Where do you come from, so early in the morning?" she would reply, "What business is it of yours?"

At the end of one month, she gave a different answer. In the evening she would say, "I am going to Jeta's park, where the Blessed One is waiting for me," and in the morning, "I have just come from Jeta's park, where I spent the night with the Blessed One." And there were some poor, credulous people who believed her and who suspected the Master of unchastity.

The sixth month, she took a piece of cloth and wrapped it around her body. "She is pregnant," they thought, and the fools maintained that the Master's virtue was only a pretense.

When the ninth month arrived, she tied a wooden ball to the thick girdle about her waist, and when she walked, she assumed a languorous gait. Finally, one night, she entered the hall where the Master was expounding the law. Boldly, she faced him, and her strident voice interrupted his speech.

"Sweet is your voice and honeyed your words as you instruct the people in the law. While I, who am pregnant because of you, I, who am soon to become a mother, have not even a place for my confinement! You would deny me the very oil and butter I need. If it would make you blush, now, to look after me, you could at least entrust me to one of your disciples, or to King Prasenajit, or to the merchant Anathapindika. But no! I am nothing to you any more, and little you care about the child that will be born! You would know all the joys of love, but the responsibilities you would ignore!"

"Is that a lie or are you telling the truth, Sinca?" asked the Master, calmly. "Only you and I know."

"You know very well I am not lying," cried Sinca.

The Master retained his composure. But Indra, who had been watching from the sky, decided it was time to expose Sinca's impudence. He had four Gods take the form of mice. They crawled under her robe and gnawed at the string that was holding the wooden ball. The ball fell to the ground.

"There, your child is born," exclaimed the Master with a laugh.

The disciples turned upon. Sinca in their rage. They reviled her; they spat in her face; they beat her. She fled. She was weeping with pain and shame and anger. Suddenly, red flames sprang up around her and enveloped her in a mantle of fire, and she, who had dared to slander the Buddha, came to a cruel and terrible end.

THE BUDDHA TAMES A WILD BUFFALO

The Master left Jeta's park. He stopped in the cities and in the villages to preach the law, and full many there were to adopt the true faith.

One day, an old man and his wife invited the Master to take his meal with them.

"My Lord," said the old man, "we have long been eager to hear your word. We are happy, now that we know the sacred truths, and among your friends you will find none more devout than we."

"I am not surprised," replied the Buddha, "for you and I were near relations in our former existences."

"Master," said the woman, "my husband and I have lived together since our early youth; we have now attained a ripe old age. Life has been kind to us. Never has the slightest quarrel come between us. We still love each other as in the days gone by, and the evening of our lives is as sweet as was the dawn. May it be granted us, my Lord, to love each other in our next existence as we have loved one another in this life."

"It will be granted," said the Master; "the Gods have protected you!"

He continued on his way. He saw an old woman drawing water from a well by the side of the road. He approached her.

"I am thirsty," said he. "Will you give me a drink?"

The old woman stared at him. She was deeply moved. She began to weep. She wanted to embrace the Master, but she was afraid. The tears coursed down her cheeks.

"Embrace me," said the Master.

The old woman ran to his arms, and she murmured:

"Now I can die happy. I have seen the Blessed One, and it was given me to embrace him."

He went on. He came to a vast forest where a herd of buffaloes lived with their keepers. One of these buffaloes was a very powerful animal. He had an ugly temper. He barely tolerated the presence of his keepers, and at the approach of a stranger he would become aggressive. When the stranger came near, he would attack him with his horns, and he would often wound him seriously. Sometimes he killed him.

The keepers saw the Blessed One walking along, quietly, and they shouted:

"Take care, traveller. Do not come near us. There is a vicious buffalo here."

But he paid no attention to the warning. He made straight for the spot where the buffalo was grazing.

All at once, the buffalo raised his head and sniffed noisily; then, lowering his horns, he rushed at the Master. The keepers trembled. "Our voices were not loud enough," they cried; "he did not hear us." But, suddenly, the animal stopped short; he knelt before the Master and began licking his feet. There was a look of pleading in his eyes.

The Master gently stroked the buffalo. He spoke to him in a quiet voice.

"Say to yourself that all earthly things are transitory, that peace is found only in nirvana. Do not weep. Believe in me, believe in my goodness, in my compassion, and your condition will change. You will not be reborn among the animals, and, in time, you will attain the sky and dwell among the Gods."

From that day, the buffalo was extremely docile. And the keepers, who had expressed their admiration for the Master and who had given him what alms they could afford, were instructed in the law, and they became known for their piety, even among the most pious.

Dissension Among the Monks

The Master arrived at the city of Kausambi, and there, at first, he was very happy. The inhabitants eagerly listened to his words, and many of them became monks. King Udayana was among the believers, and he allowed his son Rashtrapala to enter the community.

Yet it was in Kausambi that the Master met with one of his great sorrows. A monk, one day, was reprimanded for committing some minor offense. He would not own himself in the wrong; so he was punished. He refused to submit to the punishment, and, as he was a pleasant man, of great wit and learning, there were many to take his part. In vain the others besought him to return to the straight path.

"Do not assume that conceited air," they said to him; "do not consider yourself incapable of making mistakes. Heed our wise advice. Address the other monks as they should be addressed who profess a faith that is also yours; they will address you as he should be addressed who professes a faith that is also theirs. The community will grow, the community will flourish, only if the monks will take counsel from one another."

"It is not for you to tell me what is right or wrong," he replied. "Stop reproving me."

"Do not say that. Your words offend against the law. You are defying discipline; you are sowing discord in the community. Come, mend your ways. Live at peace with the community. Avoid these quarrels, and be faithful to the law."

It was useless. They then decided to expel the rebel, but, once again, he refused to obey. He would remain in the community: since he was innocent, there was no need to submit to an unjust punishment.

The Master finally intervened. He tried to pacify the monks; he pleaded with them to forget their grievances and to unite, as before, in the performance of their sacred duties, but no one paid any attention. And, one day, a monk even had the audacity to say to him:

"Keep still, O Master; do not bother us with your speeches. You have arrived at a knowledge of the law; meditate upon it. You will find your meditations quite delightful. As for us, we shall know where to go; our quarrels will not keep us from finding the way. Meditate, and be quiet."

The Master was not angry. He tried to speak, but it was impossible, He saw then that he could never convince the monks of Kausambi; they seemed to be possessed with some sudden folly. The Master decided to forsake them, but first he said to them:

"Happy is he who has a faithful friend; happy is he who has a discerning friend. What obstacles could two wise and virtuous friends not overcome? But he who has no faithful friend resembles a king without a country: he must roam in solitude, like the elephant in the wild forest. Yet it is better to travel alone than in the company of a fool. The wise man should follow a lonely path; he should avoid evil and should preserve his serenity, like the elephant in the wild forest."

He left. No one tried to stop him. He went to a village where he knew he would find his disciple Bhrigu. Bhrigu was overjoyed to see him, and the Master was not a little comforted. Then, Anuruddha, Nanda and Kimbala joined him. They gave him every proof of their respect and friendship, and they lived at peace with one another. And the Master thought, "So there are some, among my disciples, who love me and who do not quarrel."

One day, as he sat down in the shade of a tree and began thinking of the troublous times in Kausambi, a herd of elephants stopped to rest not far from him. The biggest elephant went down to the river and drew water which he brought back to the others. They drank; then, instead of thanking him for doing them this service, they abused him, they beat him with their trunks, and, finally, they drove him away.

And the Master saw that his own experience was not unlike that of the elephant: they were both victims of gross ingratitude. The elephant noticed the sadness in his face; he drew near and looked at him tenderly; then left, to go in search of food and drink for him.

The Master finally returned to Cravasti and rested in Jeta's park.

But it still grieved him to think of the cruel monks of Kausambi. One morning, however, he saw them enter the park. They were in great distress: alms had been denied them, for every one was indignant at their treatment of the Master. They had come to beg his forgiveness. The guilty monk confessed himself to have been in the wrong, and his punishment was light. His adversaries, as well as his friends, admitted the error of their ways, and all promised strictly to obey the rules. And the Master was happy: there was no longer any dissension in the community.

Kuvalaya the Dancer

One day, he returned to the country of Rajagriha.

In a field, not far from the city, he came upon a Brahman named Bharadvaja. It was the harvest season, and the Brahman and his servants were joyously celebrating. They were laughing and singing as the Master went by. He held out his alms-bowl, and those who recognized him, greeted him and made him many friendly offerings. This displeased Bharadvaja. He went up to the Master, and he said to him in a loud voice:

"Monk, tarry not in our midst; you set an evil example. We work, we that are here, and with watchful eyes, we observe the changes of seasons. When it is time to plow, my servants plow; when it is time to sow, they sow; and I plow and sow with them. Then the day comes when we harvest the fruit of our labour. We provide our own food, and when it is stored away, we have good reason to rest and play. While you, you roam the streets and walk the roads, and the only trouble you deign to take is to hold out a bowl to those you meet. It would be better far for you to work; it would be better far to plow and sow."

The Master smiled and answered:

"Friend, like you I plow and sow, and when my work is done, I eat."

"You plow? You sow?" said Bharadvaja. "How can I believe

that? Where are your cattle? Where is your grain? Where is your plow?"

The Master said:

"Purity of understanding, that is the glorious seed I sow. Works of holiness are the rain that falls upon the fertile earth where the seed sprouts and ripens. And mine is a mighty plow: it has wisdom for its plowshare, the law for its handles, and an active faith is the powerful bullock yoked to its pole. Desire is uprooted like weeds in the fields I plow, and I gather in the richest of harvests, nirvana."

He continued on his way. But the Brahman Bharadvaja followed him; he would now hear the sacred word.

They entered the city. On the public square, a large crowd was watching a troop of dancers. The daughter of the leader-was attracting particular attention. Such grace and beauty had seldom been seen, and, whenever she appeared, those who were not master of their passions burned with the desire to possess her. Her name was Kuvalaya.

She had just finished dancing. Ardent eyes were still fastened upon her. She was aware of her power, and full of pride and audacity, she shouted 'to the crowd:

"Admire me, my lords! In all Rajagriha is there one who can surpass Kuvalaya in beauty, are there any who can even equal her?"

"Yes, woman," replied the Brahman Bharadvaja. "What is your beauty when compared with the beauty of the Master?"

"I would see this Master whose beauty you praise," said Kuvalaya; "lead me to him."

"Here he is," said the Blessed One.

And he came forward.

The dancer stared at him.

"You are beautiful," she said at last. "I shall dance for you."

Kuvalaya danced. The dance began slowly. She had wrapped all her veils about her, even covering her face, and the beauty once so boldly flaunted was now only a dim promise. She was like the moon, hiding behind soft clouds from the gaze of night. A cloud flew away; a faint ray escaped through the rift. The dance became more rapid; one by one the veils fell away, and the queen of the stars appeared in all her glory. Faster and faster she whirled; suddenly, a blinding light flashed in her eyes, and she stopped. She was naked. The crowd gasped and surged forward.

"Unhappy woman!" said the Buddha.

He looked at her intently. Whereupon Kuvalaya's cheeks became sunken, her forehead wrinkled and her eyes grew dull. Only a few ugly teeth were left in her mouth; only a few thin strands of grey hair still hung from her head, and she was stooped as with age. The Blessed One had punished her as he had once punished Mara's daughters when they had tried to tempt him; he had changed the beautiful dancer into a shrivelled old woman.

She sighed:

"Master, I know the great wrong I have done. An ephemeral beauty had made me vain. You taught me a bitter lesson, but I feel that some day I shall be happy to have received it. Let me learn the sacred truths; then may I be released for ever from this body that, even when it was the delight of men, was nothing but a loathsome corpse."

The Master granted Kuvalaya's request, and she became one of the most devout of the Buddha's faithful followers.

THE GOD ALAVAKA DEFEATED BY THE BUDDHA

In the city of Atavi there ruled a king who was very fond of hunting. One day, he saw an enormous deer and started in pursuit. The deer was fleet of foot, and in the heat of the chase, the king lost sight of the other hunters. Finally, the prey escaped, and weary and discouraged, the king sat down under a tree. He fell asleep.

It happened that a wicked God named Alavaka lived in the tree. He liked to feed on human flesh, and he killed and devoured all who came near him. He saw the king; he rejoiced, and the poor hunter was about to be dealt a severe blow when a noise fortunately awoke him. He realized that his life was threatened; he made an attempt to rise, but the God took him by the throat and held him down. Then the king tried to plead with him.

"Spare me, my lord!" said he. "By your terrifying appearance, I know you to be one of the Gods that eat human flesh. Oh, deign to be kind to me. You will have no cause to regret your mercy. I shall reward you with magnificent gifts."

"What care I for gifts!" replied Alavaka. "It is your flesh I want; it will appease my hunger."

"My lord," replied the king, "if you let me return to Atavi, I shall send you a man every day to satisfy your hunger."

"When you get back to your home, you will forget this promise."

"No," said the king, "I never forget a promise. Besides, if I should once fail to make this daily offering, you have only to come to my palace and tell me of your grievance, and, immediately, without resisting, I shall follow you, and you may devour me."

The God allowed himself to be persuaded, and the king returned to the city of Atavi. But he kept thinking of his cruel promise; there was no way he could evade it, and henceforth he would have to he a hard and ruthless master.

He sent for his minister and told him what had happened. The minister considered for a moment, then said to the king:

> *"My lord, in the prison of Atavi there are criminals who have been condemned to death. We can send them to the God. When he sees that you are keeping faith with him, perhaps he will relieve you of your promise."*

The king approved of the suggestion. Guards were sent to the prison, and to those whose days were numbered they said:

> *"Not far from the city there is a tree inhabited by a God who is very fond of rice. Whoever leaves a plate of rice for him at the foot of the tree will be granted a full pardon."*

Whereupon, each day, one of these men, carrying a plate of rice, joyously set out for the tree, never to return.

Presently, there were no men condemned to death left in prison. The minister ordered the judges to be extremely severe and to acquit no one accused of murder except on irrefutable proof of his innocence, but it was in vain; some new way had to be found for appeasing the hunger of the God. Then they began to sacrifice the thieves.

In spite of all their efforts to apprehend the guilty, the prison was again empty, and the king and his minister were compelled to look for victims among the worthy inhabitants of the city. Old people were carried off and forcibly led to the tree, and if the guards were not fleet-footed, the God would sometimes devour them and the victims as well.

A vague uneasiness possessed the city of Atavi. The old people were seen to disappear; no one knew what became of them. And, each day, the king's remorse grew more poignant. But he lacked the courage to sacrifice his life to the welfare of his people. He thought:

> *"Will no one come to my assistance? There lives in Cravasti, and sometimes in Rajagriha, I have been told, a man of great power, a Buddha, whose prodigies are loudly praised. They say he is fond of travelling. Why, then, does he not come into my kingdom?"*

By his power of divination, the Buddha knew of the king's desire. He flew through the air and came to Alavaka's tree. There, he sat down.

The God saw him. He started walking toward him, but, suddenly, he became powerless. His knees trembled. Fury seized him.

"Who are you?" he asked, fiercely.

"A being far more powerful than yourself," replied the Buddha.

Alavaka was in a terrible rage. He would have liked to torture this man who was sitting on the ground in front of him, this man whom he could not reach; he would have liked to torture him to death. The Buddha never lost his composure.

Alavaka finally managed to control himself. He thought that cunning would perhaps succeed where strength had failed, and in a pleasant voice he said:

"I see you are a wise man, my Lord; it is always a pleasure for me to interrogate men of wisdom. I ask them four questions. If they can answer, they are free to go wherever they please; if they can not answer, they remain my prisoners, and I devour them when I feel so disposed."

"Ask me the four questions," said the Buddha.

"I must warn you," said Alavaka, "that no one has ever answered them. You will find scattered around the bones of those I interrogated in the past."

"Ask me the four questions," repeated the Buddha.

"Well then," said Alavaka, "how can man avoid the river of passions? How can he cross the sea of existences and find safe harbour? How can he escape the tempests of evil? How can he be left untouched by the storm of desires?"

In a quiet voice, the Buddha replied:

"Man avoids the river of passions if he believes in the Buddha, in the law and in the community; he crosses the sea of existences and finds safe harbour if he understands works of holiness; he will escape the tempests of evil if he performs works of holiness; he will be left untouched by the storm of desires if he knows the sacred path that leads to deliverance."

When Alavaka heard the Master's answers, he fell at his feet and worshipped him, and he promised to change his savage ways. Then, together, they went to Atavi, to the palace of the king. "King," said the God, "I release you from your pledge."

The king was happier than he had ever been before. When he knew who had saved him, he cried:

"I believe in you, my Lord, who have saved me and saved my people; I believe in you, and I shall dedicate my life to proclaiming your glory, the glory of the law and the glory of the community."

Devadatta Expelled from the Community

The monk Devadatta was possessed of an arrogant nature. He was impatient of any restraint. He aspired to supplant the Buddha, but the monks, he knew, would not join him in an open revolt. For that he needed the support of some king or prince.

"King Bimbasara is an old man," he said to himself, one day; "Prince Ajatashatru, who is young and brave, is eager to succeed him to the throne. I could advise the prince to his advantage, and, in return, he could help me to become the head of the community."

He went to see Ajatashatru. He addressed him in flattering terms; he praised his strength, his courage, his beauty.

"Oh, if you were king," said he, "what glory would come to Rajagriha! You would conquer the neighboring states; all the sovereigns of the world would pay you homage: you would be the omnipotent master, and you would be worshipped like a God."

With such words as these, Devadatta won Ajatashatru's confidence. He received many precious gifts, and he became still more arrogant.

Maudgalyayana noticed Devadatta's frequent visits to the prince. He decided to warn the Blessed One.

"My Lord," he began, "Devadatta is very friendly with Prince Ajatashatru."

The Blessed One interrupted him.

"Let Devadatta do as he pleases; we shall soon know the truth. I am aware that Ajatashatru pays him homage; it does not advance him a single step in the path of virtue. Let Devadatta glory in his arrogance! It will be his ruin. As the banana-tree and the bamboo-tree bear fruit only to die, so will the honours Devadatta is receiving simply hasten his downfall."

Devadatta soon reached the height of vanity. He could not abide the Buddha's grandeur, and, one day, he made bold to say to him:

"Master, you are now well along in years; it is a great hardship for you to rule the monks; you should retire. Meditate in peace upon the sublime law you have discovered, and the community let me take charge of."

The Master smiled quizzically.

"Be not concerned about me, Devadatta; you are too kind. I shall know when it is time to retire. For the present, I shall stay in charge of the community.

Besides, when the time does come, I shall not give it even to Sariputra or Maudgalyayana, those two great minds that are like blazing torches, and you want it, Devadatta, you who have such a mediocre intelligence, you who shed even less light than a night-lamp!"

Devadatta bowed respectfully before the Master, but he could not hide the fire of anger in his eyes.

The Master then sent for learned Sariputra.

"Sariputra," said he, "go through the city of Rajagriha and cry in a loud voice: 'Beware of Devadatta! He has strayed from the path of righteousness. The Buddha is not responsible for his words or for his actions; the law no longer inspires him, the community no longer interests him. Henceforth, Devadatta speaks only for himself.'"

It grieved Sariputra to have such a painful mission to perform; however, he understood the Master's reasons, and he went through the city crying Devadatta's shame. The inhabitants stopped to listen, and some thought, "The monks envy Devadatta his friendship for Prince Ajatashatru." But the others said, "Devadatta must have committed a serious offense, for the Blessed One thus publicly to denounce him."

Ajatashatru's Treachery

Devadatta was musing: "Siddhartha thought to humiliate me by making light of my intelligence. I shall show him he is mistaken. My glory will overshadow his: the night-lamp will become the sun. But King Bimbasara is his faithful friend; he protects him. As long as the king is living, I can do nothing.

Prince Ajatashatru, on the other hand, honours me and holds me in high esteem; he reposes implicit confidence in me. If he were to reign, I would get everything I desire."

He went to Ajatashatru's palace.

"Oh, prince," said he, "we are living in an unfortunate age! They that are best fitted to govern are likely to die without ever having reigned. Human life is so brief a thing! Your father's longevity causes me no little concern for you."

He kept on talking, and he was presently giving the prince most evil advice. The prince was weak; he listened. Before long, he had decided to kill his father."

Night and day, now, Ajatashatru wandered through the palace, watching for an opportunity to slip into his father's apartments and make away with him. But he could not escape the vigilance of the guards. His restlessness puzzled them, and they said to King Bimbasara:

"O king, your son Ajatashatru has been behaving strangely of late. Could he be planning an evil deed?"

"Be silent," replied the king. "My son is a man of noble character. It would not occur to him to do anything base."

"You ought to send for him, O king, and question him."

"Be silent, guards. Do not accuse my son lightly."

The guards continued to keep a close watch, and at the end of a few days, they again spoke to the king. To convince them that they were mistaken, the king summoned Ajatashatru. The prince appeared before his father. He was trembling.

"My lord," said he, "why did you send for me?"

"Son," said Bimbasara, "my guards say that you have been behaving strangely of late. They tell me you wander through the palace, acting mysteriously, and that you shun the gaze of those you meet. Son, are they not lying?"

"They are not lying, father," said Ajatashatru

Remorse suddenly overwhelmed him. He fell at the king's feet, and out of the depths of his shame, he cried:

"Father, I wanted to kill you."

Bimbasara shuddered. In a voice full of anguish, he asked: *"Why did you want to kill me?"*

"In order to reign."

"Then reign," cried the king. "Royalty is not worth a son's enmity."

Ajatashatru was proclaimed king the next day.

The first thing he did was to have great honours paid to his father. But Devadatta still feared the old king's authority; he decided to use his influence against him.

"As long as your father is allowed his freedom," he said to Ajatashatru, "you are in danger of losing your power. He still retains many followers; you must take measures to intimidate them."

Devadatta again was able to impose his will on Ajatashatru, and poor Bimbasara was thrown into prison. Ajatashatru presently decided to starve him to death, and he allowed no one to take him any food.

But Queen Vaidehi was sometimes permitted to visit Bimbasara in his prison, and she would take rice to him which he ate ravenously. Ajatashatru, however, soon put a stop to this; he ordered the guards to search her each time she went to see the prisoner. She then tried to hide the food in her hair, and when this, too, was discovered, she had to use great ingenuity to save the king from dying of hunger. But she was repeatedly found out, and Ajatashatru, finally, denied her access to the prison.

In the meanwhile, he was persecuting the Buddha's faithful followers. They were forbidden to look after the temple where Bimbasara, formerly, had placed a lock of the Master's hair and the parings of his finger-nails. No longer were flowers or perfume left there as pious offerings, and the temple was not even cleaned or swept.

In Ajatashatru's palace there dwelt a woman named Srimati. She was very devout. It grieved her to be unable to perform works of holiness, and she wondered how, in these sad times, she could prove to the Master that she had kept her faith. Passing in front of the temple, she complained bitterly to see it so deserted, and when she noticed how unclean it was, she wept.

"The Master shall know that there is still one woman in this house who would honour him," thought Srimati, and at the risk of her life, she swept out the temple and decorated it with a bright garland.

Ajatashatru saw the garland. He was greatly incensed and wanted to know who had dared to disobey him. Srimati did not try to hide; of her own accord, she appeared before the king.

"Why did you defy my orders?" asked Ajatashatru.

"If I defied your orders," she replied, "I respected those of your father, King Bimbasara."

Ajatashatru did not wait to hear further. Pale with fury, he rushed at Srimati and stabbed her with his dagger. She fell, mortally wounded; but her eyes were shining with joy, and in a happy voice, she sang:

> *"My eyes have seen the protector of the worlds; my eyes have seen the light of the worlds, and for him, in the night, I have lighted the lamps. For him who dissipates the darkness, I have dissipated the darkness. His brilliance is greater than the brilliance of the sun; his rays are purer than the rays of the sun, and my rapt gaze is dazzled by the splendour. For him who dissipates the darkness, I have dissipated the darkness."*

And, dead, she seemed to glow with the light of sanctity.

The Death of Devadatta

Devadatta was eager to succeed the Buddha as head of the community. One day, he said to King Ajatashatru: "My lord, the Buddha holds you in contempt. He hates you. You must put him to death, for your glory is at stake. Send some men to the Bamboo Grove with orders to kill him; I shall lead the way."

Ajatashatru was easily persuaded. The assassins came to the Bamboo Grove, but when they saw the Master, they fell at his feet and worshipped him. This added fuel to Devadatta's rage. He went to the royal stables where a savage elephant was kept, and he bribed the guards to release him when the Master passed by, so that the animal could gore him with his tusks or trample him underfoot. But at the sight of the Master, the elephant became quite gentle, and going up to him, with his trunk he brushed the dust from the sacred robes. And the Master smiled and said:

"This is the second time, thanks to Devadatta, that an elephant has paid homage to me."

Then Devadatta himself tried to do harm to the Master. He saw him meditating in the shade of a tree; and he had the audacity to throw a sharp stone at him. It struck him in the foot; the wound began to bleed. The Master said:

"You have committed a serious offense, Devadatta; the punishment will be terrible. Vain are your criminal attempts upon the life of the Blessed One; he will not meet with an untimely death. The Blessed One will pass away of his own accord, and at the hour he chooses."

Devadatta fled. He decided he would no longer obey the rules of the community, and, wherever he could, he would seek followers of his own.

In the meanwhile, Bimbasara was starving. But he did not die. A mysterious force sustained him. His son finally decided to have him put to death, and he gave orders to burn the soles of his feet, to slash his limbs and to pour boiling oil and salt on the open wounds. The executioner obeyed, and even he wept to see an old man tortured.

A son was born to Ajatashatru on the day he issued the order for his father's death. When he saw the child, a great joy came to him; he relented, and he hurriedly sent guards to the prison to stop the execution. But they arrived too late; King Bimbasara had died amid frightful suffering.

Then Ajatashatru began to repent. One day, he heard Queen Vaidehi saying to the infant prince, as she carried him in her arms:

"May your father be as kind to you as his father was to him. Once, when he was a child, he had a sore on his finger; it hurt him, and he cried; no ointment would heal it; so Bimbasara put the finger to his lips and drew out the pus, and Ajatashatru was able to laugh again and play. Oh, love your father, little child; do not punish him with your cruelty for having been cruel to Bimbasara."

Ajatashatru shed bitter tears. He was overwhelmed with remorse. At night, in his dreams, he saw his father, bleeding from his wounds, and he heard him moan. He was seized with a burning fever, and the physician Jivaka was summoned to attend him.

"I can do nothing for you," said Jivaka. "Your body is not sick. Go to the Perfect Master, the Blessed One, the Buddha; he alone knows the words of consolation that will restore you to health."

Ajatashatru took Jivaka's advice. He went to the Blessed One; he confessed his misdeeds and his crimes, and he found peace.

"Your father," the Buddha said to him, "has been reborn among the most powerful Gods; he knows of your repentance, and he forgives you. Heed me, King Ajatashatru; know the law, and cease to suffer."

Ajatashatru issued a proclamation, banishing Devadatta from the kingdom, and ordering the inhabitants to close their doors to him if he were to seek refuge in their homes.

Devadatta was then near Cravasti where he hoped to be received by King Prasenajit, but he was scornfully denied an audience and was told to leave the kingdom. Thwarted in his attempts to enlist followers, he finally set out for Kapilavastu.

He entered the city as night was falling. The streets were dark, almost deserted; no one recognized him as he passed, for how could this lean, wretched monk, slinking in the shadow of the walls, be identified with the proud Devadatta? He went straight to the palace where princess Gopa dwelt in solitude.

He was admitted to her presence.

"Monk," said Gopa, "why do you wish to see me? Do you bring me a message of happiness? Do you come with orders from a husband I deeply reverence?"

"Your husband! Little he cares about you! Think of the time he wickedly deserted you!"

"He deserted me for the world's salvation." "Do you still love him?"

"My love would defile the purity of his life."

"Then hate him with all your heart."

"With all my heart I respect him."

"Woman, he spurned you; take your revenge."

"Be quiet, monk. Your words are evil."

"Do you not recognize me? I am Devadatta, who loves you."

"Devadatta, Devadatta, I knew you were false and evil; I knew you would be a faithless monk, but I never suspected the depths of your villainy."

"Gopa, Gopa, I love you! Your husband scorned you, he was cruel. Take your revenge. Love me!"

Gopa blushed. From her gentle eyes fell tears of shame.

"It is you who scorn me! Your love would be an insult if it were sincere, but you lie when you say you love me. You seldom noticed me in the days when I was young, in the days when I was beautiful! And now that you see me, an old woman, worn out by my austere duties, you tell me of your love, of your guilty love! You are the most contemptible of men, Devadatta! Go away! Go away!"

In his rage he sprang at her. She put out her hand to protect herself, and he fell to the ground. As he rolled over, blood gushed from his mouth.

He fled. The Sakyas heard that he was in Kapilavastu; they made him leave the city under an escort of guards, and he was taken to the Buddha who was to decide his fate. He pretended to be repentant, but he had dipped his nails in a deadly poison, and as he lay prostrate before the Maser, he tried to scratch his ankle. The Master pushed him away with his toe; then the ground opened; fierce flames burst forth, and they swallowed up the infamous Devadatta.

Prasenajit and Ajatashatru

Although the Buddha had chastened Ajatashatru's spirit, there were times when the king still gave way to anger. One day, because of a quarrel between a man from Rajagriha and one from Cravasti, he declared war on King Prasenajit.

He collected a vast army. There were foot-soldiers and horsemen; there were some mounted on chariots, others enclosed in towers carried by elephants, and swords and lances flashed in the sun as they marched into battle.

King Prasenajit also assembled his troops. He too had chariots and horses and elephants, and he advanced to meet Ajatashatru.

It was a terrible battle. It lasted four days. The first day Prasenajit lost his elephants; the second day he lost his horses; on the third, his chariots were destroyed; and on the fourth, his foot-soldiers were killed or made prisoners; and Prasenajit himself, defeated and panic-stricken, fled in the only chariot that had been saved in the disaster and escaped to Cravasti.

There, in a small, unlighted hall, he flung himself down on a low couch. He was silent, a prey to his melancholy thoughts. He never stirred; he appeared to be dead, except for the tears that coursed down his cheeks.

A man entered; it was the merchant Anathapindika.

"My lord," said he, "long may you live, and may the tide of victory turn!"

"My soldiers are dead," the king lamented, "all my soldiers are dead! My soldiers! My soldiers!"

"Grieve not, O king. Raise another army."

"I lost my fortune when I lost my army."

"King," said Anathapindika, "I shall give you the gold you need, and you will be victorious."

Prasenajit sprang to his feet.

"You have saved me, Anathapindika!" he exclaimed. "I am grateful."

With Anathapindika's gold, Prasenajit raised a formidable host. He marched against Ajatashatru.

When the two armies met, the din terrified the Gods themselves. Prasenajit used a battle array he had been taught by men from a distant land. He attacked swiftly; Ajatashatru had no defense. He, in turn, was defeated, and he was captured.

"Kill me," he cried to Prasenajit.

"I shall spare your life," said Prasenajit. "I shall take you to the Blessed Master, and he will decide your fate."

The Master had recently arrived at Jeta's park. Prasenajit said to him:

> *"Behold, O Blessed One! King Ajatashatru is my prisoner. He hates me, though I bear him no ill will. He attacked me, for some trivial reason, and defeated me at first, but now he is at my mercy. I do not wish to kill him, O Blessed One. For the sake of his father, Bimbasara, who was my friend, I would like to set him free."*

"Then set him free," said the Master. "Victory begets hatred; defeat begets suffering. They that are wise will forgo both victory and defeat. Insult is born of insult, anger of anger. They that are wise will forgo both victory and defeat. Every murderer is struck down by a murderer; every conqueror is struck down by a conqueror. They that are wise will forgo both victory and defeat."

In the presence of the Master, Ajatashatru promised to be a faithful friend to Prasenajit.

"And," he added, "let us be more than friends. I have a son, as you know, and you have a daughter, Kshema, who is still unmarried. Will you give your daughter to my son?"

"So be it," said Prasenajit. "And may this happy marriage be the earnest of our happy friendship."

The Master approved. The two kings ever after lived at peace with each other, and Ajatashatru became known for his gentleness.

THE BUDDHA TEACHES THE DOCTRINE

The Master was growing old. When he was in Rajagriha, he called the monks together, and he spoke to them at great length:

"Monks, do not forget the precepts I have given you. Observe them carefully. You will assemble twice a month, and you will confess your transgressions to one another. If you feel that you have done evil, and you keep it to yourself, you will be guilty of a lie. Admit your transgressions: the confession will bring you rest and peace. The four gravest sins a monk can commit are, as you know: to have intercourse with a woman; to steal anything whatsoever; to kill a human being or instigate a murder; and to pretend to possess a superhuman power that he knows he does not possess.

A monk who has committed one of these four sins must be expelled from the community. Monks, do not bandy words with women, and do not corrupt them. Do not bear false witness against your brothers. Do not try to sow discord in the community. Do not strive to evade a reprimand. Never lie, and insult no one. Observe carefully, O monks, all the precepts I have given you."

He said further:

"Seriousness is the province of immortality; frivolity, the province of death. They that are serious do not die; they that are frivolous are always dead. Therefore would the wise be serious. The wise attain the supreme blessing, nirvana. He sees his glory increase who is energetic and can remember, who thinks honestly and acts deliberately, who is continent, who lives within the law, and who is serious. It is frivolity the fools and the weak-minded pursue; the wise treasure seriousness as a miser his gold. The

monk who would be serious, who sees the danger of frivolity, shakes the evil law like the wind does the leaves; he tears asunder the bonds that bind him to the world; he is close to nirvana. Standing on the terrace of wisdom, released from all suffering, the serious man who has conquered frivolity looks out over the unhappy multitude, as, from the summit of a mountain, one might gaze upon the crowd in the plains below."

The Buddha and the Shepherd

Before he died, the Blessed One decided to go on a long journey. He wanted to visit certain of his disciples and exhort them to observe his teachings with scrupulous care. With only Ananda for a companion, he left the city of Rajagriha.

One day, while he was resting in the corner of a field, he said to Ananda:

"There will come a time when men will wonder why I once entered a woman's womb. They will question the perfect purity of my birth, and they will doubt whether I ever had supreme power. These benighted men will never understand that, for him who devotes his life to works of holiness, the body is free from the impurity of birth. He who would seek supreme knowledge must enter a woman's womb; he must, out of pity for mankind, be born into the world of men. For if he were a God, how could he set in motion the wheel of the law? Imagine the Buddha as a God, Ananda; men would soon lose heart. They would say, 'The Buddha, who is a God, has happiness, holiness, perfection; but we, how can we hope to attain them?' And they would be in deep despair. Oh, let them keep still, these benighted creatures! Let them not try to steal the law, for they would use it ill. Rather, let them consider the Buddha's nature incomprehensible, these men who will never be able to gauge my eminence!"

A shepherd was crossing the field. He had the serenity of a man who is quietly performing a labour of joy.

"Who are you, shepherd?" the Master asked him.

"My name is Dhaniya," replied the shepherd.

"Where are you going?" asked the Master.

"I am going home to my wife and children."

"You seem to know pure happiness, shepherd?"

"I have boiled my rice, I have milked my cows," said the shepherd Dhaniya; "I live with my family on the banks of the river; my house is well roofed, my fire is lighted; so fall if you will, O rain of the sky.

"I am rid of anger, I am rid of stubbornness," said the Master; "I bide for a night on the banks of the river; my house has no roof, the fire of passions is quenched in my being; so fall if you will, O rain of the sky."

"The gadflies never torment my herd," said the shepherd Dhaniya; "my cows roam in the grassy meadows; they can abide the coming rain; so fall if you will, O rain of the sky."

"I built a sturdy raft, I set sail for nirvana," said the Master; "I crossed the torrent of passions and I reached the saintly shores; I need the raft no longer; so fall if you will, O rain of the sky."

"My wife is obedient, she is chaste and good," said the shepherd Dhaniya; "she has lived with me these many years; she is pleasant and kindly, no one speaks ill of her; so fall if you will, O rain of the sky."

"My mind is obedient, it is loosed from all bonds," said the Master; "I have trained it these many years; it is quite docile, no evil is left in me; so fall if you will, O rain of the sky."

"I myself pay my servants their wages," said the shepherd Dhaniya; "my children receive wholesome food at my board; no one has ever tried to speak ill of them; so fall if you will, O rain of the sky."

"I am the servant of no one," said the Master; "with what I earn I travel the whole world; there is for me no need of a servant; so fall if you will, O rain of the sky."

"I have cows, I have calves, I have heifers," said the shepherd Dhaniya, "and I have a dog that is lord of my herd; so fall if you will, O rain of the sky.

"I have neither cows nor calves nor heifers," said the Master, "and I have no dog to be on guard; so fall if you will, O rain of the sky."

"The stakes are driven deep in the ground, nothing can move them," said the shepherd Dhaniya; the ropes are new and made of strong grasses; the cows will never break them now; so fall if you will, O rain of the sky."

"Like the dog that has broken his chain," said the Master, "like the elephant that has broken his shackles, never again will I enter a womb; so fall if you will, O rain of the sky."

The shepherd Dhaniya bowed before the Master and said:

> *"I know now who you are, O Blessed One; come with me to my home."*

As they were about to enter the house, the rain fell in torrents and formed little streams that trickled over the ground. When Dhaniya heard the rain, he spoke these words:

> *"Verily, we have acquired great riches since we have seen the Buddha. O Master, you are our refuge, you who have looked at us with the eyes of wisdom. Be our protector, O Saint! We are obedient, my wife and I; if we lead a life of holiness, we shall conquer birth and death, and we shall have done with suffering."*

Then a voice was heard, and Mara, the Evil One, stood before them. No one had seen him come.

"He who has sons is happy to see his sons," said Mara, the Evil One; "he who has cows is happy to see his cows; happy is the man of substance, and he who has no substance has no happiness."

"He who has sons is worried to see his sons," said the Master; "he who has cows is worried to see his cows; worried is the man of substance, and he who has no substance has no worries."

But Mara had fled. Dhaniya and his wife were listening to the Master speak.

6

A Misreading of Buddha

Set forth in as few words as possible, Buddha's message to man is an appeal to him to find his true self, with all that this can give him—joy, peace, knowledge, love—by suppressing egoism, with all the desires and delusions on which it feeds, and breaking, one by one, the fetters of the surface life and the lower self.

Those who have followed me thus far will, I think, admit that Buddha's scheme of life coincides, at all its vital points, with the scheme that I worked out by drawing practical deductions from the master ideas of that deeply spiritual philosophy which found its highest expression in the Upanishads. One who accepted the central idea of that philosophy—the idea that the Universal Soul is the real self of each one of us—and realized its spiritual consequences, and who at the same time saw clearly that none of the current modes of apprehending it—the metaphysical, the intuitional, the poetical, the symbolical—was available for ordinary, unenlightened, undeveloped men, would probably come to the conclusion that, if the world at large was to be brought under the influence of that great spiritual idea, a practical interpretation of it must be presented to and followed by the rank and file of mankind. Such a teacher would begin by appealing to the very sense which it was his most cherished desire to cultivate,—the sense of reality, which is present in embryo in every breast. He would tell men that life is full of suffering, and that the chief cause of suffering is the impermanence—and therefore the unreality—of the objects of man's desire; and he would expect them to assent to these propositions.

This is what Buddha did.

He would explain to them that the desire for unreal things not only caused suffering in this or that earth-life, but also caused the suffering to be reproduced in other earth-lives,—desire for the shadows and illusions of earth being the subjective side of the attractive force by which earth draws the unemancipated soul back to itself again and again; and he would ask them to infer from this that deliverance from suffering (now and in the future) was to be won by the subjugation, and at last by the extinction of desire,—not of desire as such, but of the base, carnal, worldly, self-seeking desires, which, by keeping the soul in ignorance of its true nature and destiny, cause it to eddy round and round in the "whirlpool of rebirth."

This is what Buddha did.

He would tell them—though not in so many words—that, if their baser desires were to be subdued, they must practise self-control and cultivate sympathy; and, with that end in view, he would give them a few simple rules for the conduct of life,—rules which would provide for the development of self-control and sympathy along the arterial lines of morality, and the authority of which would therefore be in a measure self-evident.

This is what Buddha did.

For those who had mastered their baser desires and passions, and who, by a parallel process, had cultivated the latent virtues of gentleness, kindness, and compassion, and, speaking generally, begun to live in the lives of others, he would make further provision; he would help them in various ways to conquer their hydra-headed enemy, the lower self; he would teach them to distinguish between the shadows and the realities of life, to rid themselves of every self-seeking desire and every self-affirming delusion, to quench lust and anger, to extend in every direction the radiating light of sympathy and good will.

This is what Buddha did.

He would tell them that, when the last taint of egoism and the last shadow of ignorance had disappeared, the happiness to which they had always had an indefeasible title, but a title which each man in turn had to make good for himself, would at last be theirs; that the Path which they had followed for so long would lead them at last to the fullness of knowledge, the fullness of peace, the fullness of love,—and therefore to unimaginable bliss.

This is what Buddha did.

But he would impress on them that they lived in a world in which causes always produce their natural and necessary effects; that the consequences of their conduct would therefore follow them wherever they went; that external rewards were not to be hoped for; that external punishments were not to be dreaded; that virtue was its own reward and vice its own punishment, in the sense that whatever is done or left undone inevitably reacts upon the character, and, through the character, affects for weal or for woe the destiny of the soul; that interference from without was in the nature of things impossible; that the whole sacrificial system was based on a delusion; that ceremonial observances were of no avail:—he would teach them, in fine, that each man in turn must take his life into his own hands and work out his destiny for himself.

This is what Buddha did.

But, while he taught them all this, he would make no attempt to explain to them the deepest mysteries of existence; he would deliberately disconnect his scheme of life, so far as his own exposition of it was concerned, from theology and metaphysics; he would keep silence as to what is "ultimate and uttermost"; for he would know that the average mind has no capacity for deep thinking, and that, if he tried to disclose to his fellow-men his ultimate reasons for the course of life which he wished them to follow, they would make nonsense, first of his philosophical teaching and then of his whole scheme of life, giving themselves wrong reasons for everything that they did or left undone, and so (in the last resort) misinterpreting and misapplying every detail of his teaching.

This too is what Buddha did (or forebore to do). That he kept silence about "great matters" is as certain as that his ethical teaching was clear, coherent, and systematic.

The coincidences between the two schemes of life—that which Buddha taught and that which follows logically (in the deeper sense of the word) from the philosophy of the Upanishads—are so many and so vital that they cannot be ascribed to chance. Even if the age in which Buddha lived had been separated by a thousand years from the age which gave birth to the stories of Brahma and the Gods, and Nachiketas and Death, we should feel justified, on internal evidence, in concluding that Buddha had somehow or other come under the influence of the ideas which those stories enshrined. But we need not trust to internal evidence only. We know that the spiritual atmosphere of India in Buddha's day was impregnated with the ideas of the Upanishads. We know that those ideas must have appealed with peculiar force to a thinker of Buddha's exalted nature, whether he ended by emancipating himself from their influence or not. We know that the teachers who had expounded those ideas had utterly failed to bring them into connection with the daily life of the ordinary man, and had thereby left a gap in the philosophical teaching of India, which was waiting to be filled by some master mind. The cumulative evidence afforded by these facts, added to the internal evidence which has already been set forth in detail, seems to point with irresistible force to one conclusion, namely that Buddha accepted the idealistic teaching of the Upanishads—accepted it at its highest level and in its purest form—and took upon himself as his life's mission to fill the obvious gap in it,—in other words, to make the spiritual ideas which had hitherto been the exclusive possession of a few select souls, available for the daily needs of mankind.

If this conclusion is correct, we shall see in Buddhism, not a revolt against the "Brahmanic" philosophy as such, but an ethical interpretation of the leading ideas of that philosophy,—

a following out of those ideas, not into the word-built systems of (so-called) thought which the metaphysicians of the day were constructing with fatal facility, but into their practical consequences in the inner life of man.

But is the conclusion correct? I must admit at once that there is a preponderance of opinion against it. The Orientalist scholars into whose hands the work of expounding the ideas and doctrines of Buddha has perforce fallen, seem to be agreed in holding that in Buddhism the mind of India broke away from the Brahmanic line of thought. Some indeed go further than this. They tell us that Buddha's teaching was directly and openly subversive of the "sovereign dogmas" of Brahmanism. They admit indeed, with considerable reluctance, that he believed in re-incarnation, but they contend that he did not believe in any re-incarnating self or ego; and they accept on his behalf all the philosophical consequences of this sweeping denial, the last of these being that Nirvana—the Buddhist effort and aspiration—is the prelude to annihilation.

Foremost among the distinguished scholars who have satisfied themselves that Buddha was a negative dogmatist—a metaphysician, whose propositions were all fundamental negations—is Dr. Rhys Davids, a writer on Buddhism whose works enjoy a well-deserved popularity, and whose influence in determining the attitude of contemporary opinion towards the Buddhist scheme of life is very great. In the following passages from his writings his own attitude is clearly defined. After expounding the hour Sacred Truths, he goes on to say, "The remarkable fact is that we have here set forth a view of religion entirely independent of the soul theories on which all the various philosophies and religions then current in India were based." Speaking of re-incarnation he says, "There is no passage of a soul or I in any sense from the one life to the other.

Their [the Buddhists'] whole view of the matter is independent of the time-honoured soul-theories held in common by all the followers of every other creed." Speaking of the interest that the Brahmans took in Buddha's speculations, he says that "his [Buddha's] rejection of the soul-theory and of all that it involved was really incompatible with the whole theology of the Vedas." Elsewhere he says that no other school of religious thought is "quite so frankly and entirely independent as Buddhism of the two theories of God and the soul." Other significant passages in his writings are the following: "The victory to be gained by the destruction of ignorance is, in Gautama's view, a victory which can be gained and enjoyed in this life and in this life only."

"Man is never the same for two consecutive moments, and there is within him no abiding principle whatever." "Another proof of the prominence of the doctrine of the non-existence of the soul is the fact that the Brahmans who have misunderstood many less important or less clearly expressed tenets of Buddhism recognize this as one of its distinctive features."

"Would it be possible in a more complete and categorical manner to deny that there is any soul—anything of any kind which continues to exist, in any manner, after death?"

If there is no soul or ego, in any sense of the word, what is the meaning of Nirvana? According to Dr. Rhys Davids, it is a state of blissful repose which precedes annihilation, with which, however, it must not be confounded. "Death, utter death, with no new life to follow, is then the result of, but it is not Nirvana."

These passages make it clear that Buddha, according to Dr. Rhys Davids' estimate of him, was a daring speculative thinker who had thought out all the master problems of existence and solved them to his own satisfaction, his solution in every case, or rather in the one case which is decisive of the rest, being an unqualified negation. The uncompromising denial of the soul, which Dr. Rhys Davids ascribes to Buddha, makes an end of all metaphysical speculation. If there is no soul, if the sense of self is wholly delusive, we may know, without further inquiry, that there is no God (in any spiritual sense of the word), no inward life, no former life, no after life. But what of the outward things which the (so-called) self perceives and, in the act of perceiving, certifies as existent, and even provisionally certifies as real?

According to Western thought these are real things; and the physical force which is behind them all, is the fundamental reality which it is the aim of speculation to discover. But, according to Buddha, outward things are all shadows and delusions; his primary aim, as a moral teacher, being to deliver men from belief in their reality,—a belief which is the source of all error, sorrow, and suffering. It is clear then that, if Dr. Rhys Davids' interpretation of Buddha's metaphysical system is correct, he (Buddha) was not a materialist, like those modern thinkers with whom he may seem to have much in common, but a philosophical nihilist, who could find no centre of reality, no principle of permanence, in that whirl and flux of phenomena which for him constituted the Universe.

It is true that in more than one passage in his American lectures Dr. Rhys Davids says that Buddha denied the existence of the soul in the Christian sense of the word: and one might infer from this that it was open to him to believe in the soul in some other sense of the word,—for example in the Brahmanic, which is diametrically opposite to the "Christian." But whether Dr. Rhys Davids has himself failed to distinguish between the Christian and the Brahmanic theories of the soul, or whether he regards the former as the only soul-theory which is in any degree compatible with mental sanity, I cannot pretend to say. What is certain is that he regards Buddha's rejection of the soul-theory as thorough-going and uncompromising. The words "There is no passage of a soul or I in any sense from the one life to the other. Their [the Buddhists'] whole view of the matter is independent of the time-honoured soul-theories held in common by all the followers of every other creed," are decisive on this point. Besides, it stands to reason that if "death, utter death," is the inevitable sequel to Nirvana, there is no room in Buddha's philosophy for the soul, in any sense of the word.

My reason for setting forth in detail Dr. Rhys Davids' interpretation of Buddha's philosophy is that it happens to be the one interpretation which has found its way into the outer world. Ask the man in the street what he knows of Buddha. He will tell you that Buddha was a pessimist and an atheist, who denied the soul, denied a supreme cause, denied that the world had any centre of reality, and taught his followers to look forward to annihilation as the final deliverance from the woes of earth. This, if not identical with Dr. Rhys Davids' teaching, is at least an echo of it. Dr. Paul Carus, who has taken upon himself to popularize Buddhism and to vindicate it from the disparaging criticism of its "Christian critics," is in the main in full agreement with Dr. Rhys Davids, but is more ready than that distinguished scholar to accept the logical consequences of the dynamically atomistic philosophy which he ascribes to Buddha.

Even the author of "The Soul of a People," a writer whose deep and delicate sympathy with, and insight into, the "soul" or inner life of a Buddhist people, besides investing his book with a charm which is all its own, entitles him to a respectful hearing whenever he speaks, in general terms, about Buddhism,—even he, when treating of the popular belief in re-incarnation, must needs shake his head over the credulity of the good, simple people, and remind them that belief in the survival of the "I" is "opposed to all Buddhism," the real teaching of Buddha—"that what survives death is not the 'I' but only the results of its action"—"being too deep for them to hold."

Such unanimity on the part of the popular exponents of Buddhism points to a large measure of unanimity on the part of its more learned interpreters and commentators. That Dr. Rhys Davids has given voice to a general consensus of opinion on the part of the Western students of Buddhism, can scarcely be doubted. From Barthelemy Saint-Hilaire to H. C. Warren, the Orientalists of Europe and America are agreed, with one or two notable exceptions, in holding that Buddha denied the Ego and regarded Nirvana as the prelude to annihilation; while the fact that the South Buddhist Church has given Dr. Paul Carus a certificate of orthodoxy suggests that on these points the general trend of official opinion in the Buddhist world itself coincides, mutatis mutandis, with the general trend of learned opinion in the West.

What evidence can Dr. Rhys Davids, and those who think with him, give in support of their thesis that Buddha was a negative dogmatist

"Who dropped his plummet down the broad

Deep Universe, and said 'No God'

There is this initial difficulty in the way of our accepting Dr. Rhys Davids' interpretation of Buddha's metaphysical—as distinguished from his ethical—philosophy, that, on our author's own showing, Buddha was a true and consistent agnostic, who was so far from dogmatizing about what is ultimate that he regarded all metaphysical speculation as vain and foolish, and all metaphysical strife as morally wrong. "There were a certain number of questions to which it was his habit to refuse to reply. These were questions the discussion of which, in his opinion, was apt to lead the mind astray, and so far from being conducive to a growth in insight, would be a hindrance to the only thing which was supremely worth aiming at—the perfect life in Arahat-ship.

Such questions as: What shall I be during the ages of the future? Do I after all exist, or am I not? are regarded as worse than unprofitable, and the Buddha not only refused to discuss them, but held that the tendency, the desire to discuss them was a weakness, and that the answers usually given were a delusion." With these words, which are to be found in Dr. Rhys Davids' American lectures on Buddhism, we may compare Dr. Oldenberg's statement that "the most serious obstacle in the way of our comprehending Buddhist dogmas is the silence with which everything is passed over which does not lead to the separation from the earthly, to the subjection of all desire, to the cessation of the transitory, to quietude, knowledge, illumination, to Nirvana."

Both writers are agreed in holding that the scheme of life which Buddhism set before its votaries was in all probability formulated by Buddha himself; but both writers are also agreed in holding that, though Buddha gave his followers what I may call the penultimate (or perhaps the ante-penultimate) reasons for entering "the Path," he not only carefully abstained from giving them the ultimate reasons, but positively forbade them to speculate as to what those reasons might be. What then becomes of Dr. Rhys Davids' confident and often repeated statement that Buddha's philosophy centred in a fundamental denial? To deny the Ego is to gather all metaphysical problems into one pregnant question, and to answer that question with an everlasting "No." In other words, it is to say the last word that can be said in metaphysical speculation. Is it possible for the same thinker to be, at the same time and on the same plane of thought, a true agnostic and an aggressive dogmatist? If this is not possible, which role are we to assign to Buddha?

The teaching of Buddha, as Dr. Rhys Davids presents it to us, may be divided into two parts,—an ethical scheme of life, and a metaphysical theory of things. Dr. Rhys Davids will scarcely contend that the authenticity of the latter is as strongly vouched for by external evidence as that of the former. That there are passages in the Buddhist Scriptures in which Buddha is represented as having authoritatively denied the Ego, may perhaps be provisionally admitted.

But surely, in the light of Dr. Rhys Davids' assertion that Buddha both abstained from and discountenanced metaphysical speculation, we are free to conjecture that, as statements of Buddha's own metaphysical teaching, these passages are entirely untrustworthy. It is surely conceivable that what is set forth in them is, not Buddha's own words or even his own opinions, but the writers' private interpretation of Buddha's deeper philosophy,—an interpretation which is based partly on what he said, partly on what he left unsaid (for his silence is both significant and suggestive), but chiefly on what the writers themselves happened to believe.

It is conceivable that the writers felt, as Dr. Rhys Davids evidently feels and as we must all feel, that behind Buddha's silence there was a living creed; and that, feeling this, they succumbed to a temptation which it is always hard to resist—the temptation to bring the ideas of a great writer into line with one's own—and ascribed to Buddha conclusions and arguments which he had never formulated, but which, in their opinion, he would certainly have endorsed.

It is conceivable, to say the least, that many of the stories and discourses in the Buddhist Scriptures are as far from setting forth the inner creed of Buddha as the writings of Christian theologians in all ages are from setting forth the inner creed of Christ. At any rate, if I am to reconcile Dr. Rhys Davids' authoritative statement that Buddha abstained on principle from metaphysical speculation with his equally authoritative exposition of Buddha's metaphysical system, I must assume that he has based the latter on internal rather than on external evidence; I must assume, in other words, that his interpretation of Buddha's philosophy is, in the main, the outcome of his study of Buddha's scheme of life, is in fact his own private attempt "to complete and to find the centre of the circle" of which Buddha has given us only a "broken arc."

If this is what Dr. Rhys Davids has attempted to do, he has set us an example which I, for one, intend to follow. The specific passages to which he appeals in support of his general thesis will be considered in due course, and an attempt will be made to show that for the most part they admit of an interpretation which is the exact opposite of that which Dr. Rhys Davids has put upon them. But as, on his own showing, the internal evidence is far more weighty than the external (which indeed he has expressly debarred himself from regarding as conclusive), and as on this point I am in full accord with him, I will now study the internal evidence in the light of his interpretation of it. He tells me that Buddha broke away, abruptly and completely, from the deeper spiritual ideas of his own age and country. That he should have done this, that any great Teacher should ever do this, is improbable in a very high degree. Christ was in open revolt against the legalism of his age and nation; but, far from rejecting the grandly poetical conception of God which Israel had evolved in the days of his spiritual greatness, and to which his sacred writings owe their charm and influence, he went back to that conception, went back to what was most spiritual and most poetical in it, reaffirmed this against the materialism and formalism of the Scribes and Pharisees, and then transformed it into a deeper and more spiritual vision of God than Israel, at his best, had ever fashioned.

The relation of Christ to Judaism may well have been paralleled by the relation of Buddha to Brahmanism. That there was much in the Brahmanism of his day which Buddha rejected and even denounced, is certain; but it does not follow from this that he had broken away from the Brahmanic teaching at its highest level. On the contrary, the fact that the Brahmanism of his day had either forgotten that high teaching or deliberately betrayed it, makes it probable that in denouncing the former he was championing the cause of the latter. And the further fact that his own scheme of life, when surveyed from the standpoint of the Brahmanic philosophy, seems to be the practical application and expression of its spiritual ideas, raises to a high degree the probability of his having been in sympathy with those ideas, and raises to a still higher degree the improbability of his having formally renounced them.

Thus at the outset we are entitled to insist that the internal evidence which Dr. Rhys Davids brings forward in support of his general position shall be convincingly strong. It happens, however, that, as an interpreter of the inner creed of an Eastern thinker, he, in common with other European exponents of Buddhism, labours under the disability of looking at "great matters" from standpoints which are exclusively Western. For example, that ultra-Stoical conception of life which makes it possible for him to say that "the true Buddhist saint does not mar the purity of his self-denial by lusting after a positive happiness, which he, himself, shall enjoy hereafter," and which gives a strong bias to the general attitude which he and others have instinctively adopted towards Buddhism, is wholly foreign to Eastern modes of thought, and is in no way countenanced by Buddha's own ethical teaching.

On this point there cannot be the shadow of a doubt. Buddha's own outlook on life, if, as all the commentators admit, it is faithfully mirrored in the "Four Sacred Truths," was not ultra-Stoical but essentially anti-Stoical. The two paramount ends which he set before his disciples, when he urged them to enter "the Path," were deliverance from suffering and the ultimate fruition of perfect bliss. In other words, his philosophy was hedonism of a pure and exalted type. It is true that he condemned the life of pleasure. But why? Not because those who led it were trying to be happy, but because they were trying to be happy in the wrong way,—because they had mistaken the shadow of happiness for the reality, because what they sowed as pleasure they were doomed to reap as pain. So far was he from condemning man's longing for happiness, that his whole scheme of life may be said to base itself on an appeal to, and resolve itself into a systematic attempt to cultivate, that instinctive desire, by teaching men to "fix their hearts" "where true joys are to be found."

More important even, and more characteristically Western, than the ultra-Stoicism which dominates Dr. Rhys Davids' own ethical philosophy is the dualism which dominates his metaphysical theory of things. This tendency affects his interpretation of Buddha's ideas in more ways than one, but chiefly in this one way. He insists on things being divided into the existent and the non-existent, which are alternatives, whereas the higher thought of India seems to have divided them into the real and the unreal, which are not alternatives but polar opposites.

Thus Dr. Rhys Davids would say that the Ego exists or does not exist, whereas the Indian thinker would concern himself with the problem of the reality of the Ego, and would see that what is real (or unreal) from one point of view may be unreal (or real) from another. The difference between the two ways of looking at things goes very deep; goes in fact to the root of most of the problems that perplex the student of Buddhism. Existence and non-existence are alternatives; and, if we are to choose between alternatives, we must provide ourselves with a criterion by which we may know the true alternative from the false. But how shall man, who is presumably not omniscient, provide himself with a criterion which will enable him to define the boundaries of the Universe? For it is this, and nothing less, that he attempts to do when he takes upon himself to divide things into the existent and the non-existent. What is the criterion or test of existence?

It is impossible to answer this question except by begging it. In other words, we must say what we mean by existence before we can attempt to distinguish between the existent and the non-existent. But in the very act of defining the word, we provide ourselves, whether we intend to do this or not, with a test of the thing. For example. We ask ourselves: Does a certain thing exist or not? Does a centaur exist or not? Does a mermaid exist or not? It is easy for us to answer these questions, so long as we agree among ourselves that the existent is that which is perceptible by man's bodily senses. In thus defining the word existent, we provide ourselves with a test of existence; and the test is valid just so long and so far as the definition is true.

But the definition is, at best, only hypothetically and provisionally true. In the ordinary affairs of everyday life it is sufficiently true to answer our practical purposes. This is all that we can say about it. To take for granted that it is absolutely true, and that the corresponding test of existence is absolutely valid, is to beg every question which this hypothesis enables us to answer: for, the moment we accept the definition as true without qualification or reserve, we commit ourselves to a vast metaphysical assumption. Does the Ego exist or does it not? "No," answers the "uninitiated" thinker, "it does not satisfy my criterion of existence.

It is not perceptible by my bodily senses." He fails to see that the question as to the existence of the Ego, which is, ex hypothesi, invisible and otherwise imperceptible, involves the further question as to the validity of his materialistic test of existence. To ask whether the Ego exists or not is to challenge, by implication, the validity of that particular test. Had the test been regarded as absolutely valid, the question as to the Ego would never have been raised. Yet it is only the thinker who has allowed the materialistic conception of existence to dominate his mind and limit his whole speculative outlook; in other words, who has allowed the practical demands of his ordinary everyday life to control the philosophical movement of his thoughts;—it is only the thinker of this crude and commonplace type, who can bring himself to ask whether the Ego exists or not. The teacher who rejects that particular test of existence knows that there is no (final) test, and he therefore abstains from asking a question which is of necessity begged in the act of being asked.

Not only must there be a recognized test of existence, if the controversy as to the existence of the Ego is to have any issue, but there must also be a tacit agreement among the disputants as to the meaning of the word Ego. In the absence of such agreement, the discussion can lead to nothing but loss of temper and confusion of thought. And as in the region of metaphysics such agreement is not to be looked for, since, if it existed, the very raison d'etre of metaphysical inquiry would be gone, one can but conclude that to debate such a question as Does the Ego exist?—a question which takes one in an instant to the ultimate limits of human thought—is not merely a mischievous waste of mental energy, but also a proof of mental blindness on the part of those who allow themselves to indulge in so futile a controversy. Even such questions as Does a centaur exist? or Does a mermaid exist? become unanswerable the moment they become metaphysical. For, though neither a centaur nor a mermaid exists, in the sense of being perceptible by man's bodily senses, each of these fabled beings does exist as a creation of the human mind. Is existence, in that sense of the word, equivalent to non-existence? Perhaps it is: but the question goes to the root of human thought; and it is impossible to answer it offhand without begging all the deeper questions which it involves.

As metaphysical controversy was wholly repugnant to Buddha's type of mind, the antecedent improbability of his having indulged in the most futile of all metaphysical controversies and authoritatively solved the meaningless problem in which that controversy finally centres, is overwhelmingly strong. Moreover, there is, as it happens, positive evidence that, when he was invited to think and teach in the category of the existent and the non-existent, he deliberately refused to do so. The story of the dialogue between Buddha and Vacchagotta will presently be told, and its meaning will be considered. Meanwhile, it is enough for our present purpose to know that, when the wandering monk Vacchagotta challenged the "Exalted One" with the question "Is there the Ego?" and then with the question "Is there not the Ego?" he was in each case answered with silence.

The more carefully one studies the teaching of Buddha, the stronger does one's conviction become that the ultimate category in which he thought was that of the real and the unreal, not that of the existent and the non-existent. The difference between these two categories is that, whereas the existent and the non-existent are (as has been already pointed out) mutually exclusive alternatives, the real and the unreal are polar opposites, and as such always coexist—except of course at the ideal points of infinity and zero—varying together in inverse proportion, or, in other words, being so related to one another that the one falls as the other rises and rises as the other falls. If we are to choose between alternatives, we must be able to apply to each of them from without (so to speak) a recognized criterion or test. When our alternatives are ultimate conceptions, such as the existent and the non-existent, it stands to reason that to apply a test from without is impossible:—

"For God alone sits high enough above

To speculate so largely."

If we are to choose between polar opposites, we must be able to measure them by a standard. This standard is always internal to, and inherent in, the movement of the two opposites from pole to counter pole. It follows that, even when our opposites are ultimate conceptions, such as the real and the unreal, a standard of measurement is available, being inherent in the very movement of our thought. For example, to ask whether the inward and spiritual side of life is existent or non-existent, is to ask a meaningless and therefore an unanswerable question. To ask whether it is real or unreal is to ask a question to which life itself, both in its universal and in its individual movement, is the abiding, though never formulated, answer. That Buddha thought in the category of the real and the unreal is suggested by the whole tenor of his teaching. If there is any one thing which his sayings make quite clear, it is that he regarded outward things and the outward side of life as unreal. But he was not so foolish as to think of them as non-existent. Which is the real pole of existence? is the question which he must have asked himself; and his scheme of life is his answer to that question.

Let us now assume, for argument's sake, that the answer which he gave to life's master question was the opposite of that which the general tenor of his teaching would seem to suggest. Let us go further. Let us assume, with most of the Western exponents of Buddhism, that Buddha was a negative dogmatist, pure and simple,—that he regarded the Ego not merely as unreal but as non-existent. What follows with regard to his scheme of life? That scheme undoubtedly centres in the doctrine of re-incarnation, the very purpose of it being to deliver men from the "whirlpool of rebirth." If there is no re-incarnating Ego, what becomes of the doctrine of re-incarnation? And if this, the keystone of the arch of Buddhist thought, is withdrawn, what becomes of Buddha's scheme of life? Dr. Rhys Davids, and those who think with him, have tried to face this difficulty.

In his first exposition of Buddhism Dr. Rhys Davids saw clearly that denial of the Ego turned the doctrine of re-incarnation into nonsense, and he accepted the consequences of this conclusion. He so expounded the Buddhist belief in re-incarnation as to make nonsense of it, and then boldly affirmed that the belief was in its essence nonsensical. Speaking of those who have trusted themselves to the seemingly stately bridge which Buddhism has tried to build over the river of the mysteries and sorrows of life, he said, "they have failed to see that the very keystone [of the bridge], the link between one life and another, is a mere word—this wonderful hypothesis, this airy nothing, this imaginary cause beyond the reach of reason—the individualized and individualizing force of Karma." But in his

American lectures he departs from this logical and intelligible position, and tries to persuade himself that the doctrine of re-incarnation, even if there be no re-incarnating Ego, is sense. "There is a real identity between a man in his present life and in the future. But the identity is not in a conscious soul which shall fly out away from his body after he is dead.

The real identity is that of cause and effect. A man thinks he began to be a few years—twenty, fifty, sixty years ago. There is some truth in that; but in a much larger, deeper, truer sense he has been (in the causes of which he is the result) for countless ages in the past; and those same causes (of which he is the temporary effect) will continue in other like temporary forms through countless ages yet to come. In that sense alone, according to Buddhism, each of us has after death a continuing life." This is an interesting statement of Dr. Rhys Davids' own ideas about human immortality, but as a statement of what Buddha taught it is utterly misleading. It is doubtless true that all the forces of Nature, operating through millions of years, meet in me; and that what I do will produce consequences which will pass on, with an ever widening lateral movement, into the remotest future.

But this is not what Buddhism teaches, in the doctrine of Karma, or has ever taught. "The peculiarity of Buddhism," says Dr. Rhys Davids himself, "lies in this, that the result of what a man is or does is held not to be dissipated, as it were, into many streams, but concentrated together in the formation of one new sentient being." What Buddhism teaches is that I reap the crop which was sowed by some one man who lived before I did, and that in like manner some one man in the future will reap the crop which I am sowing now; and so on, both backwards and forwards. It teaches, in other words, that the current of moral cause and effect flows in the narrow channel of a succession of individual lives (or rather in a number of such channels), whereas modern science, to which Dr. Rhys Davids seems to look for inspiration and guidance, teaches that there is always a dual movement,—from the collective life into the individual, and from the individual life into the collective.

The difference between these two conceptions of moral causation, and between the two derivative conceptions of human immortality, is as wide as it is deep. The question which we have to ask ourselves with regard to the Buddhist conception is a simple one: Is the identity between me and the inheritor of my Karma, or again between me and the man whose Karma I inherit, as real as the identity between the me of today and the me of twenty years hence (if I shall be living then), or again between the me of today and the me of my boyhood? If it is not as real, the doctrine of re-incarnation is pure nonsense from both points of view,—from that of Eastern idealism and of Western science. But if it is as real, the doctrine is sound sense in the eyes of Eastern idealism; and though Western science cannot countenance it, it is equally certain that it cannot reject it, for the matter is one which necessarily eludes its grasp.

Now, strange as it may seem, there is nothing in the Buddhist Scriptures to show that even those thinkers who are supposed to have declared war against the Ego regarded the identity between man and man, in a given line of Karmic succession, as less real than the identity between what a man is today and what he was twenty years ago, or will be twenty years hence. The author of the Milinda dialogues, for example, is supposed to have argued against the Ego. I doubt if he really did. It is quite possible, I think, that his dialogues have a different aim and admit of a different interpretation.

But let us assume that, in theory at least, he denied the Ego, and that in this respect he falls into line with the modern votaries of metaphysical atomism. What then? I cannot find anything in any of his dialogues to show that his belief in individual re-incarnation was other than real. I cannot find anything to show that he regarded the identity between A, who is living now, and B, the future inheritor of his Karma, as in any way different from the identity between the A of today and the A of twenty years ago or twenty years hence. Thoroughgoing denial of the Ego destroys the identity of a man from moment to moment as effectually as from life to life. But—to quote Pascal's words—*"la nature soutient la raison impuissante et l'empeche d'extravaguer jusqu'a ce point."* Even Dr. Paul Carus, whose intense antipathy to the Ego makes him the protagonist of the metaphysical atomists, would probably admit, as a working hypothesis, that he was the same being as Dr. Paul Carus of twenty years ago, just as he would speak of self-culture, self-development, self-control, though all the while he regards the sense of self as entirely delusive. And, in like manner, the author of the Milinda dialogues would have accepted, as a working hypothesis, the identity of himself with the next inheritor of his Karma, even though he regarded (according to our provisional assumption) the sense of self as entirely delusive.

But between these two concessions, which seem to have so much in common, there is a great gulf fixed,—the very gulf which separates Western from Eastern thought. Dr. Paul Carus, who is steeped in the science of the West, would never admit, even as a working hypothesis, that A, who is living now, was the same being as a certain B, who appeared on earth one hundred years ago (or whatever the number of intervening years might be). The idea of one man inheriting all the Karma of another man is one which he could not possibly entertain. The author of the Milinda dialogues might well have said, "I have lived on earth many times already, and shall probably live many times more, but of course there is no I in the case at all." But Dr. Paul Carus could not say this, though he might well say, "I have lived on earth for so many years, and may possibly live for so many more, but of course there is no I in the case at all."

There is nothing, then, to show that the Buddhist of the anti-Ego school is not as sure of his identity from life to life as Dr. Paul Carus is of his identity from year to year, or from day to day. In each case the sense of assurance sinks in theory to zero, but in practice it is strong enough for all the practical purposes of life. In other words, the denial is in each case academic (or "notional") whereas the belief is practical (or "real"). But the difference between the respective ranges of the "real" belief of a Buddhist and the "real" belief of Dr. Paul

Carus is immense, and has far-reaching consequences. Within the limits of his own earth life, Dr. Paul Carus combines academic denial with "real" belief; but the moment those limits are passed, the denial ceases to be academic and becomes intensely "real." The Buddhist, who is much more logical, sees no reason for drawing a hard and fast line at either birth or death. Backward and forward, as far as the eye of his thought can reach, his denial of the Ego, however sweeping and uncompromising it may be, is always "notional," whereas his belief in it is always "real." We shall presently learn that the monk Yamaka, who identified Nirvana with annihilation, was persuaded to abandon this "wicked heresy" by a fellow-monk, who reminded him that the arguments against the reality of the Nirvanic life of the "Saint" were not a whit stronger than the arguments against the reality of the true life of the "Saint" whilst on earth. The moral of this story is surely obvious and significant.

I have spoken at some length on this point because I wish to make it clear that, if denial of the Ego is real, if its meaning is fully pressed home, the doctrine of re-incarnation, which is undoubtedly the keystone of the whole arch of Buddhist thought, becomes pure nonsense. The essence of the doctrine is that B inherits the whole of A's Karma, C the whole of B's, and so on. Unless the identity of A with B, of B with C, and so on, is as real as the identity, within the limits of each earth life, of the child with the youth and the youth with the man, the doctrine loses its meaning, and the arch of thought which it holds together becomes a ruinous heap. We must therefore either assume that the arch of Buddhist thought and doctrine had no keystone, or that the Buddhist denial of the "Ego" was "notional" rather than "real." Of these alternative assumptions, reason and common sense alike demand that we should adopt the latter.

Whichever assumption we adopt, we are at liberty to say that the attempts which Dr. Rhys Davids, Dr. Paul Carus and other Western interpreters of Buddhism make to bring the doctrine of re-incarnation into line with the scientific doctrines of heredity, of physical causation, and the like, are sophistical and inconclusive. I have not made an exhaustive study of the eschatology of the modern "religion of science"; but I understand that it recognizes three kinds of immortality. The first is that of living in the lives of our direct descendants,—an immortality which one can enjoy, while still on earth, down to the second or third of the after generations (for a man may live to see his great-grandchildren), but which bachelors, old maids, and other persons who die without issue are not allowed to share. The second is the immortality of fame (or notoriety)—the immortality of a Marcus Aurelius (or a John Lackland)—an immortality which few persons are privileged to enjoy, and which, with very rare exceptions, is of brief duration.

The third is the immortality of living in the consequences of one's actions, so far as these affect for good or for evil the lives of other men. The immortality to which Buddha taught his disciples to look forward has nothing in common with any of these. The immortality of living in the ever-widening consequences of one's conduct is real enough, and the contemplation of it may give satisfaction to certain minds. But the immortality which the law of Karma makes possible is wholly different from this. The Karmic consequences of action are in the main inward and spiritual,—the effect on the doer of what he habitually does. Hence it is that the doctrine of re-incarnation, when divorced from the doctrine of a re-incarnating soul or Ego, loses its meaning and its value, and becomes as wildly fantastic as Western thought too readily assumes it to be. It stands to reason that, if there is no Ego, the inward consequences of a man's conduct will end abruptly at his death. What then? Are we to suppose that the outward consequences of his conduct, which have diffused themselves far and wide during his lifetime, will after his death—perhaps long after his death, for the return to earth may be long delayed—be reunited in the channel of a single human life?

The supposition is not merely incredible, but absolutely unthinkable. The alternative supposition that B, the inheritor of A's Karma, will be rewarded (or punished)—presumably by an omnipotent magician—for A's conduct while on earth is worse than unthinkable. It does violence to one's sense of law on every plane of thought. But when the doctrine of Karma is supported and elucidated by the conception of a re-incarnating soul or Ego, it at once becomes intelligible, even from the point of view of denial of the Ego. To say that conduct always reacts upon character, and that the departing soul will therefore take away with it from earth the inward consequences of its action and bring these back to earth, with all their possible ulterior consequences, at its next incarnation, is to say what is certainly disputable and perhaps untrue but at any rate has the merit of making coherent sense.

The inherent unreasonableness of the doctrine of Karma, as Western orientalists choose to interpret it, will become more apparent when we consider it in its relation to the motives which Buddha set before his followers. The paramount motive was the prospect of escaping from the "whirlpool of rebirth" and attaining to the bliss of Nirvana. That this goal should be won within the limits of a single earth-life, however virtuous, was not—we may rest assured—contemplated by Buddha, or by any of those thinkers who carried on the tradition of his teaching. This is a general statement which admits of isolated exceptions. A man of abnormal spiritual development, like Buddha himself—a man whom a long series of virtuous lives had brought to the threshold of Nirvana—might conceivably cross that threshold before he died, and return to earth no more.

But for the rank and file of mankind the goal of deliverance was a "far-off divine event" to which the journey was in any case long and toilsome, though it might be materially shortened if the Path which Buddha pointed out to mankind—the path of sympathy and self-control—was resolutely entered and faithfully followed. "The Buddhist," says Dr. Rhys Davids, "hopes to enter, even though he will not reach the end of, the Path in this life; and if he once enters therein, he is certain in some future existence, perhaps under less material conditions, to arrive at the goal of salvation, at the calm and rest of Nirvana." "He is certain." But is it he who will arrive at the goal, or someone else? Why does the life of sympathy and self-control tend to shorten the journey to Nirvana? Obviously, because it makes for the spiritual development of the man who leads it; because it strengthens his character, deepens his insight, expands his consciousness, purifies his soul. But what if there is to be no identity between A, who is now walking in the Path, and B, the next inheritor of his Karma? From the point of view of the goal which Buddha set before men, the inward consequences of A's conduct—the reaction of what he does on what he is—are of supreme importance.

But if there is no self, no Ego to return to earth, the inward consequences will, as I have lately pointed out, end abruptly at A's death, and there will be no character—developed, expanded, purified—for A to transmit to B, his new self. We must at any rate assume, if we are to see any meaning in Buddha's appeal to mankind, that the identity between A and B is as real as the identity between the A of this year and the A of next year, however real (or unreal) that identity may be. And this, I think, is what the accredited exponents of Buddhism, including those who may have denied the Ego in theory, have always taken for granted. There is nothing to show that, when Buddhism expounds and enforces the doctrine of natural retribution, it has any doubt as to B inheriting the inward consequences of A's conduct. But the inward consequences of A's conduct are summed up in his character; and if he transmits his character to B, he transmits himself.

It is here that Buddhism parts company with those Western interpreters of it who try, like Dr. Paul Carus, to affiliate it to the (so-called) "religion of science." Whatever theory Dr. Paul Carus may hold as to the identity (or non-identity) of the man of sixty or seventy years with the same man (as we must call him) at the age of twenty or thirty, he would admit, without hesitation, that it was both reasonable and just that the old man should suffer because the young man had sinned. Similarly, whatever theory the author of the Milinda Dialogues may have held as to the identity (or non-identity) of B with A, he would have admitted, without hesitation, that it was both reasonable and just that B should suffer because A had sinned. But Dr. Paul Carus could never bring himself to admit this: he could never in any way recognize individual re-incarnation.

Let us, however, suppose that Buddha and his followers were in full accord with Dr. Paul Carus. Let us suppose that their denial of the Ego, as an entity which survives death, was not academic, but practical and real. In that case what would become of the paramount motive which they set before their fellow-men? If it were possible for each man, in his own lifetime on earth, to attain to Nirvana, there would be a meaning, even for those who denied the Ego, in the promise of deliverance, though in that case the fulfilment of the Buddhist Law would involve the early extinction of the whole human race. But as, apart from a few isolated cases, the possibility of a man attaining to Nirvana in his own earth-life has never been contemplated by Buddhism, the promise of deliverance, when coupled with an authoritative denial of the Ego, must be regarded as the hollowest of mockeries.

What sense is there in telling me to live virtuously now in order that, if my successors in that line of earth-lives to which I happen to belong are equally virtuous, someone who would otherwise appear on earth 100,000 years hence (let us say) may not be born; and in order that someone else—his immediate predecessor in the given line of lives—may enjoy the evanescent bliss of Nirvana? To tell A to be virtuous in order that, somewhere in the remote future, Y may be supremely happy for a few years and Z may not be born, is to set him a meaningless task. It is difficult to say which sense is the more deeply outraged by such a doctrine of moral retribution,—one's sense of justice or (for the chain of cause and effect is obviously broken at each successive death) one's sense of natural law.

I will now set forth as briefly as possible my reasons for calling the current interpretation of Buddha's ideas a "misreading of Buddha."

The antecedent improbability of a great Teacher breaking away completely from the highest and deepest thought of his nation and his age, is very great. The great Teacher is always a reformer as well as an innovator; and to reform is to go back to an ideal which had been forgotten, or otherwise obscured. The chances are, then, that Buddha, who was unquestionably one of the greatest of all moral teachers, went back from what was corrupt and degenerate in the thought and the consequent practice of his age to what was pure and spiritual. This much we may say before we begin to study his scheme of life.

But when we study that scheme, and find, as we certainly do, that it is the practical application and embodiment of the great ideas of Indian idealism—so much so, indeed, that we may actually deduce from those ideas (given a practical aim on the part of their votary) the leading features of the Buddhist "Law"—we cannot but feel that the probability of the Founder of Buddhism having been an idealist (in the truest sense of the word) at heart—at the heart of his own deep silence—is raised to a very high degree.

And when, having for argument's sake assumed the opposite of this, assumed that the teaching of Buddha was directly and fundamentally subversive of the ideas which found utterance in the Upanishads, we find that the whole system falls to pieces and the wisdom of it becomes unthinkable nonsense, then what has hitherto been probability of a very high degree seems to approach the level of certainty. At any rate, if we may not yet say that the creed which Buddha held but did not openly profess, was the spiritual idealism of ancient India, we may say that the counter-hypothesis—that Buddha's creed was the direct negation of that lofty faith—can easily be disproved. The efforts that are made to bring the teaching of Buddha into line with the negative dogmatism of the "religion of science" would be ludicrous if they were not, in a sense, pathetic. For, in truth, they prove nothing except the depth of the abyss that separates Eastern from Western thought.

THE PESSIMISM OF BUDDHA

In each of the charges that it brings against the teaching of Buddha, the West delimits with precision the range of its own thought. When it attempts to prove that Buddha denied the Ego, what it succeeds in proving is that its own conception of the Ego is as narrow and commonplace as that of the materialists and semi-materialists of Buddha's day. For the only reason that it gives for ascribing to Buddha denial of the Ego is that he refused to identify it with any of the things—form, sensation, and the like—of which the "ignorant, unconverted man" says, "This is mine; this am I."

So, too, when the West accuses Buddha of atheism, it tells us, by implication, how crudely anthropomorphic is its own conception of God. Buddha, who refused to individualize the Ego, would have been false to his deepest convictions had he allowed himself, in any respect or degree, to individualize the Supreme Reality. But because he kept silence about God rather than use words which might seem (however figuratively) to individualize him, he is held to have "denied the Divine." This means that if the West may not worship the Jewish Jehovah or some kindred deity, it will reject as untenable the whole idea of God.

Let us now consider the charge of pessimism which is so often brought against Buddha. In formulating this charge, the West defines with precision the limits of its own conceptions, first of happiness and then of the Universe. The true pessimist—who is also the true atheist—is he who sees darkness, and darkness only, at the heart of the Universe. Was Buddha a pessimist in this sense of the word? That he regarded the earth life as full of sorrow is undeniable. Does this convict him of pessimism? Not unless the earth-life is the only life, and the visible world the "all of being."

The impermanence of everything earthly seems to have impressed itself deeply on Indian thought. In the West we live, and are content to live, from year to year, and even from day to day; and we regard as permanent things that will last unchanged for a few generations, or even for a few years. But the far-sighted Indian mind, looking backward and forward through vast stretches of time, saw that sooner or later everything outward, however secure of life it might seem to be, must change and fade and pass away. To the Brahmanic thinkers the impermanence of things was a proof of their unreality. But Buddha, who made his appeal, first and foremost, to the "general heart of man," saw that impermanence reveals itself to the many, not as unreality but as sorrow. He saw also that the connection between impermanence and sorrow is the outcome of the widespread tendency to mistake the impermanent for the real. Men cling to shadows and lean on reeds. The shadows fail them, and so cause disappointment and disillusionment. The reeds "pierce their bosoms," "and then they bleed." Seeing that this was so and must be so, Buddha did what he could to make men realize that this life, as they conceived it, was full of suffering. But he did this, not because he despaired of Nature, but because he had unbounded trust in her.

Far from teaching men that life was intrinsically evil, he taught them that the evil in it, the suffering which seemed to be of its essence, was in large measure the result of their own ignorance—their "ignorance of the true being and the true value of the Universe"—and that those who could detach themselves from whatever was impermanent and changeable might, even while on earth, enjoy a happiness higher and purer than any that the soul of man could consciously desire. So far was he from being a pessimist, in the deeper and darker sense of the word, that at the heart of Nature he could see nothing but light. If that light dazzled his eyes and blinded him to the lesser light that plays over the surface of life, his blindness was a proof, not of the despair of his soul, but of the very excess of its optimistic faith.

There are passages in the "Imitation of Christ" which might have been written by the Sages of the Upanishads. Such are "Amor ex Deo natus est; nec potest nisi in Deo requiescere." "Fili, ego debeo esse finis tuus supremus et ultimus, si vere desideras esse beatus." "Omnia vanitas præter amare Deum et isti soli servire." If Indian idealism is pessimistic, so is the outlook on earth and on life which finds expression in these inspired aphorisms. But surely it is not pessimism but abounding optimism which makes a man pitch his standard of happiness immeasurably high, and yet believe that the resources of the Universe are more than equal to any demand that the aspiring heart may make upon them.

He who could say to his followers: "What you deem happiness is unworthy of the name. There are better things than this in store for you. There are treasures of happiness in store for you,—pure, perfect, imperishable, real. These will be given to you freely if you will but win them for yourselves":—he who could say this (or the equivalent of this) had reached the highest conceivable level of optimism. To accuse him of pessimism is to make confession of one's own lack of imagination, of insight, and of faith. Those who believe that the surface life is the only life and that its pleasures are the beginning and end of happiness, and who assume that Buddha's faith coincided with their own, may well regard him, when they learn that he saw nothing but sorrow and suffering in the surface life and its pleasures, as the gloomiest and most uncompromising of pessimists. But the charge that they bring against him recoils upon themselves. If the surface life is the only life, and if its pleasures are the beginning and end of happiness, then indeed there is darkness—the darkness of death—at the heart of the Universe. But Buddha's conception of life, if he was true, as he believed himself to be, to "the spirit of the ancient faith," was the exact opposite of this; and what he saw at the heart of the Universe was, not the darkness of death, but the glory of Nirvana.

THE EGOISM OF BUDDHA

On this point the Western critics of Buddhism are divided. Some of them, including Dr. Rhys Davids, Dr. Paul Carus, and other enemies of the Ego, contend that Buddha's teaching was ultra-stoical, in that he bade men do right for right's sake only, the sole reward which the doer was allowed to look forward to being the enjoyment of inward peace during that twilight hour which should precede the final extinction of his life. Others, including the critics who seek to depreciate Buddhism in the supposed interest of Christianity, contend that Buddha was an egoistic hedonist, who taught each man in turn to think of himself and his own welfare only, and whose conception of happiness had so little in it of idealism or aspiration that it scarcely rose above the level of providing for humanity an early escape from sorrow and pain.

The answer to those who regard Buddha as ultra-stoical is that, as a matter of plain historical fact, what he set before men, when he bade them enter the Path, was the prospect, not of doing right for right's sake (he would probably have seen no meaning in those words) but of winning release from suffering—the suffering of those who struggle in the whirlpool of rebirth,—and of entering into bliss—the bliss of those who will return to earth no more.

In giving this answer I may seem to justify the critics who brand Buddha's scheme of life as egoistic. But no. Buddha's scheme of life was as far from being egoistic as from being ultra-stoical. It is the word self that misleads us. With the doubtful exception of the word Nature, there is no word in which there are so many pitfalls. When we ask whether a given scheme of life is egoistic or not, our answer will entirely depend on the range of the self for which the scheme in question makes provision. To get away from self is impossible; but it may be possible to widen self till it loses its individuality and becomes wholly selfless. Long before that ideal point has been reached, long before the individual has become one with the Universal Self, the word egoistic will have lost its accepted meaning.

That Buddha's teaching was entirely free from the cant of altruism may be admitted without hesitation. Accepting as a fact, which can neither be gainsaid nor ignored, that every man naturally and instinctively seeks his own happiness, and that therefore in the last resort the desire for happiness is the only motive to which the moralist can appeal, Buddha took upon himself to teach men to distinguish the semblance of happiness from the reality, to detach themselves from the former and to win their way to the latter. "Tous les hommes," says Pascal, "recherchent d'etre heureux: cela est sans exception. Quelques differents moyens qu'ils y emploient, ils tendent tous a ce but.

C'est le motif de toutes les actions de tous les hommes, jusqu'a ceux qui vont se pendre." It is impossible for me to prefer my neighbour's happiness to my own; for if I am asked why I take such pains to make him happy, I can but answer (in the last resort) that it makes me happy to do so.

Buddha's teaching is equally free from the cant of Stoicism. To bid men do right for right's sake "in the scorn of consequence," is as though a doctor should order his patients to eat the right sort of food for the sake of its rightness, and without regard to its effect on the health of the eater. What is it that constitutes rightness in food,—and in conduct? The right food (from a doctor's point of view) is presumably the food that ministers most effectively to the health of the patient; and it is in the interest of his health, and not of any abstract conception of rightness, that the patient is advised to eat it. It is the same, mutatis mutandis, with right conduct. The exhortation to do right for right's sake is saved from being meaningless only by the tacit assumption that right doing makes, on the whole and in the long run, for the happiness of the doer.

Indeed, it is because such and such courses of action make for the true happiness of him who follows them, and for no other reason, that we call them right. In other words, the epithet right, as applied to conduct, withholds its meaning from us until we define it in terms of happiness. That being so, it is surely better that the moralist should make his appeal (as Buddha openly did) to man's unquenchable desire for happiness than to a motive which would be utterly ineffective were it not that its air of sublime disinterestedness is, in the nature of things, a hollow sham.

But, while Buddha steered clear of the quick-sands of altruism and pseudo-stoicism, he took care not to wreck his scheme of life on the less dangerous, because more plainly visible, rock of egoism. It is when we begin to study the details of the scheme, that we see how little it deserves to be called egoistic. Based as it is on the conviction that the Ego—the real self—is not to be identified with "form," with "sensation," with "perception," or with anything else that is impermanent and changeable, it keeps one aim steadily in view,—to detach man, by a course of self-discipline which may last through many lives, from each of his apparent or lower selves, and to help him to find his true self.

As it is attachment to the apparent or lower self—that tendency to identify oneself with what is impermanent and changeable, which makes one say of this thing and of that, "This is mine: this am I: this is my Ego"—as it is this clinging, grasping, self-asserting frame of mind which is the root of all selfishness (to use a homelier word than egoism), it is clear that Buddha's scheme of life, far from, being egoistic or self-regarding, was in its essence a scheme for the extirpation of "self."

Buddha did not say to his disciples, what the altruist professes to say, "Thou shalt love thy neighbour better than thyself." He did not even say to them in so many words, "Thou shalt love thy neighbour as thyself." But he bade them enter a path which, if faithfully followed, would lead each man at last to love all men as himself. For if one is to escape from the impermanent, one must take refuge in the Eternal; and the Eternal and the Universal are the same fundamental reality looked at from different points of view. Every precept that Buddha gave has one positive aim in view,—to help the soul to expand its life or, in a word, to grow. But to the process of soul-growth there are no assignable limits. The soul has not attained to maturity, has not fulfilled its destiny, has not found its true self, until (according to the sublime conception which is at the heart of the "ancient faith") it has become one with the Universal Self, and in becoming one with it has become one with all men and all things. When that stage has been reached, when the Ego has become all-embracing, the last trace of "egoism" will have vanished, and the precept, "Thou shalt love thy neighbour as thyself" (the real meaning of which will not till then have been apprehended) will at last have been fulfilled. So, too, will the desire of the heart for happiness.

It is by the Christian, the professed follower of Christ, that the charge of egoism is most frequently brought against the teaching of Buddha. It is strange that such a charge should come from such a quarter. Will the Christian consent to brand as egoistic the teaching of his own Master? The conception of life which underlies Christ's searching question: "What is a man profited if he shall gain the whole world and lose his own soul?" is, according to the view that we are able to take of it, either ignobly selfish or sublimely self-forgetful. On this point opinions may differ. What is certain is that the gospel of Buddha is neither more nor less "egoistic" than the Gospel of Christ. For at the heart of each gospel is the same overmastering conviction that it is better for a man to find "his own soul"—his own true self—than to "gain the whole world."

In conclusion. The desire for unreal happiness—the Protean desire which Buddha sought to extinguish—leads us into all the highways and byways of selfishness, and into every haunt of error and delusion; and the phantom which is ever flitting before us ends by eluding our grasp. But the desire for real happiness—the desire which Buddha at once appealed to and strove to foster—is the desire (self-justifying and self-fulfilling) for oneness with the All; nor will that "egoistic" desire have found final fulfilment till it has provided an escape for the soul from the prison-house of "self" into the boundless ether of love.

THE NIHILISM OF BUDDHA

The supreme end of Buddhist endeavour, the last term in its ascending "series," is Nirvana. When the Path has been followed to its goal, when the victory over self has been fully won, when the prize of victory has been fully earned, the emancipated soul (if I may use that word "without prejudice") passes away from earth, passes beyond the vision of "Gods and men" and enters the bliss of Nirvana. What does this mean? The "Perfect One" has disappeared from the eye of thought behind the veil of human experience. What is there behind that veil? What is there behind the last of the many veils which life (as we who are living on earth understand the word) hangs before our eyes? The question as to the destiny of the Perfect One and the question as to the real life of those who are now on earth are (as Sariputta saw clearly) one and the same. What is the answer to them? The answer which the learned criticism of the West ordinarily gives, and which the popular criticism of the West faithfully echoes, is, in a word, Nothing. "Tout se reunit," says Barthelemy Saint-Hilaire, "pour demontrer que le Nirvana n'est au fond que l'aneantissement definitif et absolu de tous les elements qui composent l'existence." According to Eugene Burnouf, "Le Nirvana est l'aneantissement complet, non seulement des elements materials de l'existence, mais de plus et surtout du principe pensant." These statements are typical, and I need not add to them.

The word Nirvana means "going out" or "extinction." But, as Dr. Rhys Davids explains with force and clearness, what is extinguished, when Nirvana is won, is not existence but passion and desire. In support of this thesis Dr. Rhys Davids appeals to some verses in one of the Sacred Books of Buddhism, in which "we have an argument based on the logical assumption that if a positive exists its negative must also exist; if there is heat, there must be cold; and so on. In one of these pairs we find existence opposed, not to Nirvana, but to non-existence; whilst in another the three fires [of lust, hatred and delusion] are opposed to Nirvana."

But, though Dr. Rhys Davids is careful to distinguish Nirvana from annihilation, he is bound by his own assumption, that Buddha denied the Ego, denied "that there is anything of any kind which continues to exist, in any manner, after death," to regard Nirvana as the prelude to annihilation. For him, then, and for those who think with him, Nirvana, on which the Buddhist writings have ever "lavished" "awe-struck and ecstatic praise," is the twilight hour that precedes the night of Nothingness,—an hour in which the "Perfect One," having at last extinguished the fires of lust, hatred and delusion, enjoys the bliss of perfect peace. "Death, utter death, with no new life to follow, is a result of but it is not Nirvana."

It matters little whether Nirvana is itself the night of Nothingness, or the twilight hour which precedes that night. The goal of the Path is, in either case, the premature annihilation of him who walks in it. When the Perfect One has lifted the last veil of illusion and passed behind it into the reality which it hides from thought, he becomes absorbed into Nothing. It follows that the self-existent Reality which underlies all appearances and which is therefore at the very heart of the Universe is, in a word, Nothing.

Did Buddha really believe this? Was it in the strength of this supreme negation that he devoted his life to the enlightenment and emancipation of his fellow-men, and won to his will the hearts of all who listened to his teaching? The hypothesis which we are invited to accept as an established conclusion, is so wildly improbable, that we have a right to ask those who formulate it to bring forward strong documentary evidence in support of it. As it happens, no such evidence is forthcoming. On the one hand, the passages in the Buddhist Scriptures on which the hypothesis has been based all admit of an entirely different interpretation,—namely, that after the death of the body the Perfect One ceases to exist, not absolutely, but only in the sense which "the ignorant, unconverted man" attaches to the word existence.

On the other hand, there are passages in the Buddhist Scriptures in which the hypothesis is directly or indirectly traversed; such as the dialogue between Yamaka and Sariputta, in which the belief that "on the dissolution of the body the monk who has lost all depravity is annihilated" is first condemned as a wicked heresy and then conclusively refuted; or, again, as the dialogue between King Pasenadi and the nun Khema, in which the question as to the existence of the Perfect One after death is shown to be unanswerable, not because the Perfect One will then have ceased to be, but because he will have passed beyond the reach of human thought.

It is worthy of note (though the point seems to have escaped the notice of the Western students of Buddhism) that the question "What becomes of the ordinary, unemancipated man when he dies?" is never asked in any Buddhist dialogue. Why is this? Evidently because the doctrine of re-incarnation is the accepted answer to the question. What interests King Pasenadi, the monk Yamaka, and others is not the general question

"What comes after death?" but the particular question, "What becomes of the Perfect One when he finally passes away from earth?" The answer to this question is always the same. "Do not ask. The question is unanswerable. The Perfect One passes, when he dies, beyond the remotest horizon of human thought; and when thought fails, words can do nothing but perplex and mislead."

The truth is that here, as elsewhere, when the West seems to be passing judgment on Buddhism, it is really delimiting the range of its own thought. To the consideration of the problem of the Perfect One's final state, as of all kindred problems, Western thought carries with it the metaphysical assumption which has obsessed it for two thousand years,—the assumption that nothing exists, in the order of Nature, except what is perceptible by man's bodily senses. The religious thought of the West has always taken refuge from the consequences of this assumption in the dream-world of the Supernatural. But the dualism of Nature and the Supernatural was (and is) entirely foreign to Indian thought. Seeing, then, that Buddha transported the Perfect One beyond the vision of Gods and men, and yet provided no asylum for him in any Supernatural heaven, the Western exponents of Buddhism find themselves driven to conclude, with the monk Yamaka, that "on the dissolution of his body" the Perfect One "is annihilated, perishes, and does not exist after death."

But it is Western, not Indian, thought which creates the vacuum that receives the Perfect One's emancipated soul. When Dr. Rhys Davids, after quoting Buddha's words, "While his body shall remain he will be seen by Gods and men, but after the termination of life, upon the dissolution of the body, neither Gods nor men will see him," asks: "Would it be possible in a more complete or categorical manner to deny that there is any soul—anything of any kind which continues to exist, in any manner, after death?" there is an obvious answer to his triumphant challenge.

It is by assuming that Buddha, too, believed in the intrinsic reality of what is perceptible and the non-existence of what is imperceptible, that he proves his point. But has he any right to make that assumption? Is not Buddha's attitude towards the problem of reality the very question which is really (though not ostensibly) in dispute? And inasmuch as Buddha devoted his life to teaching men that the perceptible is the unreal, is it not rash, to say the least, to assume offhand that his mind was ruled by the fundamental postulate of Western thought? Yet, unless his mind was ruled by that postulate, the words on which Dr. Rhys Davids lays so much stress can be shown to have another meaning than that which he ascribes to them, and the conclusion—that Buddha regarded death as the end of life—instead of being obviously true, becomes demonstrably false.

What Buddha meant (if we may argue from the general tenor of his teaching) when he said that, upon the dissolution of the Perfect One's body, neither Gods nor men would see him, was not that the Perfect One would then pass into non-existence, but rather that then at last he would attain to absolute reality. For the perceptible world, as Buddha conceived of it, is the world of dreams and shadows; and it is therefore clear that, until the Perfect One has passed, wholly and irrevocably, beyond the horizon of perception, he has not found rest in the Real.

Let us now attempt, in defiance of Buddha's express prohibition, to penetrate the mystery of Nirvana. The mystery is, in a sense, final. The Path ends—for good and all—in Nirvana. The Western hypothesis that Nirvana is not the final state of the Perfect One, but the prelude to that state, is wholly gratuitous.

Not a word is said in any of the passages with which the students of Buddhism have made us familiar, which might seem to suggest that the Nirvanic state ends with the death of the Perfect One's body, or that there is any state of existence (or non-existence) beyond it. That Buddha, who turned the prying mind back on the hither brink of Nirvana, should have looked beyond Nirvana and told men what was awaiting them on its farther shore, is in the highest degree improbable. The progress of the Perfect One is followed till Nirvana begins:

"But there sight fails. No heart may know
The bliss when life is done."

The question, then, which we have to ask ourselves is this: What goal would he be likely to reach who followed the Path to the end? This question suggests a second: What is the Path supposed to do for him who walks in it?

The answer to this question is embodied in Buddha's scheme of life. The Path detaches him who walks in it from the impermanent, the changeable, the phenomenal.

But it does this, not by the ascetic curtailment of the range of his life, but by the progressive expansion of his consciousness. It will be remembered that Buddha told his disciples in the earliest of his discourses that they were to steer a middle course between the "unworthy and unreal" paths of pleasure on the one side, and mortification on the other. It will also be remembered that the precepts which he gave them aimed, to make a general statement, at the cultivation of two faculties,—self-control and sympathy.

The function of self-control is, on the one hand, to train the will for the task that awaits it,—the task of directing the process of soul-growth; and, on the other hand, to prevent the lower and narrower self from becoming so aggressive as to arrest the outgrowth of the higher and larger self. And the function of sympathy, which carries a man out of himself into the lives of others, is to promote the outgrowth of the higher and larger self, by raising the level and widening the range of one's life.

hus the Path detaches men from the phenomenal, not by cutting it out of their lives or otherwise blinding them to its existence, but by giving them the power (through the expansion of their consciousness) of seeing it in its true proportions and its true light.

It is possible for one who walks in the Path to take an interest and a pleasure in the ephemeral concerns of life, and yet to hold on to them by the very lightest of threads. There is nothing of Puritanical gloom or sourness in the teaching of

Buddha. The foreglow of Nirvana falls on the Path and throws its rays on either side of it, till those who walk in it learn at last to take an innocent delight even in the things which they know to be phantasmal.

Now the goal of the Path is the natural consummation of it,—not a reward which will be given by an omnipotent onlooker to those who have kept to the Path and obeyed its commandments, but the end to which the Path naturally and inevitably leads; an end which is not merely pre-figured by the Path, even in its earlier stages, but is also, in some sort, present in promise and potency in those earlier (and all subsequent) stages, just as the full-grown oak is present in promise and potency in the acorn and the sapling, or the ripened peach in the fruit-bud and the blossom.

And inasmuch as the function of the Path is to detach men from the phenomenal by expanding their consciousness, and to expand their consciousness by fostering the growth of their souls, it seems to follow that the goal of the Path will be the ideal perfection of him who walks in it, and that when this ideal state has been reached the consciousness of the Perfect One (as we may now call him) will have become all-embracing, and his detachment from the phenomenal complete.

We are now in a position to give this tentative and provisional answer to the question, What is Nirvana? Nirvana is a state of ideal spiritual perfection, in which the soul, having completely detached itself—by the force of its own natural expansion—from what is individual, impermanent, and phenomenal, embraces and becomes one with the Universal, the Eternal, and the Real. In other words, the essence of Nirvana is the finding of the ideal self, in and through the attainment to oneness—living, conscious oneness—with the All and the Divine.

It is true that Buddha spoke of consciousness as one of the five things from which the "learned and noble disciple" must strive to detach himself; but he obviously meant by consciousness what his audience, composed for the most part of ordinary unenlightened men, would have understood the word to mean,—

that sense of selfhood which is based on the sense of difference from other things, In the Nirvanic consciousness the sense of selfhood is based on the sense of oneness with other things, or rather of oneness with the vital essence of all things,—with the living Whole. 'When we predicate consciousness of him who has passed into Nirvana, what we mean is that the Nirvanic state of being is on the farther, not on the hither, side of consciousness; that it enormously transcends what we, with our limited range of perception and thought, understand by consciousness, but that it is reached by the continuance of the same process of growth by which consciousness itself has been evolved.

The Western mind, which is dominated, even in its seasons of speculative activity, by mathematical and mechanical conceptions, understands by oneness with the Divine a quasi-material absorption into the Whole, which involves the complete extinction of consciousness in him who "Slips into the shining sea."

The Indian conception of oneness with the Divine is the polar opposite of this. If soul is to mingle with soul it must do so as soul, preserving, yet raising to an infinite power, all the characteristics of soul life,—its freedom and self-compulsion (which it now realizes as infinite energy), its thought (which it now realizes as infinite wisdom), its desire (which it now realizes as infinite love).

Such, in shadowy outline, is the conception of Nirvana which my study of Buddha's teaching, from the standpoint of Indian idealism, has forced upon my mind.

That I carried the conception with me is undeniable, and that I should eventually work round to it was no doubt pre-ordained.

But the curve of thought which I have completed has helped me to enrich and deepen the conception, for it has enabled me to trace the steps by which the genius and practical wisdom of one gifted Teacher could transform a philosophical idea into a master principle of action, and so make it available for the daily needs of mankind.

To the Sages of the Upanishads re-union with the Divine was the goal of meditative aspiration,—a goal which few could hope to reach, for the path to it was one which few could find and fewer still could follow. Buddha saw that it was also the goal of spiritual growth, and that as such it could be reached—in the fullness of time—by the lowliest and most ignorant of men. But he saw also that, as the goal of spiritual growth (and therefore of spiritual endeavour), it must be pursued unconsciously; that the path to it must be clearly defined, but that of the goal itself nothing was to be predicated except that it was the home of happiness and peace.

Dr. Oldenberg complains that Buddha's teaching is a "fragment of a circle to complete which and to find the centre of which is forbidden by the Thinker." But if we place at the centre of the circle the sovereign dogma of Indian idealism, if we assume that Nirvana, the admitted end of Buddhist desire and endeavour, is a state of self-realization through union with the Divine or Universal Soul, the circle will complete itself: for we shall see a meaning in every precept that Buddha gave, and in every argument that he used; we shall see a meaning in every discourse and dialogue which Western thought has (on this hypothesis) misunderstood; we shall see a meaning in the Western misunderstanding of Buddha's teaching; we shall see a meaning in Buddha's mysterious silence; and we shall see that his scheme of life was a "perfect round,"—a coherent and consistent whole. Nor are we making a random guess when we fix that particular centre for Buddha's circle of thought. "Of all plane figures the circle alone has the same curvature at every point." If Buddha's ethical teaching was indeed a fragment of a circle, then it is possible for those who care to do so, both to complete the circle and to find its centre. But we must be allowed to assume, before we undertake this task, that the fragment which is before us is part of a circle and not of any less perfect curve.

The conception which Western critics, in their desire to claim Buddha as of their own school of thought, place at the centre of his philosophy, has the grave demerit of turning what is supposed to be the fragment of a circle into a fragment, or series of fragments, of one of the wildest and most lawless of curves.

But if we assume that Buddha's scheme of life, as it existed in his mind, was a "perfect round," and that what he chose to formulate was a fragment of that "perfect round," we shall find that there is only one possible centre to it,—the conception which history, psychology, and common-sense unite in suggesting to us as central,—the conception that the Universal Self is the true self of each one of us, and that to realize the true self is the destiny and the duty of man.

7

Siddhartha Disciples and Knowledge

SIDDHARTHA DESERTED BY HIS FIRST DISCIPLES

The clear waters of the Nairanjana flowed through a rich and fertile land. Little villages drowsed in the shade of magnificent trees, and great meadows stretched away into the distance. The hero thought, "How pleasant it is here; what an inviting spot in which to meditate! Perhaps, here, I shall find the path to wisdom. Here I shall dwell."

He became deeply absorbed in contemplation. He was so engrossed with his thoughts that he stopped breathing, and, one day, he fell into a swoon. The Gods, who were watching him from the sky, thought he was dead, and they cried:

"Is he dead, this child of the Sakyas? Has he died and left the world to its suffering?"

Maya, the hero's mother, lived among the Gods. She heard their cries and plaints, and she feared for the life of her son. Attended by a host of Apsarases, she descended to the banks of the Nairanjana, and when she saw Siddhartha, so stiff, so inert, she wept.

She said:

"When you were born in the garden, I was assured, O my son, that you would behold the truth. And later, Asita predicted that

you would set the world free. But they were all lies, these predictions. You did not win fame by any royal conquest, you did not attain supreme knowledge! You died, pitifully and alone. Who will help you, O my son? Who will bring you back to life? For ten moons I carried you in my womb, O my jewel, and now I can only grieve."

She scattered flowers over the body of her son, whereupon he stirred and spoke to her in a gentle voice:

"Have no fear, mother; your labour was not in vain; Asita told you no lie. Even if the earth crumble into dust, even if Meru sink below the waters, even if the stars fall like rain upon the earth, I shall not die. I, alone, of all men, will survive the world's ruin! Do not weep, mother! The time is approaching when I shall attain supreme knowledge."

Maya smiled at her son's words; three times she bowed, then ascended to the sky, to the music of celestial lutes.

For six years, the hero remained on the banks of the river and meditated. He never sought shelter from the wind, from the sun or from the rain; he allowed the gadflies, the mosquitoes and the serpents to sting him. He was oblivious to the boys and girls, the shepherds and woodcutters, who jeered at him as they passed by and who sometimes threw dust or mud at him. He hardly ate: a fruit and a few grains of rice or of sesame composed his fare. He became very thin; his bones showed prominently. But under his gaunt forehead, his dilated eyes shone like stars.

And yet true knowledge did not come to him. He felt he was becoming very weak, and he realized that if he wasted away, he would never reach the goal he had set for himself. So he decided to take more nourishment.

There was a village called Uruvilva near the spot where Siddhartha spent long hours in meditation. The head man of this village had ten daughters. They revered the hero, and they brought him grain and fruit by way of alms. He rarely touched these gifts, but, one day, the girls noticed that he had eaten all they had offered him. The next day, they came with a large dish full of boiled rice, and he emptied that. The following day, each one brought a different delicacy, and the hero ate them all. He began to gain flesh, and, presently, he started going to the village to beg his food. The inhabitants vied with one another in giving him alms, and, before long, he had regained his strength and his beauty.

But the five disciples who had joined him said to each other:

"His austerities did not lead him into the path of true knowledge, and now he has ceased to practice them. He takes abundant nourishment; he seeks comfort. He no longer thinks of doing holy deeds. How can he, now, attain true knowledge? We considered him a wise man, but we were mistaken: he is a madman and a fool."

And they left him and went to Benares.

MARA'S DEFEAT

The light emanating from the hero's body reached even to those realms where Mara, the Evil One, reigned supreme. It dazzled Mara, and he seemed to hear a voice saying:

"The hero who has renounced royalty, the son of Suddhodana, is now seated under the tree of knowledge. He is concentrating his mind, he is making the supreme effort, and soon he will bring to all creatures the help which they need. The road he will have taken, others will take. Once set free, he will set others free. Once he has found peace, he will bring peace to others. He will enter nirvana, and he will cause others to enter. He will find wisdom and happiness, and he will give them to others. Because of him, the city of the Gods will be crowded; because of him, the city of the Evil One will be deserted. And you, Mara, a commander without an army, a king without subjects, will not know where to take refuge."

Mara was filled with apprehension. He tried to sleep, but his slumber was disturbed by terrible dreams. He awoke and summoned his servants and his soldiers. When they saw him, they became alarmed, and Sarthavaha, one of his sons, said to him:

> *"Father, you look pale and unhappy; your heart beats fast and your limbs tremble. What have you heard? What have you seen? Speak."*

"Son," replied Mara, "the days of my pride are over. I heard a voice crying in the light, and it told me that the son of the Sakyas was seated under the tree of knowledge. And I had horrible dreams. A black cloud of dust settled over my palace. My gardens were bare of leaves, of flowers and of fruit. My ponds had dried up, and my swans and peacocks had their wings clipped. And I felt alone, amid this desolation. You had all deserted me. My queen was beating her breast and tearing her hair, as though haunted by remorse. My daughters were crying out in their anguish, and you, my son, were bowing before this man who meditated under the tree of knowledge! I wanted to fight my enemy, but I could not draw my sword from the scabbard. All my subjects fled in horror. Impenetrable darkness closed in upon me, and I heard my palace crashing to the ground."

Sarthavaha said:

> *"Father, it is disheartening to lose a battle. If you have seen these omens, bide your time, and do not run the chance of being ingloriously defeated."*

But Mara, at the sight of the legions that surrounded him, felt his courage return. He said to his son:

> *"To the man of energy, a battle can end only in victory. We are brave; we will surely win. What strength can this man have? He is alone. I shall advance against him with a vast army, and I shall strike him down at the foot of the tree."*
>
> *"Mere numbers do not make the strength of an army," said Sarthavaha, "The sun can outshine a myriad of glowworms. If wisdom is the source of his power, a single hero can defeat countless soldiers."*

But Mara paid no heed. He ordered the army to advance at once, and Sarthavaha thought:

> *"He who is insane with pride will never recover."*

Mara's army was a fearful sight. It bristled with pikes, with arrows and with swords; many carried enormous battle-axes and heavy clubs. The soldiers were black, blue, yellow, red, and their faces were terrifying. Their eyes were cruel flames; their mouths spewed blood. Some had the ears of a goat, others the ears of a pig or of an elephant. Many had bodies shaped like a jug. One had the paws of a tiger, the hump of a camel and the head of a donkey; another had a lion's mane, a rhinoceros' horn and a monkey's tail. There were many with two, four and five heads, and others with ten, twelve and twenty arms. In place of ornaments, they wore jawbones, skulls and withered human fingers. And shaking their hairy heads, they advanced with hideous laughter and savage cries:

"I can shoot a hundred arrows at one time; I shall seize the body of the monk." "My hand can crumple up the sun, the moon and the stars; how easy it will be to crush this man and his tree." "My eyes are full of poison: they would dry up the sea; I shall look at him, and he will burn to a cinder."

Sarthavaha kept to himself. A few friends had gathered around him, and they were saying:

"Fools! You think he is mad because he meditates; you think he is craven because he is calm. It is you who are madmen, it is you who are cowards. You do not know his power; because of his great wisdom he will defeat you all. Were your numbers as infinite as the grains of sand on the banks of the Ganges, you would not disturb a single hair of his head. And you believe you can kill him! Oh, turn back! Do not try to harm him; bow before him in reverence. His reign has come. The jackals howl in the forests when the lion is away, but when the lion roars, the jackals scamper off in terror. Fools, fools! You shout with pride while the master is silent, but when the lion speaks you will take to your heels,"

The army listened with contempt to these words of wisdom spoken by Sarthavaha and his friends. It kept advancing.

Before attacking the hero, Mara sought to frighten him. He roused against him the fury of the winds. Fierce gales rushed toward him from the horizon, uprooting trees, devastating villages, shaking mountains, but the hero never moved; not a single fold of his robe was disturbed.

The Evil One summoned the rains. They fell with great violence, submerging cities and scarring the surface of the earth, but the hero never moved; not a single thread of his robe was wet.

The Evil One made blazing rocks and hurled them at the hero. They sped through the air but changed when they came near the tree, and fell, not as rocks, but flowers.

Mara then commanded his army to loose their arrows at his enemy, but the arrows, also, turned into flowers. The army rushed at the hero, but the light he diffused acted as a shield to protect him; swords were shivered, battle-axes were dented by it, and whenever a weapon fell to the ground, it, too, at once changed into a flower.

And, suddenly, filled with terror at the sight of these prodigies, the soldiers of the Evil One fled.

And Mara wrung his hands in anguish, and he cried:

"What have I done that this man should defeat me? For they are not a few, those whose desires I have granted! I have often been kind and generous! Those cowards who are fleeing could bear witness to that."

The troops that were still within hearing answered:

"Yes, you have been kind and generous. We will bear witness to that."

"And he, what proof has he given of his generosity?" continued Mara. "What sacrifices has he made? Who will bear witness to his kindness?"

Whereupon a voice came out of the earth, and it said:

"I will bear witness to his generosity."

Mara was struck dumb with astonishment. The voice continued:

"Yes, I, the Earth, I, the mother of all beings, will bear witness to his generosity. A hundred times, a thousand times, in the

course of his previous existences, his hands, his eyes, his head, his whole body have been at the service of others. And in the course of this existence, which will be the last, he will destroy old age, sickness and death. As he excels you in strength, Mara, even so does he surpass you in generosity."

And the Evil One saw a woman of great beauty emerge from the earth, up to her waist. She bowed before the hero, and clasping her hands, she said: "O most holy of men, I bear witness to your generosity."

Then she disappeared.

And Mara, the Evil One, wept because he had been defeated.

SIDDHARTHA UNDER THE TREE OF KNOWLEDGE

The hero's clothes had become threadbare in the six years he had been wearing them, and he thought: "It would be well if I had some new clothes; otherwise I shall have to go naked, and that would be immodest."

Now, Sujata, the most devout of the ten young girls who had been bringing him food, had a slave who had just died. She had wrapped the body in a shroud made of a reddish material and had it carried to the cemetery. The dead slave was lying in the dust. The hero saw the body as he passed; he went over to it and removed the shroud.

It was very dusty, and the hero had no water in which to wash it. Sakra, from the sky, saw his perplexity. Coming down to earth he struck the ground, and a pool appeared before the eyes of the Saint.

"Good," said he, "here is water, but I still need a wash-stone."

Sakra made a stone and set it down on the edge of the pool.

"Man of virtue," said the God, "give me the shroud; I shall wash it for you."

"No, no," replied the Saint. "I know the duties of a monk; I myself shall wash the shroud."

When it was clean, he bathed. Now, Mara, the Evil One, had been watching for him for some time. He suddenly raised the banks of the pool, making them very steep. The Saint was unable to climb out of the water. Fortunately, there was a tall tree growing near the pool, and the Saint addressed a prayer to the Goddess who lived in it.

"O Goddess, may a branch of this tree bend over me!"

A branch immediately bent over the pool. The Saint caught hold of it and pulled himself out of the water. Then he went and sat down under the tree, and he began to sew on the shroud and make a new garment for himself.

Night came on. He fell asleep, and he had five dreams.

First, he saw himself lying in a large bed that was the whole earth; under his head, there was a cushion which was the Himalaya; his right hand rested on the western sea, his left hand on the eastern sea, and his feet touched the southern sea.

Then he saw a reed coming out of his navel, and the reed grew so fast that it soon reached the sky.

Then he saw worms crawling up his legs and completely covering them.

Then he saw birds flying toward him from all points of the horizon, and when the birds were near his head, they seemed to be of gold.

Finally, he saw himself at the foot of a mountain of filth and excrement; he climbed the mountain; he reached the summit; he descended, and neither the filth nor the excrement had defiled him.

He awoke, and from these dreams he knew that the day had come when, having attained supreme knowledge, he would become a Buddha.

He rose and set out for the village of Uruvilva, to beg.

Sujata had just finished milking eight wonderful cows that she owned. The milk they gave was rich, oily and of a delicate savour. She added honey and rice flour to it, then set the mixture to boil in a new pot, on a new stove. Huge bubbles began to form and kept floating off to the right, without the liquid rising or spilling a single drop. The stove did not even smoke. Sujata was astonished, and she said to Purna, her servant:

"Puma, the Gods are favouring us today. Go and see if the holy man is approaching the house."

Purna, from the doorstep, saw the hero walking toward Sujata's house. He was diffusing a brilliant light, a golden light. Puma was dazzled. She ran back to her mistress.

"Mistress, he is coming! He is coming! And your eyes will be blinded by his splendour!"

"Let him come! Oh, let him come!" cried Sujata. "It is for him that I have prepared this wonderful milk."

She poured the milk mixed with honey and flour into a golden bowl, and she awaited the hero.

He entered. The house was lighted up by his presence. Sujata, to do him honour, bowed seven times. He sat down. Sujata kneeled and bathed his feet in sweet-scented water; then she offered him the golden bowl full of milk mixed with rice flour and honey. He thought:

"The Buddhas of old, it is said, had their last meal served to them in a golden bowl, before attaining supreme knowledge. Since Sujata offers me this milk and honey in a golden bowl, the time has come for me to be a Buddha."

Then he asked the young girl:

"Sister, what must I do with this golden bowl?"

"It belongs to you," she replied.

"I have no use for such a bowl," said he.

"Then do as you please with it," said Sujata. "It would be contemptible of me to offer the food and not offer the bowl."

He left, carrying the bowl in his hands, and he walked to the banks of the river. He bathed; he ate. When the bowl was empty, he threw it into the water, and he said:

"If I am to become Buddha this very day, may the bowl go upstream; if not, may it go with the current."

The bowl floated out to the middle of the river, then rapidly started upstream. It disappeared in a whirlpool, and the hero heard the muffled ring as it landed, in the subterranean world, among those other bowls the former Buddhas had emptied and thrown away.

The hero sauntered along the banks of the river. Night slowly descended. The flowers wearily closed their petals; a sweet fragrance rose from the fields and gardens; the birds timidly rehearsed their evensongs.

It was then the hero walked toward the tree of knowledge.

The road was sprinkled with gold-dust; rare palms, covered with precious stones, lined the way. He skirted the edge of a pool whose blessed waters exhaled an intoxicating perfume. White, yellow, blue and red lotuses spread their massive petals over the surface, and the air rang with the clear songs of the swans. Near the pool, under the palms, Apsarases were dancing, while in the sky the Gods were admiring the hero.

He approached the tree. On the side of the road, he saw Svastika, the reaper.

"They are tender, these grasses you are mowing, Svastika. Give me some grass; I want to cover the seat I shall occupy when I attain supreme knowledge. They are green, these grasses you are mowing, Svastika. Give me some grass, and you will know the law some day, for I shall teach it to you, and you may teach it to others."

The reaper gave the Saint eight handfuls of grass.

There stood the tree of knowledge. The hero went to the east of it and bowed seven times. He threw the handfuls of grass on the ground, and, suddenly, a great seat appeared. The soft grass covered it like a carpet.

The hero sat down, his head and shoulders erect, his face turned to the east. Then he said in a solemn voice:

"Even if my skin should parch, even if my hand should wither, even if my bones should crumble into dust, until I have attained supreme knowledge I shall not move from this seat."

And he crossed his legs.

SIDDHARTHA BECOMES THE BUDDHA

By sunset the army of the Evil One had fled. Nothing had disturbed the hero's meditation, and, in the first watch of the night, he arrived at the knowledge of all that had transpired in previous existences. In the second watch, he learned the present state of all beings. In the third, he understood the chain of causes and effects. He now clearly saw all creatures being continually reborn, and, whether of high or of low caste, in the path of virtue or of evil, he saw them going through the round of existences, at the mercy of their actions. And the hero thought:

"How miserable is this world that is born, grows old and dies, then is reborn only to grow old and die again! And man knows no way out!"

And in profound meditation, he said to himself:

"What is the cause of old age and death? There is old age and death because there is birth. Old age and death are due to birth. What is the cause of birth? There is birth because there is existence. Birth is due to existence. What is the cause of existence? There is existence because there are ties. Existence is due to ties. What is the cause of ties? There are ties because there is desire. Ties are due to desire. What is the cause of desire? There is desire because there is sensation. Desire is due to sensation. What is the cause of sensation? There is sensation because there is contact. Sensation is due to contact. What is the cause of contact? There is contact because there are six senses. Contact is due to the six senses. What is the cause of the six senses? There are six senses because there is name and form. The six senses are due to name and form. What is the cause of name and form? There is name and form because there is perception. Name and form are due to perception. What is the cause of perception? There is perception because there is impression. Perception is due to impression. What is the cause of impression? There is impression because there is ignorance. Impression is due to ignorance."

And he thought:

"Thus does ignorance lie at the root of death, of old age, of suffering, of despair. To suppress ignorance is to suppress

impression. To suppress impression is to suppress perception. To suppress perception is to suppress name and form. To suppress name and form is to suppress the six senses. To suppress the six senses is to suppress contact. To suppress contact is to suppress sensation. To suppress sensation is to suppress desire. To suppress desire is to suppress ties. To suppress ties is to suppress existence. To suppress existence is to suppress birth. To suppress birth is to suppress old age and death. To exist is to suffer. Desire leads from birth to rebirth, from suffering to further suffering. By stifling desire, we prevent birth, we prevent suffering. By leading a life of holiness, desire is stifled, and we cease to endure birth and suffering."

When dawn appeared, this most noble of men was a Buddha. He exclaimed:

"I have had numerous births. In vain have I sought the builder of the house. Oh, the torment of perpetual rebirth! But I have seen you at last, O builder of the house. You no longer build the house. The rafters are broken; the old walls are down. The ancient mountain crumbles; the mind attains to nirvana; birth is no more for desire is no more."

Twelve times the earth shook; the world was like a great flower. The Gods sang:

"He has come, he who brings light into the world; he has come, he who protects the world! Long blinded, the eye of the world has opened, and the eye of the world is dazzled by the light.

O conqueror, you will give all beings that which they hunger after. Guided by the sublime light of the law, all creatures will reach the shores of deliverance. You hold the lamp; go now and dispel the darkness!"

THE BUDDHA FINDS HIS FORMER DISCIPLES

The Blessed One entered the great city of Benares. He wandered through the streets, asking for alms; he ate the food that was given him, then he went to the Deer Park where he knew he would find Rudraka's former disciples.

The five disciples saw him in the distance. They thought they recognized him, and they said to each other:

"Do we not know this man, walking toward us? Is he not the one whose austerities, formerly, used to astonish us, and who, one day, revolted against the severe self-discipline he had been observing? If his mortifications did not show him the way to supreme knowledge then, how can his thoughts profit us today when he is swayed by greed and cowardice? Let us not go and meet him, or rise when he approaches; let us not relieve him of his cloak or of his alms-bowl; let us not even offer him a seat. We will say to him, 'All the seats here are taken.' And we will give him nothing to eat or drink."

Thus did they decide. But the Blessed One kept drawing nearer, and the closer he came the more uncomfortable they felt. They were seized with a great desire to rise from their seats. They were like birds frantically trying to escape from a cage under which a fire has been kindled. They were restless; they seemed to be ill. Finally, they broke their resolution. They rose as one man; they ran to the Blessed One, and they greeted him. One took his alms-bowl, another his cloak; a third offered him a seat. They brought him water to bathe his feet, and with one voice they cried:

"Welcome, friend, welcome. Take a seat in our midst."

The Blessed One sat down and bathed his feet. Then he said to the five hermits:

"Do not address me as friend, O monks. I am the Saint, the Perfect One, the supreme Buddha. Open your ears, O monks; the path is discovered that leads to deliverance. I will show you the path; I will teach you the law. Listen well, and you will learn the sacred truth."

But they answered:

"Formerly, in spite of your austere practises, you did not arrive at perfect knowledge, so how could you have attained it, now that you lead a life of self-indulgence?"

"O monks," replied the Blessed One, "I do not lead a life of self-indulgence; I have renounced none of the blessings to which I aspired. I am the Saint, the Perfect One, the supreme Buddha. Open your ears, O monks; the path is discovered that leads to deliverance. I will show you the path; I will teach you the law. Listen well, and you will learn the sacred truth."

He added, "O monks, will you admit that I have never before addressed you in this manner?" "We admit it, Master."

"I say unto you: I am the Saint, the Perfect One, the supreme Buddha. Open your ears, O monks; the path is discovered that leads to deliverance. Listen well."

And the five monks listened as he spoke.

"There are two extremes that he must avoid who would lead a life governed by his intelligence. Some devote themselves to pleasure; their lives are a constant round of dissipations; they seek only to gratify their senses. Such beings are contemptible; their conduct is ignoble and futile; it is unworthy of him who would acquire intelligence. Others devote themselves to self-mortification; they deprive themselves of everything; their conduct is gloomy and futile; it is unworthy of him who would acquire intelligence. From these two extremes, O monks, the Perfect One stands aloof. He has discovered the middle path, the path that opens the eyes and opens the mind, the path that leads to rest, to knowledge, to nirvana. This sacred path, O monks, has eight branches: right faith, right resolve, right speech, right action, right living, right effort, right thought, right meditation. This, O monks, is the middle path, the path that I, the Perfect One, discovered, the path that leads to rest, to knowledge, to nirvana."

All five held their breath, the better to hear him. He paused a moment, then continued:

> *"O monks, I will tell you the truth about suffering. Suffering is birth, suffering is old age, suffering is sickness, suffering is death. You are bound to that which you hate: suffering; you are separated from that which you love: suffering; you do not obtain that which you desire: suffering. To cling to bodies, to sensations, to forms, to impressions, to perceptions: suffering, suffering, suffering. O monks, I will tell you the truth about the origin*

of suffering. The thirst for existence leads from rebirth to rebirth; lust and pleasure follow. Power alone can satisfy lust. The thirst for power, the thirst for pleasure, the thirst for existence; there, O monks, is the origin of suffering. O monks, I will tell you the truth about the suppression of suffering. Quench your thirst by annihilating desire. Drive away desire. Forgo desire. Free yourselves of desire. Be ignorant of desire. O monks, I will tell you the truth about the path that leads to the extinction of suffering. It is the sacred path, the noble eight-fold path: right faith, right resolve, right speech, right action, right living, right effort, right thought, right meditation. O monks, you know the sacred truth about suffering; no one before me had discovered it; my eyes opened, and suffering was revealed to me.

I understood the truth about suffering; you, O monks, must now understand it. O monks, you know the sacred truth about the origin of suffering; no one before me had discovered it; my eyes opened, and the origin of suffering was revealed to me. I understood the truth about the origin of suffering; you, O monks, must now understand it. O monks, you know the sacred truth about the suppression of suffering; no one before me had discovered it; my eyes opened, and the suppression of suffering was revealed to me.

I understood the truth about the suppression of suffering; you, O monks, must now understand it. O monks, you know the sacred truth about the path that leads to the extinction of suffering; no one before me had discovered it; my eyes opened, and the path that leads to the extinction of suffering was revealed to me. I understood the truth about the path that leads to the extinction of suffering; you must now understand it, O monks."

The five disciples listened with rapture to the words of the Blessed One. He spoke again:

"O monks, as long as I did not have a complete understanding of these four truths, I knew that neither in this world nor in the world of the Gods, in Mara's world nor in Brahma's world I knew that among all beings, men, Gods, hermits or Brahmans, I had not attained the supreme rank of Buddha. But, O monks,

now that I have a complete understanding of these four truths, I know that in this world as in the world of the Gods, in Mara's world and in Brahma's world, I know that among all beings, men, Gods, hermits or Brahmans, I have attained the supreme rank of Buddha. I am for ever set free: for me there will be no new birth."

Thus spoke the Blessed One, and the five monks joyfully acclaimed him and glorified him.

THE BUDDHA IS PREPARED TO PREACH THE DOCTRINE

The Buddha began to wonder how he would propagate the knowledge. He said to himself:

"I have discovered a profound truth. It was difficult to perceive; it will be difficult to understand; only the wise will grasp it. In a world full of confusion, men lead restless lives, yet men enjoy living in a world full of confusion. How then can they understand the chain of causes and effects? How can they understand the law? They will never be able to stifle their desires; they will never break away from earthly pleasures; they will never enter nirvana. If I preach the doctrine, I shall not be understood. Perhaps no one will even listen to me. What is the use of revealing to mankind the truth I had to fight to win? Truth stays hidden from those controlled by desire and hatred. Truth is hard to find; it remains ever a mystery. The vulgar mind will never grasp it. He will never know truth whose mind is lost in darkness, who is a prey to earthly desires."

And the Blessed One was not inclined to preach the doctrine.

Then Brahma, by virtue of his supreme intelligence, knew of the doubts that beset the Blessed One. He became frightened. "The world is lost," he said to himself, "the world is undone, if the Perfect One, the Holy One, the Buddha, now stands aloof, if he does not go among men to preach the doctrine and propagate the knowledge."

And he left the sky. It took him less time to reach the earth than it takes a strong man to bend or stretch his arm, and he appeared before the Blessed One. To show his deep reverence, he uncovered one shoulder, then kneeling, he raised his folded hands to the Blessed One and said:

> *"Deign to teach the knowledge, O Master, deign to teach the knowledge, O Blessed One. There are men of great purity in the world, men whom no filth has ever defiled, but, if they are not instructed in the knowledge, how will they find salvation? They must be saved, these men; oh, save them! They will listen to you; they will be your disciples."*

Thus spoke Brahma. The Blessed One remained silent. Brahma continued:

> *"Till now an evil law has prevailed in the world. It has led men into sin. It behooves you to destroy it. O Man of Wisdom, open for us the gates of eternity; tell us what you have found, O Saviour! You are he who has climbed the mountain, you stand on the rocky summit, and you survey mankind from afar.*
>
> *Have pity, O Saviour; think of the unhappy peoples who suffer the anguish of birth and of old age. Go, conquering hero, go! Travel through the world, be the light and the guide. Speak, teach; there will be many to understand your word."*

And the Blessed One answered:

> *"Profound is the law that I have established; it is subtile and hard to understand; it lies beyond ordinary reasoning. The world will scoff at it; only a few wise men perhaps will grasp the meaning and decide to accept it. If I set out, if I speak and am not understood, I risk an ignominious defeat. I shall stay here, Brahma; men are the sport of ignorance."*

But Brahma spoke again:

> *"You have attained sublime wisdom; the rays of your light reach even into space, yet you are indifferent, O Sun! No, such conduct is unworthy of you; your silence is reprehensible; you must speak. Rise up! Beat the drums, sound the gong! Let the law blaze like a burning torch, or like refreshing rain, let it fall upon the parched earth. Deliver those who are tormented by evil; bring peace to those consumed by a vicious fire! You, who are like a star among men, you alone can destroy birth and*

death. See, I fall at your feet and implore you, in the name of all the Gods!"

Then the Blessed One thought:

"Among the blue and white lotuses that flower in a pool, there are some that stay under water, others that rise to the surface, and still others that grow so tall that their petals are not even wet. And in the world I see good men and evil men; some have sharp minds and others are dull; some are noble, others ignoble; some will understand me, others will not; but I shall take pity on them all. I shall consider the lotus that opens under water as well as the lotus that flaunts its great beauty."

And he said to Brahma:

"May the gates of eternity be open to all! May all who have ears hear the word and believe! I was thinking of the weariness in store for me and fearing the effort would come to nothing, but my pity outweighs these considerations. I rise, O Brahma, and I shall preach the law to all creatures."

3. The Buddha Leaves for Benares

The Blessed One wondered who was worthy of being the first to hear the word of salvation. "Where is there a man of virtue, intelligence and energy, to whom I can teach the law?" he asked himself. "His heart must be innocent of hatred, his mind must be tranquil, and he must not keep the knowledge to himself as if it were some dark secret."

He thought of Rudraka, son of Rama. He remembered that he had been free from hatred and had tried to lead a life of virtue, and that he was not the sort of man who would make a secret of the knowledge. He decided to teach him the law, and this question arose in his mind: "Where is Rudraka, now?" Then he learned that Rudraka, son of Rama, had been dead seven days, and he said:

"It is a great pity that Rudraka, son of Rama, should have died without hearing the law. He would have understood it, and he, in turn, could have taught it."

He thought of Arata Kalama. He remembered his clear intellect and his virtuous life, and he decided that Arata Kalama would be glad to propagate the knowledge. And this question arose in his mind: "Where is Arata Kalama now?" Then he learned that Arata Kalama had been dead three days, and he said:

"Arata Kalama died without hearing the law; great is Arata Kalama's loss."

He thought again, and he remembered Rudraka's five disciples who had once joined him. They were virtuous; they were energetic; they would certainly understand the law. The Blessed One knew, by virtue of his intelligence, that Rudraka's five disciples were living in the Deer Park at Benares. So he set out for Bernares.

At Mount Gaya he met a monk named Upaka. At the sight of the Blessed One, Upaka uttered a cry of admiration.

"How beautiful you are!" he exclaimed. "Your face is radiant. Fruit that has ripened in the sun has less bloom. Yours is the beauty of a clear autumn. My Lord, may I ask who your master was?"

"I had no master," answered the Blessed One. "There is no one like me. I alone am wise, calm, incorruptible."

"What a great master you must be!" said Upaka. "Yes, I am the only master in this world; my

equal can not be found on earth or in the sky." "Where are you going?" asked Upaka.

"I am going to Benares," said the Blessed One, "and there I shall light the lamp that will bring light into the world, a light that will dazzle even the eyes of the blind. I am going to Benares, and there I shall beat the drums that will awaken mankind, the drums that will sound even in the ears of the deaf. I am going to Benares, and there I shall teach the law."

He continued on his way, and he came to the banks of the Ganges. The river was high, and the Blessed One looked for a boatman to take him across. He found one and said to him:

"Friend, will you take me across the river?"

"Certainly," replied the boatman, "but first pay me for the trip."

"I have no money," said the Blessed One.

And he flew through the air to the opposite bank.

The boatman was heart-broken. He cried, "I did not take him across the river, he who was such a saintly man! Oh, woe is me!" And he rolled on the ground in his great distress.

TRAPUSHA AND BHALLIKA

The Buddha never moved. He remained under the tree, his legs crossed. He was filled with bliss at having attained perfect knowledge. He thought, "I have found deliverance." One whole week he remained under the tree of knowledge, without moving.

The second week he went on a long journey; he travelled through all the worlds.

The third week he again remained under the tree of knowledge, and he never once blinked his eyes.

The fourth week he went on a short journey, from the eastern sea to the western sea.

It was then that Mara, whom defeat had left inconsolable, went to the Buddha and spoke these evil words:

"Blessed One, why do you tarry, you who know the path to deliverance? Blow out the lamp, quench the flame; enter nirvana, O Blessed One; the hour has come."

But the Blessed One answered:

"No, Mara, I shall not quench the flame, I shall not enter nirvana. I must first gain many disciples, and they, in turn, must win others over to my law. By word and by deed I must silence my adversaries. No, Mara, I shall not enter nirvana until the Buddha is glorified throughout the world, until his beneficent law is recognized."

Mara left him. He was crestfallen, and he seemed to hear divine voices mocking him.

"You have been defeated, Mara," they were saying, "and you stand wrapped in thought, like an old heron. You are powerless, Mara, like an aged elephant stuck fast in a swamp. You thought you were a hero, and you are weaker than a sick man abandoned in a forest. Of what avail were your insolent words? They were as futile as the chattering of crows."

He picked up a piece of dead wood, and began drawing figures in the sand. His three daughters, Rati, Arati and Trishna, saw him. They were taken aback at the sight of his grief.

"Father, why are you so melancholy?" asked Rati.

"I have been defeated by a saintly man," replied Mara. "He is proof against my strength and my cunning."

"Father," said Trishna, "we are beautiful; we have seductive ways."

"We shall go to this man," continued Arati; "we shall bind him with the chains of love, and we shall bring him to you, humbled and craven."

They went to the Buddha, and they sang:

"Spring is here, friend, the loveliest of the seasons. The trees are in blossom; we must be merry. Your eyes are beautiful, they shine with a lovely light, and you bear the marks of omnipotence. Look at us: we were made to give pleasure and happiness to both men and Gods. Rise and join us, friend; make the most of your shining youth; dismiss all solemn thoughts from your mind. Look at our hair, see how soft it is; flowers lend their fragrance to its silkiness. See our eyes wherein slumbers the sweetness of love. See our warm lips, like fruit ripened in the sun. See our firm, rounded breasts. We glide with the stately grace of swans; we know songs that charm and please, and when we dance, hearts beat faster and pulses throb. Come, friend, do not spurn us; he is foolish, indeed, who would throw away a treasure. Look at us, dear Lord; we are your slaves."

But the Blessed One was unmoved by the song. He frowned at the young girls, and they turned into hags.

In despair they returned to their father. "Father," cried Rati, "see what he has done to our youth and our beauty."

"Love will never hurt him," said Trishna, "for he was able to resist our charms."

"Oh," sighed Arati, "how cruelly he has punished us."

"Father," implored Trishna, "cure us of this hideous old age."

"Give us back our youth," cried Rati.

"Give us back our beauty," cried Arati.

"My poor daughters," replied Mara, "I grieve for you. Yes, he has defeated love; he is beyond my power, and I am sad. You plead with me to give you back your youth and your beauty, but how can I? The Buddha alone can undo what the Buddha has done. Return to him; admit that you were blameworthy; tell him that you are repentant, and perhaps he will give you back your charms."

They implored the Buddha.

"Blessed One," said they, "forgive us our offense. Our eyes were blind to the light, and we were foolish. Forgive us!"

"Yes, you were foolish," replied the Blessed One; "you were trying to destroy a mountain with your finger-nails, you were trying to bite through iron with your teeth. But you acknowledge your offense; that already is a sign of wisdom. O maidens, I forgive you."

And the three daughters of the Evil One left his presence, more beautiful than ever before.

The fifth week the Blessed One remained under the tree. But, suddenly, there blew a bitter wind, and a cold rain fell. Then Mucilinda, the serpent-king, said to himself: "The Blessed One must not suffer from the rain or from the cold." He left his home. Seven times he coiled himself around the Buddha, and he spread his hood above the Buddha's head to shelter him. And thus the Buddha suffered not at all during this period of bad weather.

The sixth week he went to a fig-tree where goatherds often forgathered. There, some Gods awaited him, and they humbly bowed as he approached. He said.

"Meekness is sweet to him who knows the law; kindness is sweet to him who can see; meekness is sweet to all creatures; kindness is sweet to all creatures. Blessed is he who has not a desire in the world; blessed is he who has conquered sin; blessed is he who has escaped the torture of the senses; blessed is he who no longer thirsts for existence!"

The seventh week he remained under the tree of knowledge.

Two brothers, Trapusha and Bhallika, were returning to the northern countries. They were merchants and had five hundred chariots in their train. As they came near the tree, the chariots stopped. In vain did the drivers try to encourage or goad the beasts that drew them; they could not advance a step. The wheels kept sinking in the mud up to the hubs. Trapusha and Bhallika became alarmed, but a God appeared who reassured them and said:

"Walk a little way, O merchants, and you will find one to whom you should do homage."

Trapusha and Bhallika saw the Blessed One. His face was radiant. "Is it the God of some river or the God of the mountain?" they wondered. "Could it be Brahma himself?"

But upon looking at his garments, they thought:

"It must be some monk. Perhaps he would like something to eat."

Trapusha and Bhallika went to the chariot that carried the provisions. They found flour and honey cakes, and they brought them to the Buddha.

"Take them, saintly man," they said, offering him the cakes, "take them and be gracious to us."

The Blessed One had no bowl in which to receive alms. He did not know what to do. The Gods, who were watching at the four quarters of the earth, saw his perplexity, and they quickly brought him bowls made of gold. But the Blessed One said to himself:

"Truly, it would be unseemly for a monk to receive alms in a golden bowl."

And he refused the golden bowls. The Gods then brought him silver bowls, which he also refused. He likewise refused emerald bowls, and he would only accept bowls made of stone.

He then received the cakes the merchants offered him. When he had finished eating, he said:

"The blessing of the Gods be with you, merchants! Prosper and be happy!"

Trapusha and Bhallika bowed, and they heard a God say to them:

"He who is before you has arrived at supreme knowledge. This was his first meal since he found the path to deliverance, and to you fell the signal honour of offering it to him. He will now go through the world and teach the true law."

Trapusha and Bhallika rejoiced, and they were the first to profess their faith in the Buddha and in the law.

RIGHT KNOWLEDGE OR KNOWLEDGE OF RELATIONS

Then Mahamati said: Pray tell us, Blessed One, about the being and the non-being of all things?

The Blessed One replied: People of this world are dependent in their thinking on one of two things: on the notion of being whereby they take pleasure in realism, or in the notion of non-being whereby they take pleasure in nihilism; in either case they imagine emancipation where there is no emancipation. Those who are dependent upon the notion of being, regard the world as rising from a causation that is really existent, and that this actually existing and becoming world does not take its rise from a causation that is non-existent.

This is the realistic view as held by some people. Then there are other people who are dependent on the notion of the non-being of all things. These people admit the existence of greed, anger and folly, and at the same time they deny the existence of the things that produce greed, anger and folly. This is not rational, for greed, anger and folly are no more to be taken hold of as real than are things; they neither have substance nor individual marks. Where there is a state of bondage, there is binding and means for binding; but where there is emancipation, as in the case of Buddhas, Bodhisattvas, masters and disciples, who have ceased to believe in both being and non-being, there is neither bondage, binding nor means for binding.

It is better to cherish the notion of an ego-substance than to entertain the notion of emptiness derived from the view of being and non-being, for those who so believe fail to understand the, fundamental fact that the external world is nothing but a manifestation of mind. Because they see things as, transient, as rising from cause and passing away from cause, now dividing, now combining into the elements which make up the aggregates of personality and its external world and now passing away, they are doomed to suffer every moment from the changes that follow one after another, and finally are doomed to ruin.

Then Mahamati asked Blessed One, saying: Tell us, Blessed One, how all things can be empty, un-born, and have no self-nature, so that we may be awakened and quickly realise highest enlightenment?

The Blessed One replied: What is emptiness, indeed! It is a term whose very self-nature is false-imagination, but because of one's attachment to false-imagination we are obliged to talk of emptiness, no-birth, and no-self-nature. There are seven kinds of emptiness: emptiness of mutuality which is non-existence; emptiness of individual marks; emptiness of self-nature; emptiness of no-work; emptiness of work; emptiness of all things in the sense that they are unpredicable; and emptiness in its highest sense of Ultimate Reality.

By the emptiness of mutuality which is non-existence is meant that when a thing is missing here, one speaks of its being empty here. For instance: in the lecture hall of Mrigarama there are no elephants present, nor bulls, nor sheep; but as to monks there are many present. We can rightly speak of the hall as being empty as far as animals are concerned. It is not asserted that the lecture hall is empty of its own characteristics, or that the monks are empty of that which makes up their monkhood, nor that in some other place there are no elephants, bulls, nor sheep to be found. In this case we are speaking of things in their aspect of individuality and generality, but from the point of view of mutuality some things do not exist somewhere. This is the lowest form of emptiness and is to be sedulously put away.

By emptiness of individual marks is meant that all things have no distinguishing marks of individuality and generality. Because of mutual relations and interactions things are superficially discriminated but when they are further and more carefully investigated and analysed they are seen to be non-existent and nothing as to individuality and generality can be predicated of them. Thus when individual marks can no longer be seen, ideas of self, otherness and bothness, no longer hold good. So it must be said that all things are empty of self-marks.

By emptiness of self-nature is meant that all things in their self-nature are un-born; therefore, is it said that things are empty as to self-nature. By emptiness of no-work is meant that the aggregate of elements that makes up personality and its external world is Nirvana itself and from the beginning there is no activity in them; therefore, one speaks of the emptiness of no-work. By emptiness of work is meant that the aggregates being devoid of an ego and its belongings, go on functioning automatically as there is mutual conjunction of causes and conditions; thus one speaks of the emptiness of work. By emptiness of all things in the sense that they are unpredicable is meant that, as the very nature of false-imagination is inexpressible, so all things are unpredicable, and, therefore, are empty in that sense. By emptiness in its highest sense of the emptiness of Ultimate Reality is meant that in the attainment of inner self-realisation of Noble Wisdom there is no trace of habit-energy generated by erroneous conceptions; thus one speaks of the highest emptiness of Ultimate Reality.

When things are examined by right knowledge there are no signs obtainable which would characterise them with marks of individuality and generality, therefore, they are said to have no self-nature. Because these signs of individuality and generality are seen both as existing and yet are known to be non-existent, are seen as going out and yet are known not to be going out, they are never annihilated. Why is this true? For this reason; because the individual signs that should make up the self-nature of all things are non-existent. Again in their self-nature things are both eternal and non-eternal. Things are not eternal because the marks of individuality appear and disappear, that is, the marks of self-nature are characterised by non-eternality. On the other hand, because things are un-born and are only mind-made, they are in a deep sense eternal. That is, things are eternal because of their very non-eternality.

Further, besides understanding the emptiness of all things both in regard to substance and self-nature, it is necessary for Bodhisattvas to clearly understand that all things are un-born. It is not asserted that things are not born in a superficial sense, but that in a deep sense they are not born of themselves. All that can be said, is this, that relatively speaking, there is a constant stream of becoming, a momentary and uninterrupted change from one state of appearance to another. When it is recognised that the world as it presents itself is no more than a manifestation of mind, then birth is seen as no-birth and all existing objects, concerning which discrimination asserts that they are and are not, are non-existent and, therefore, un-born; being devoid of agent and action things are un-born.

If things are not born of being and non-being, but are simply manifestations of mind itself, they have no reality, no self-nature:—they are like the horns of a hare, a horse, a donkey, a camel. But the ignorant and the simple-minded, who are given over to their false and erroneous imaginings, discriminate things where they are not. To the ignorant the characteristic marks of the self-nature of body-property-and-abode seem to be fundamental and rooted in the very nature of the mind itself, so they discriminate their multitudinousness and become attached to them.

There are two kinds of attachment: attachment to objects as having self-nature, and attachment to words as having self-nature. The first takes place by not knowing that the external world is only a manifestation of the mind itself; and the second arises from one's clinging to words and names by reason of habit-energy in the teaching of no-birth, causation is out of place because, seeing that all things are like maya and a dream, one does not discriminate individual signs. That all things are un-born and have no self-nature because they are like maya is asserted to meet the thesis of the philosophers that birth is by causation. They foster the notion that the birth of all things is derived from the concept of being and non-being, and fail to regard it as it truly is,—as caused by attachment to the multitudinousness which arises from discriminations of the mind itself.

Those who believe in the birth of something that has never been in existence and, coming into existence, vanishes away, are obliged to assert that things come to exist and vanish away by causation—such people find no foothold in my teachings. When it is realised that there is nothing born, and nothing passes away, then there is no way to admit being and non-being, and the mind becomes quiescent.

Then Mahamati said to the Blessed One: The philosophers declare that the world rises from causal agencies according to a law of causation; they state that their cause is unborn and is not to be annihilated. They mention nine primary elements: Ishvara the Creator, the Creation, atoms, etc., which being elementary are unborn and not to be annihilated. The Blessed One, while teaching that all things are un-born and that there is no annihilation, also declares that the world takes its rise from ignorance, discrimination, attachment, deed, etc., working according to a law of causation. Though the two sets of elements may differ in form and name, there does not appear to be any essential difference between the two positions. If there is anything that is distinctive and superior in the Blessed One's teaching, pray tell us, Blessed One, what it is?

The Blessed One replied: My teaching of no-birth and no-annihilation is not like that of the philosophers, nor is it like their doctrine of birth and impermanency. That to which the philosophers ascribe the characteristic of no-birth and no-annihilation is the self-nature of all things, which causes them to fall into the dualism of being and non-being. My teaching transcends the whole conception of being and non-being; it has nothing to do with birth, abiding and destruction; nor with existence and non-existence. I teach that the multitudinousness of objects have no reality in themselves but are only seen of the mind and, therefore, are of the nature of maya and a dream. I teach the non-existence of things because they carry no signs of any inherent self-nature. It is true that in one sense they are seen and discriminated by the senses as individualised objects; but in another sense, because of the absence of any characteristic marks of self-nature, they are not seen but are only imagined. In one sense they are graspable, but in another sense, they are not graspable. When it is clearly understood that there is nothing in the world but what is seen of the mind itself, discrimination no more rises, and the wise are established in their true abode which is the realm of quietude.

The ignorant discriminate and work trying to adjust themselves to external conditions, and are constantly perturbed in mind; unrealities are imagined and discriminated, while realities are unseen and ignored. It is not so with the wise. To illustrate: What the ignorant see is like the magically-created city of the Gandharvas, where children are shown streets and houses, and phantom merchants, and people going in and coming out. This imaginary city with its streets and houses and people going in and coming out, are not thought of as being born or being annihilated, because in their case there is no question as to their existence or non-existence.

In like manner, I teach, that there is nothing made nor unmade; that there is nothing that has connection with birth and destruction except as the ignorant cherish falsely imagined notions as to the reality of the external world. When objects are not seen and judged as they truly are in themselves, there is discrimination and clinging to the notions of being and non-being, and individualised self-nature, and. as long as these notions of individuality and self-nature persist, the philosophers are bound to explain the external world by a law of causation.

This position raises the question of a first cause which the philosophers meet by asserting that their first cause, Ishvara and the primal elements, are un-born and un-annihilate; which position is without evidence and is irrational.

Ignorant people and worldly philosophers cherish a kind of no-birth, but it is not the no-birth which I teach. I teach the un-bornness of the un-born essence of all things which teaching is established in the minds of the wise by their self-realisation of Noble Wisdom. A ladle, clay, a vessel, a wheel, or seeds, or elements—these are external conditions; ignorance discrimination, attachment, habit, karma,—these are inner conditions. When this entire universe is regarded as concatenation and as nothing else but concatenation, then the mind, by its patient acceptance of the truth that all things are un-born, gains tranquillity.

PERFECT KNOWLEDGE, OR KNOWLEDGE OF REALITY

Hen Mahamati asked the Blessed one: Pray tell us, Blessed One, about the five Dharmas, so that we may fully understand Perfect Knowledge?

The Blessed One replied: The five Dharmas are: appearance, name, discrimination, right-knowledge and Reality. By appearance is meant that which reveals itself to the senses and to the discriminating-mind and is perceived as form, sound, odour, taste, and touch. Out of these appearances ideas are formed, such as clay, water, jar, etc., by which one says: this is such and such a thing and is no other,—this is name. When appearances are contrasted and names compared, as when we say: this is an elephant, this is a horse, a cart, a pedestrian, a man, a woman, or, this is mind and what belongs to it,—the things thus named are said to be discriminated. As these discriminations come to be seen as mutually conditioning, as empty of self-substance, as un-born, and thus come to be seen as they truly are, that is, as manifestations of the mind itself,—this is right-knowledge. By it the wise cease to regard appearances and names as realities.

When appearances and names are put away and all discrimination ceases, that which remains is the true and essential nature of things and, as nothing can be predicated as to the nature of essence, it is called the "Suchness" of Reality. This universal, undifferentiated, inscrutable, "Suchness" is the only Reality but it is variously characterised as Truth, Mind-essence, Transcendental Intelligence, Noble Wisdom, etc. This Dharma of the imagelessness of the Essence-nature of Ultimate Reality is the Dharma which has been proclaimed by all the Buddhas, and when all things are understood in full agreement with it, one is in possession of Perfect Knowledge, and is on his way to the attainment of the Transcendental Intelligence of the Tathagatas.

Then Mahamati said to the Blessed One: Are the three self-natures, of things, ideas, and Reality, to be considered as included in the Five Dharmas, or as having their own characteristics complete in themselves.

The Blessed One replied: The three self-natures, the eightfold mind-system, and the twofold egolessness are all included in the Five Dharmas. The self-natures of things, of ideas, and of the sixfold mind-system, correspond with the Dharmas of appearance, name and discrimination; the self-nature of Universal Mind and Reality corresponds to the Dharmas of right-knowledge and "Suchness."

By becoming attached to what is seen of the mind itself, there is an activity awakened which is perpetuated by habit-energy that becomes manifest in the mind-system. From the activities of the mind-system there rises the notion of an ego-soul and its belongings; the discriminations, attachments, and notion of an ego-soul, rising simultaneously like the sun and its rays of light.

By the egolessness of things is meant that the elements that make up the aggregates of personality and its objective world being characterised by the nature of maya and destitute of anything that can be called ego-substance, are therefore unborn and have no self-nature. How can things be said to have an ego-soul? By the egolessness of persons is meant that in the aggregates that make up personality there is no ego-substance, nor anything that is like ego-substance nor that belongs to it. The mind-system, which is the most characteristic mark of personality, originated in ignorance, discrimination, desire and deed; and its activities are perpetuated by perceiving, grasping and becoming attached to objects as if they were real.

The memory of these discriminations, desires, attachments and deeds is stored in Universal Mind since beginningless time, and is still being accumulated where it conditions the appearance of personality and its environment and brings about constant change and destruction from moment to moment. The manifestations are like a river, a seed, a lamp, a cloud, the wind; Universal mind in its voraciousness to store up everything, is like a monkey never at rest, like a fly ever in search of food and without partiality, like a fire that is never satisfied, like a water-lifting machine that goes on rolling. Universal mind as defiled by habit-energy is like a magician that causes phantom things and people to appear and move about. A thorough understanding of these things is necessary to an understanding of the egolessness of persons.

There are four kinds of Knowledge: Appearance-knowledge, relative-knowledge, perfect-knowledge, and Transcendental Intelligence. Appearance-knowledge belongs to the ignorant and simple-minded who are addicted to the notion of being and non-being, and who are frightened at the thought of being unborn.

It is produced by the concordance of the triple combination and attaches itself to the multiplicities of objects; it is characterised by attainability and accumulation; it is subject to birth and destruction. Appearance-knowledge belongs to word-mongers who revel in discriminations, assertions and negations.

Relative-knowledge belongs to the mind-world of the philosophers. It rises from the mind's ability to consider the relations which appearances bear to each other and to the mind considering them, it rises from the mind's ability to arrange, combine and analyse these relations by its powers of discursive logic and imagination, by reason of which it is able to peer into the meaning and significance of things.

Perfect-knowledge belongs to the world of the Bodhisattvas who recognise that all things are but manifestations of mind; who clearly understand the emptiness, the un-bornness, the egolessness of all things; and who have entered into an understanding of the Five Dharmas, the twofold egolessness, and into the truth of imagelessness. Perfect-knowledge differentiates the Bodhisattva stages, and is the pathway and the entrance into the exalted state of self-realisation of Noble Wisdom.

Perfect-knowledge (*jnana*) belongs to the Bodhisattvas who are entirely free from the dualisms of being and non-being, no-birth and no-annihilation, all assertions and negations, and who, by reason of self-realisation, have gained an insight into the truths of egolessness and imagelessness. They no longer discriminate the world as subject to causation: they regard the causation that rules the world as something like the fabled city of the Gandharvas. To them the world is like a vision and a dream, it is like the birth and death of a barren-woman's child; to them there is nothing evolving and nothing disappearing.

The wise who cherish Perfect-knowledge, may be divided into three classes: disciples, masters and Arhats. Common disciples are separated from masters as common disciples continue to cherish the notion of individuality and generality; masters rise from common disciples when, forsaking the error of individuality and generality, they still cling to the notion of an ego-soul by reason of which they go off by themselves into retirement and solitude. Arhats rise when the error of all discrimination is realised. Error being discriminated by the wise turns into Truth by virtue of the "turning-about" that takes place within the deepest consciousness. Mind, thus emancipated, enters into perfect self-realisation of Noble Wisdom.

But, Mahamati, if you *assert* that there is such a thing as Noble Wisdom, it no longer holds good, because anything of which something is asserted thereby partakes of the nature of being and is thus characterised with the quality of birth. The very assertion: "All things are un-born" destroys the truthfulness of it. The same is true of the statements: "All things are empty," and "All things have no self-nature,"—both are untenable when put in the form of assertions. But when it is pointed out that all things are like a dream and a vision, it means that in one way things are perceived, and in another way they are not perceived; that is, in ignorance they are perceived but in Perfect-knowledge they are not perceived. All assertions and negations being thought-constructions are un-born. Even the assertion that Universal Mind and Noble Wisdom are Ultimate Reality, is thought construction and, therefore, is un-born. As "things" there is no Universal Mind, there is no Noble Wisdom, there is no Ultimate Reality. The insight of the wise who move about in the realm of imagelessness and its solitude is pure. That is, for the wise all "things" are wiped away and even the state of imagelessness ceases to exist.

THE MIND SYSTEM

Then Mahamati said to the Blessed One: Pray tell us, Blessed One, what is meant by the mind (*citta*)?

The Blessed One replied: All things of this world, be they seemingly good or bad, faulty or faultless, effect-producing or not effect-producing, receptive or non-receptive, may be divided into two classes: evil out-flowings and the non out-flowing good. The five grasping elements that make up the aggregates of personality, namely, form, sensation, perception, discrimination, and consciousness, and that are imagined to be good and bad, have their rise in the habit-energy of the mind-system,—they are the evil out-flowings of life. The spiritual attainments and the joys of the Samadhis and the fruitage of the Samapattis that come to the wise through their self-realisation of Noble Wisdom and that culminate in their return and participation in the relations of the triple world are called the non out-flowing good.

The mind-system which is the source of the evil out-flowings consists of the five sense-organs and their accompanying sense-minds (*vijnanas*) all of which are unified in the discriminating-mind (*manovijnana*). There is an unending succession of sense-concepts flowing into this discriminating or thinking-mind which combines them and discriminates them and passes judgement upon them as to their goodness or badness.

Then follows aversion to or desire for them and attachment and deed; thus the entire system moves on continuously and closely bound together. But it fails to see and understand that what it sees and discriminates and grasps is only a manifestation of its own activity and has no other basis, and so the mind goes on erroneously perceiving and discriminating differences of forms and qualities, not remaining still even for a minit.

In the mind-system there are three modes of activity distinguishable: the sense-minds functioning while remaining in their original nature, the sense-minds as producing effects, and the sense-minds as evolving. By normal functioning the sense-minds grasp appropriate elements of their external world, by which sensation and perception arise at once and by degrees in every sense-organ and every sense-mind, in the pores of the skin, and even in the atoms that make up the body, by which the whole field is apprehended like a mirror reflecting objects, and not realising that the external world itself is only a manifestation of mind.

The second mode of activity produces effects by which these sensations react on the discriminating mind to produce perceptions, attractions, aversions, grasping, deed and habit. The third mode of activity has to do with the growth, development and passing of the mind-system, that is, the mind-system is in subjection to its own habit-energy accumulated from beginningless time, as for instance: the "eyeness" in the eye that predisposes it to grasp and become attached to multiple forms and appearances. In this way the activities of the evolving mind-system by reason of its habit-energy stirs up waves of objectivity on the face of Universal Mind which in turn conditions the activities and evolvement of the mind-system. Appearances, perception, attraction, grasping, deed, habit, reaction, condition one another incessantly, and the functioning sense-minds, the discriminating-mind and Universal Mind are thus bound up together.

Thus, by reason of discrimination of that which by nature is maya-like and unreal false-imagination and erroneous reasoning takes place, action follows and its habit-energy accumulates thereby defiling the pure face of Universal Mind, and as a result the mind-system comes into functioning and the physical body has its genesis.

But the discriminating-mind has no thought that by its discriminations and attachments it is conditioning the whole body and so the sense-minds and the discriminating-mind go on mutually related and mutually conditioned in a most intimate manner and building up a world of representations out of the activities of its own imagination. As a mirror reflects forms, the perceiving senses perceive appearances which the discriminating-mind gathers together and proceeds to discriminate, to name and become attached to. Between these two functions there is no gap, nevertheless, they are mutually conditioning. The perceiving senses grasp that for which they have an affinity, and there is a transformation takes place in their structure by reason of which the mind proceeds to combine, discriminate, apprise, and act; then follows habit-energy and the establishing of the mind and its continuance.

The discriminating-mind because of its capacity to discriminate, judge, select and reason about, is also called the thinking, or intellectual-mind. There are three divisions of its mental activity: mentation which functions in connection with attachment to objects and ideas, mentation that functions in connection with general ideas, and mentation that examines into the validity of these general ideas.

The mentation which functions in connection with attachment to objects and ideas derived from discrimination, discriminates the mind from its mental processes and accepts the ideas from it as being real and becomes attached to them. A variety of false judgements are thus arrived at as to being, multiplicity, individuality, value, etc., a strong grasping takes place which is perpetuated by habit-energy and thus discrimination goes on asserting itself.

These mental processes give rise to general conceptions of warmth, fluidity, motility, and solidity, as characterising the objects of discrimination, while the tenacious holding to these general ideas gives rise to proposition, reason, definition, and illustration, all of which lead to the assertions of relative knowledge and the establishment of confidence in birth, self-nature, and an ego-soul.

By mentation as an examining function is meant the intellectual act of examining into these general conclusions as to their validity, significance, and truthfulness. This is the faculty that leads to understanding, right-knowledge and points the way to self-realisation.

Then Mahamati said to the Blessed One: Pray tell us, Blessed One, what relation ego-personality bears to the mind-system?

The Blessed One replied: To explain it, it is first necessary to speak of the self-nature of the five grasping aggregates that make up personality, although as I have already shown they are empty, un-born, and without self-nature. These five grasping aggregates are: form, sensation, perception, discrimination, consciousness. Of these, form belongs to what is made of the so-called primary elements, whatever they may be. The four remaining aggregates are without form and ought not to be reckoned as four, because they merge imperceptibly into one another. They are like space which cannot be numbered; it is only due to imagination that they are discriminated and likened to space. Because things are endowed with appearances of being, characteristic-marks, perceivableness, abode, work, one can say that they are born of effect-producing causes, but this can not be said of these four intangible aggregates for they are without form and marks.

These four mental aggregates that make up personality are beyond calculability, they are beyond the four propositions, they are not to be predicated as existing nor as not existing, but together they constitute what is known as mortal-mind. They are even more maya-like and dream-like than are things, nevertheless, as discriminating mortal-mind they obstruct the self-realisation of Noble Wisdom. But it is only by the ignorant that they are enumerated and thought of as an ego-personality; the wise do not do so. This discrimination of the five aggregates that make up personality and that serve as a basis for an ego-soul and ground for its desires and self-interests must be given up, and in its place the truth of imagelessness and solitude should be established.

Then said Mahamati to the Blessed One: Pray tell us, Blessed One, about Universal Mind and its relation to the lower mind-system?

The Blessed One replied: The sense-minds and their centralised discriminating-mind are related to the external world which is a manifestation of itself and is given over to perceiving, discriminating, and grasping its maya-like appearances. Universal Mind (Alaya-vijnana) transcends all individuation and limits. Universal Mind is thoroughly pure in its essential nature, subsisting unchanged and free from faults of impermanence, undisturbed by egoism, unruffled by distinctions, desires and aversions. Universal Mind is like a great ocean, its surface ruffled by waves and surges but its depths remaining forever unmoved. In itself it is devoid of personality and all that belongs to it, but by reason of the defilement upon its face it is like an actor and plays a variety of parts, among which a mutual functioning takes place and the mind-system arises. The principle of intellection becomes divided and mind, the functions of mind, the evil out-flowings of mind, take on individuation. The sevenfold gradation of mind appears: namely, intuitive self-realisation, thinking-desiring-discriminating, seeing, hearing, tasting, smelling, touching, and all their interactions and reactions take their rise.

The discriminating-mind is the cause of the sense-minds and is their support and with them is kept functioning as it describes and becomes attached to a world of objects, and then, by means of its habit-energy, it defiles the face of Universal Mind. Thus Universal Mind becomes the storage and clearing house of all the accumulated products of mentation and action since beginningless time.

Between Universal Mind and the individual discriminating-mind is the intuitive-mind (*manas*) which is dependent upon Universal Mind for its cause and support and enters into relations with both. It partakes of the universality of Universal Mind, shares its purity, and like it, is above form and momentariness. It is through the intuitive-mind that the good non out-flowings emerge, are manifested and are realised. Fortunate it is that intuition is not momentary for if the enlightenment which comes by intuition were momentary the wise would lose their "wiseness" which they do not. But the intuitive-mind enters into relations with the lower mind-system, shares its experiences and reflects upon its activities.

Intuitive-mind is one with Universal Mind by reason of its participation in Transcendental Intelligence (*Arya-jnana*), and is one with the mind-system by its comprehension of differentiated knowledge (*vijnana*). Intuitive-mind has no body of its own nor any marks by which it can be differentiated. Universal Mind is its cause and support but it is evolved along with the notion of an ego and what belongs to it, to which it clings and upon which it reflects. Through intuitive-mind, by the faculty of intuition which is a mingling of both identity and perceiving, the inconceivable wisdom of Universal Mind is revealed and made realisable. Like Universal Mind it can not be the source of error.

The discriminating-mind is a dancer and a magician with the objective world as his stage. Intuitive-mind is the wise jester who travels with the magician and reflects upon his emptiness and transiency. Universal Mind keeps the record and knows what must be and what may be. It is because of the activities of the discriminating-mind that error rises and an objective world evolves and the notion of an ego-soul becomes established. If and when the discriminating-mind can be gotten rid of, the whole mind-system will cease to function and

Universal Mind will alone remain. Getting rid of the discriminating-mind removes the cause of all error.

Then said Mahamati to the Blessed One: Pray tell us, Blessed One, what is meant by the cessation of the mind-system?

The Blessed One replied: The five sense-functions and their discriminating and thinking function have their risings and complete endings from moment to moment.

They are born with discrimination as cause, with form and appearance and objectivity closely linked together as condition. The will-to-live is the mother, ignorance is the father.

By setting up names and forms greed is multiplied and thus the mind goes mutually conditioning and being conditioned. By becoming attached to names and forms, not realising that they have no more basis than the activities of the mind itself, error rises, false-imagination as-to pleasure and pain rises, and the way to emancipation is blocked.

The lower system of sense-minds and the discriminating-mind do not really suffer pleasure and pain-they only imagine they do. Pleasure and pain are the deceptive reactions of mortal-mind as it grasps an imaginary objective world.

There are two ways in which the ceasing of the mind-system may take place: as regards form, and as regards continuation.

The sense-organs function as regards form by the interaction of form, contact and grasping; and they cease to function when this contact is broken. As regards continuation,—when these interactions of form, contact and grasping cease, there is no more continuation of the seeing, hearing and other sense functions; with the ceasing of these sense functions, the discriminations, graspings and attachments of the discriminating-mind cease; and with their ceasing act and deed and their habit-energy cease, and there is no more accumulation of karma-defilement on the face of Universal Mind.

If the evolving mortal-mind were of the same nature as Universal Mind the cessation of the lower mind-system would mean the cessation of Universal Mind, but they are different for Universal Mind is not the cause of mortal-mind.

There is no cessation of Universal Mind in its pure and essence-nature.

What ceases to function is not Universal Mind in its essence-nature, but is the cessation of the effect-producing defilements upon its face that have been caused by the accumulation of the habit-energy of the activities of the discriminating and thinking mortal-mind. There is no cessation of Divine Mind which, in itself, is the abode of Reality and the Womb of Truth.

By the cessation of the sense-minds is meant, not the cessation of their perceiving functions, but the cessation of their discriminating and naming activities which are centralised in the discriminating mortal-mind.

By the cessation of the mind-system as a whole is meant, the cessation of discrimination, the clearing away of the various attachments, and, therefore, the clearing away of the defilements of habit-energy on the face of Universal Mind which have been accumulating since beginningless time by reason of these discriminations, attachments, erroneous reasonings, and following acts.

The cessation of the continuation aspect of the mind-system as a whole, takes place when there is the cessation of that which supports the mind-system, namely, the discriminating mortal-mind. With the cessation of mortal-mind the entire world of maya and desire disappears. Getting rid of the discriminating mortal-mind is Nirvana.

But the cessation of the discriminating-mind can not take place until there has been a "turning-about" in the deepest seat of consciousness.

The mental habit of looking outward by the discriminating-mind upon an external objective world must be given up, and a new habit if realising Truth within the intuitive-mind by becoming one with Truth itself must be established. Until this intuitive self-realisation of Noble Wisdom is attained, the evolving mind-system will go on. But when an insight into the five Ḋharmas, the three self-natures, and the twofold egolessness is attained, then the way will be opened for this "turning-about" to take place. With the ending of pleasure and pain, of conflicting ideas, of the disturbing interests of egoism, a state of tranquillisation will be attained in which the truths of emancipation will be fully understood and there will be no further evil outflowings of the mind-system to interfere with the perfect self-realisation of Noble Wisdom.

Bibliography

Adikaram, E. W.: *Early History of Buddhism in Ceylon,* D. S. Puswella, Migoda, 1946.

Ahmad, Imtiaz: *State and Foreign Policy: India's Role in South Asia,* Vikas, New Delhi, 1993.

Aiyar, R. Krishnaswami: *Outlines of Vedaanta,* Chetana, Bombay, 1978.

Archer, W. G.: *The Kama Sutra,* Unwin Hyman, London, 1990.

Aurobindo, Sri: *Vyasa and Valmiki,* Acharya Press, Pondicherry, 1956.

Avalon, Arthur and Ellen: *Hymns to the Goddess,* Ganesh and Co., Madras, 1964.

Bagchi, P. C.: *Studies in Dharmashastra,* University of Calcutta Press, Calcutta, 1939.

Banerjea, J. N.: *Pauranic and Vedanta Religion,* University of Calcutta, Calcutta, 1996.

Bankimchandra, C.: *Essentials of Dharma,* Sanskrit Book Depot, Calcutta 1979.

Basu, Manoranjan: *Dharmashastra: A General Study,* Shrimati Mira Basu, Calcutta, 1976.

Bhattacharyya, B.: *Nispannayogavali of Mahapandita Abhyakara Gupta,* Oriental Institute, Baroda, 1949.

Bose, D. N.: *Dharmashastra: Their Philosophy and Occult Secrets,* Kali Press, Calcutta, 1965.

Bromley, D.: *Krishna Consciousness in the West,* Bucknell University Press, Lewisburg, 1989.

Coomeraswamy, Ananda K.: *Buddha and the Gospel of Buddhism,* MacMillan, London, 1928.

Dargyay, Eva M.: *The Rise of Esoteric Buddhism in Tibet,* Delhi, Motilal Banarsidass, 1977.

Davids, T. W. Rhys: *Buddhist India,* Delhi, Motilal Banaradass, 1980.

Dayal, Har: *The Bodhisattva Doctrine in Buddhist Sanskrit Literature,* London, Kegan Paul, 1932.

Donat, K.: *Meditate the Tantric Yoga Way*, George Allen and Unwin, London, 1973.

Doniger, W.: *The Rig Veda: An Anthology*, Penguin, New York, 1981.

Dowman, Keith: *Masters of Mahamudra: Songs and Histories of the Eighty-Four Buddhist Siddhas,* Albany, SUNY Press, 1985.

Dresser, Marianne: *Buddhist Women on the Edge: Contemporary Perspectives from the Western Frontier,* Berkeley, North Atlantic Books, 1996.

Duboi, Abbe: *Hindu Manners, Customs and Ceremonies*, Fifth Indian Impression, CUP, 1985.

Dutt, Nalinaksha, *Aspects of Mahayana Buddhism.* London: Luzac, 1930.

Eppsteiner, Fred: *The Path of Compassion: Writings on Socially Engaged Buddhism,* Berkeley, Parallax Press, 1988.

Frauwallner, E.: *The Earliest Vinaya and the Beginnings of Buddhist Literature,* Rome, Istituto Italiano per il Medio ed Estremo Oriente, 1956.

Gambhirananda, S.: *Brahma Sutra Shamkar Bhasya,* Adavita Ashrama, Calcutta, 1977.

George, Christopher S.: *The Candamaharosana Tantra,* New Haven, American Oriental Society, 1974.

Gethin, R. M. L.: *The Buddhist Path to Awakening: A Study of the Bodhi-Pakkhiya Dhamma,* Leiden, E. J. Brill, 1992.

Gombrich, Richard F.: *Buddhist Precept and Practice,* Delhi, Motilal Banarsidass, 1991.

Gonda, Jan: *Vedic Literature: Samhitas and Brahmanas,* Wiesbaden, 1975.

Gross, Rita M.: *Buddhism after Patriarchy: A Feminist History, Analysis, and Reconstruction of Buddhism,* Albany, SUNY Press, 1993.

Growse, F. S.: *The Ramayana of Tulasidasa*, Motilal Banarsidass, Delhi, 1995.

Guenther, Herbert V.: *Philosophy and Psychology in the Abhidharma,* Berkeley, Shambhala, 1976.

Hakeda, Yoshito S.: *Kukai, Major Works,* New York, Columbia University Press, 1972.

Haldar, J. R.: *Early Buddhist Mythology,* New Delhi, Manohar, 1977.

Hixon, L.: *Mother of the Universe: Visions of the Goddess, Tantric Hymns of Enlightenment*, Quest Books, Wheaton, 1994.

Irene, S.: *Vedic Heritage Teaching Program*. Arsha Vidya Gurukulam, Coimbatore, 1994.

Jacob, K.: *Religion and Ethics in Advaita*, C.M.S. Press, Kottayam, 1982.

Jean, M.: *Tantrik Yoga*, The Aquarian Press, Wellingborough, 1970.

Karmarkar, D.: *Sankara's Advaita*, Karnatak University, Dharwar, 1976.

Keith, A.B. : *Rigveda Brahmanas*, Harvard University Press, Cambridge, 1920.

Knipe, M.: *Hinduism: Experiments in the Sacred*, Harper, San Francisco, 1991.

Knott, K.: *Hinduism, A Very Short Introduction,* Oxford University Press, New York, 1998.

Kuiper, F.B.J. : *Aryans in the Rigveda*, Rodopi, Amsterdam, 1991.

Strauss, L.: *Political Philosophy*, The Bobbs Merrill Co., New York, 1975.

Tejomayananda, Swami: *Hindu Culture: An Introduction,* Chinmaya Publications, Piercy, 1993.

Utpat, V.N.: *Riddles of Buddha and Ambedkar,* Itihas Patrika Prakashan, Thane 1988.

Index

❑❑❑